OTR

PUBLICATIONS

PRESENTS

A Celebration of Rare Breeds

APPEARING ON THE FRONT COVER:

(Top Left) **FINNISH SPITZ:** Champion Jayenn's Auburn Anow, owner Joan Grant, Golden, B.C., Canada.
(Top Right) **ANATOLIAN SHEPHERD DOG:** Duman of Arkadas, owners Wallace and Maureen Austin, Alpine, California. (Wallace Austin photo)
(Bottom Left) **NEAPOLITAN MASTIFF:** Thundermugs Cinzia, owners Garry and Lynn Travers, Cheltenham, Ontario, Canada.
(Bottom Right) **CAVALIER KING CHARLES SPANIEL:** Champion Glencroft Captain Cook of Kilspindie, owner Elizabeth Spalding, Falmouth, Maine.

APPEARING ON THE BACK COVER:

(Top Left) **AMERICAN ESKIMOS:** Grand Champion "PR" Shamrck's Daybrk Shandale and Champion "PR" Shamroc's Nordic Scandal, owner Brenda O'Sullivan, Reno, Nevada.
(Top Right) **POLISH OWCZAREK NIZINNY:** Vladja Z Elzbieta, owner E. Jane Brown, Bowie, Maryland.
(Bottom Left) **AUSTRALIAN KELPIE:** Australian Champion Happyvalley Ocker, owner Ms. Gill Rogers, Australia.
(Bottom Right) **TOY FOX TERRIERS:** Grand Champion Gorden's Stamper Lil's Fantasia and Grand Champion Gorden's Shamrock Lad, owners Doug and Betty Gorden, Crosby, Texas.

This charming Cavalier King Charles Spaniel puppy would brighten up anyone's Christmas morning. This little beauty is owned by Elizabeth Spalding, Kilspindie Cavaliers, Falmouth, Maine.

A Celebration of Rare Breeds

by

Cathy J. Flamholtz

OTR PUBLICATIONS

P.O. Box 1243

Ft. Payne, Alabama 35967

DEDICATION

To Harvey, who massaged my shoulders when I couldn't
type another word, who gave me pep talks when I was
down and who always believed in me and the project.
He made the high times higher and the low times not so low.

Kilspindie Cheer Up, a Best in Show winner and dam of champions, Owner Elizabeth Spalding, Kilspindie Cavaliers, Falmouth, Maine.

Preface

This book is the culmination of a life long interest in all breeds of dogs. The credit for this project belongs not to me, but to all the dedicated owners of rare breeds who generously and warmly shared their information, their experiences, the results of their own research, their photographs and their love of their dogs. They selflessly took time out from their busy lives to share their knowledge with me. Since no single person can claim to be an expert on every one of these breeds, I have, whenever possible, preferred to let them speak with their own words. Without their support and encouragement, this book would have been impossible.

In the course of research for this book, I contacted more than 1,000 rare breed fanciers. I've corresponded with hundreds of people, both in this country and abroad. They have loaned me books written in other languages, and some have volunteered their services and talents as translators. A project of this nature makes you realize just how fantastic dog people are and that, regardless of where we make our homes, we all share a strong bond. I've made some wonderful friends.

It has been my intent to provide a glimpse of the glorious history of these rare breeds and to tell you what they are like to live with on a day-to-day basis. I have also tried to introduce you to some of the people involved with these breeds. The appendix lists the names and addresses of breed clubs which will be glad to provide you with additional information. They will certainly send you a copy of the standard. Since these standards are available in magazines and dog encyclopedias, I have not included them here. I felt that discussions of the personalities and characters of these breeds would be more valuable and interesting.

In the past few years, we have entered a new and very exciting phase in the ownership of purebred dogs. Perhaps, in another ten years, some of the breeds listed in this book will have faded from view. However, many will have become a firm part of the purebred world in this country. There are many other breeds that have recently arrived on these shores, and other new imports are expected shortly. I am sorry that I could not include all of them. To the owners of the Berger Picardy, the Bergamese Shepherd, the Bolognese, the Drever, the German Longhaired Pointer, the Kraski Ovcar, the Mexican Hairless, the Munsterlander (large and small), the Peruvian Inca Orchid, the Pudelpointer, the Rat Terrier, the Spanish Mastiff, the Spinone Italiani, the Wachtelhund, the Wire-haired Vizsla and the Xoloitzcuintli, I must apologize for not having enough space to include them in this book. While there was plenty of information available for chapters on these breeds, the book would have been much too long. Perhaps, it will be possible, in the coming years, to celebrate with a second volume.

The beautiful Champion Myra de la Sylvade was the top all-breed obedience champion of the Netherlands in 1980 and 1981. She is owned by Mrs. Truus Manders, of Holland.

Table of Contents

Chapter 1

Why A Rare Breed?

We are in the midst of one of the most exciting periods in American dog history. Never before have so many rare breeds appeared on the dog scene at one time. The rare breed movement in this country is gaining momentum at an extraordinary rate. Articles on rare breeds, published in American dog magazines, have generated overwhelming response. Rare breed clubs, both all-breed and specialty groups, have sprung up all across the country. They serve an invaluable function as a network for fans of these uncommon dogs.

In recent years, Americans have travelled to more and more international shows, where they have had the opportunity to see breeds that are unknown in this country. These shows have afforded many dog enthusiasts a chance to meet foreign breeders. It is fascinating to learn of their work with breeds that are new to us. Lasting friendships have developed and we have discovered that dog lovers the world over share a common bond.

In years past, the person who voiced an interest in a rare breed was likely to be confronted with the question, "Why on earth would you want to own a breed that isn't recognized by the American Kennel Club?" Such questions are rarely heard today. We have discovered that there is much to applaud about these rare breeds, and that owning and working with them can be every bit as challenging, if not more so, as involvement with an A.K.C. registered breed.

There is no single profile of a rare breed owner. These pioneers, however, all have several qualities in common. Love, respect and boundless enthusiasm for their chosen breeds are common denominators. Rare breed owners don't shy away from a challenge. They have learned that these uncommon dogs have many attributes that would be appreciated by a variety of dog lovers. It takes missonary zeal to introduce and popularize a little known breed. It also takes vigilance and dedication to wisely guide the future of a new breed. In the past, we have seen that mushrooming popularity can be devastating. Slow, steady progress, coupled with education, is the key to ensuring a breed's future. Wisely promoting a rare breed requires incredible dedication, perseverance, the ability to cope with set-backs, discipline and organization. It also requires a selfless attitude. Breeds which remain solely under the control of a single person, are not likely to prosper. It is essential to build on the abilities and the talents of many owners to achieve goals for the good of the breed. More and more dog enthusiasts are finding that the results are worth the effort. "Nothing has been more gratifying or satisfying than my work with rare breeds," one dedicated owner says.

The reasons for selecting a rare breed are as many and varied as there are dog lovers. Some rare breed owners gave little thought to their breed's unrecognized status. "When I saw my first Australian Shepherd, in 1970, I had no idea what they were," says Alice Ward. "I spotted the first one at a horse show. He was just tagging along after a cowboy. That guy (the dog) was so friendly that it's a wonder someone didn't permanently 'borrow' him. Most of the first dogs I saw were not registered, although I do believe many of them were purebred. I was intrigued by their looks, but inspired by their devotion."

"My interest in a rare breed came about more or less by accident," says Margie Lachs, a Canaan Dog owner. "I have had dogs my entire life, but became interested in purebreds in 1940 when I acquired a

Eight week old Canaan Dog puppies, bred by Terry Bagley, Terramara Kennels, Grand Centre, Canada.

Cocker Spaniel. Eventually, for no special reason, I became involved with Standard Poodles. They were my hobby for about twenty-five years and I showed them in breed and obedience." One of Mrs. Lachs' Poodles had earned a Utility Dog degree and she then became interested in tracking. "My Poodle did not share my interest." Mrs. Lachs' became attracted to the working breeds. She read an article on the Canaan Dog by Ursula Berkowitz. She contacted Mrs. Berkowitz and learned that the Canaan was a working breed. "I was, by this time, getting sick and tired of hair and grooming, and wanted nothing more than to throw my clippers as far as I could," she says. Marguerite Lachs visited Mrs. Berkowitz and came home with a charming Canaan puppy.

"I absolutely fell in love with the first Jack Russell Terrier that I met," says Catherine Doran. "I didn't know it was a rare breed because it is commonly owned by people who keep horses for fox hunting. I've owned other breeds and shown horses, but never have I had the fun that my Jack Russells give me."

By contrast, other rare breed owners made a conscientious and careful decision to acquire an uncommon dog. "I chose the Australian Shepherd for its intelligence and herding abilities," says Patricia Headley. "I live on a farm and I try to place my Aussies in working environments. I also raise Border Collies. While I find that the Aussie is not as capable with sheep as the Border Collie, they make excellent cow and horse dogs."

"We selected a rare breed because we were looking for a breed that had not been bred for show," explain David Sims and Orysia Dawydiak of their decision to raise Akbash Dogs. Their dogs are working livestock guardians who watch over the couple's sheep and goats. "We were definitely not interested in American Kennel Club acceptance of our breed. We want to preserve the working qualities of the Akbash Dog."

"We raise angora goats as well as white and colored sheep," says Sue Drummond. "Many farmers here have had problems with domestic and wild dogs. Since angora goats are rather 'pricey,' we decided to investigate the possibility of getting one of the breeds called guardian dogs. We began reading about guardian dogs in general. We talked with people who were actually using them, spoke with breeders, and read reports from livestock dog projects in this and other countries. We began to zero in on the Great Pyrenees and the Maremma because of their reputations for being more friendly with humans. Because we wanted working dogs and most Pyrenees have been raised for show, we chose the Maremma."

One of the most inspiring reasons for selecting a rare breed is a sense of pride in one's heritage. The characterization of the United States as a "melting pot" now seems overused and trite, but it is nonetheless true. Ours is a country of varied cultural influences, a rich patchwork of ethnic diversity and tradition. Immigrants to these shores have enriched the lives of all Americans. We are now seeing a new wave of canine immigrants that promises to further enrich our lives.

Ursula Berkowitz, importer of the first Canaan Dogs to enter this country, was proud of her Jewish heritage. She embarked on a one-woman crusade to introduce this Israeli breed to American dog lovers. Similarly, it was a respect for their Polish traditions that guided and inspired Kaz and Betty Augustowski in their efforts to familiarize dog fanciers with the Polish Owczarek Nizinny. Joseph and Maya Schîn are equally proud of their Slovakian background. This wonderful couple has devoted countless hours to bring the Slovak Tchouvatch to the attention of North American dog lovers. Graciela Hoff is the leading promotor of the Argentine Dogo in this country. "I love the United States," she says, "but I was born and raised in Argentina, and I still have family there. I want so much to share this wonderful breed from my homeland with Americans." I believe this attitude says something heartwarming and very positive about the United States.

"I think the reason people switch to rare breeds and participate in rare breed shows is that they can't cut it with A.K.C. breeds," says one critic of the current movement. "You can't make it in the A-league, but in rare breeds you can become a big duck in a little pond." Perhaps there are a few rare breed enthusiasts to which this applies, but there are many more who have achieved notable and outstanding success with recognized breeds. Mrs. Anne Snelling, an ardent supporter of the Petit Basset Griffon Vendéen, would certainly qualify as extraordinarily successful in anyone's book. Her Irish Water Spaniel, Ch. Oaktree's Irishtocrat, one of history's most superb showmen, won Best in Show at Westminster in 1979. In 1982, her charming Ch. St. Aubrey Dragonora of Elsdon, a Pekingnese, also took Best in Show at Westminster, America's premier dog event.

Barbara J. Andrews, a Miniature Bull Terrier enthusiast, is another example of a tremendously successful breeder who is active in the rare breed movement. No discussion of the Akita would be complete without citing the contributions of Mrs. Andrews. Her Ch. Sachmo is the breed's all-time top producing sire, and her Ch. Ko-Go is the top producing Akita bitch. 76 A.K.C. champions, including Group and Specialty winners, hail from her O'B.J.'s Kennel.

While some rare breed owners are novices, many

have been involved with other breeds. An increasing number of very experienced, long time fanciers are turning their talents to rare breeds. Sometimes it is the association with recognized breeds that spurs their interest in these less common dogs. "I had no particular interest in a rare breed," says Mrs. B.J. Andrews, a Miniature Bull Terrier breeder. "We bred standard Bull Terriers, but decided we preferred the smaller variety." Ms. Donly Chorn would certainly understand. "Miniature Bull Terriers were a natural extension of the Standard Bull Terriers I already raised."

Many Akita fanciers were attracted to the Japanese Shiba. "The Shiba just seemed to be a natural choice since we owned and loved Akitas, and were looking for a smaller breed," says Julie Jennings. Many Shiba kennels raise both of these Japanese breeds. Indeed, the tremendous growth of interest in the impressive Akita seems to have spurred interest in the smaller Shiba.

"I selected the Shar-Pei because I found the breed unusual, but that wasn't my sole reason," says Gayle Gold. "We were involved with Airedales and Soft-Coated Wheaten Terriers. We got our first Wheaten the year they were recognized by the A.K.C. After talking with people who saw them through to recognition, we felt it would be fun to see a breed through the miscellaneous classes. I also preferred to show my own dogs rather than sending them out with handlers. In some other breeds, it's extremely difficult to compete if you're not a professional handler."

"I saw my first Shar-Pei at a dog show approximately six years ago," says Tommie Sue Mason. "I was so very awed by this wrinkled wonder. It was totally different from every other breed." Ms. Mason is not alone. Many dog owners step to the beat of their own drum. They like the unique, the unusual, the distinctive. " I've never wanted to be just like everybody else," Tommie Sue says, "I've always liked the unusual. It's a good feeling to know you have something different, and the attention it draws is fun!"

"I like owning an unusual dog," says a New York stockbroker. "I enjoy owning the distinctive, and there's a certain status in rare breeds. I work very hard and I've been successful. My financial success allows me to buy the best. I drive a Mercedes rather than a Ford, I buy designer clothes and, when I began to look for a breed of dog, I wanted something unique and different. Anyone can own a German Shepherd or a Doberman. Most people can't afford to import a unique dog from a foreign country. I can."

"I used to breed German Shepherds," says an Australian Shepherd fancier. "I became disgusted with the decline in quality within the breed. The truly sound German Shepherd became a rarity and the breed was riddled with hip dysplasia. I felt that judges selected for tremendously sloping toplines and over angulated rears. The magnificent old German Shepherds would, I am afraid, stand little chance in today's show rings."

Other rare breed fanciers share this concern with the changes that have occurred in recognized breeds. "I began more than fifteen years ago with a sporting breed. I became an avid student of this particular breed. I read everything I could get my hands on, including purchasing old out of print books. I tried to learn as much as possible about definitive breed type. You know, those essential qualities that differentiated this breed from any other. However, over the years, there was a change in the breed that I did not feel was correct. Breeders, anxious for success in the show rings, modified the breed into a more elegant, refined, and wholly different breed. Not everyone applauded the changes. Some breeders would tell me that they did not think a top winner had correct type, but they would breed to him, just the same, because that was the style that was winning. It just wasn't the same breed I fell in love with."

"I considered dog shows a great hobby," says a former Rottweiler breeder. "They were a wonderful activity for me and my family. When I started, twenty years ago, the atmosphere was very friendly and I considered a dog show great fun. The Rott has became so popular that it seemed everyone was breeding them. While there are a greater number of outstanding Rottweilers, there are also more poor ones. Years ago, I felt that all of those breeding and showing Rotts were one big happy family. Now, there is much more competition and the atmosphere is more cut-throat. The ring is filled with professional handlers and it's just not as much fun."

"We raised Boxers for years," says Betsy Davison, a Chinese Shar-Pei breeder, "then wanted something smaller and less obstreperous, but with personality and charm. We didn't show our Boxers." A friend of he Davisons did take one of their puppies into the ring. "But," says Betsy, "she was the old-type of Boxer--big, heavy boned, a real working class dog. It was just what we wanted, and people who bought our pups loved them. 'Just like the Boxer I had when I was a kid,' they'd say. For the last few years, the Boxer is smaller, finer boned, and even more hyper."

It's often said that one picture is worth a thousand words, but we sometimes forget what a lasting impression a photograph can make. "My husband first saw a photograph of the Chinook in a 1946 issue of *National Geographic Magazine*," says Marra Wollpert. "He remembered that photo and, in 1969, decided that he was ready to purchase his first

Chinook."

It was also a photograph that attracted Jody Nathan. "When I was looking for a breed, I saw a picture of the Telomian and fell in love. I was looking for a dog of that size and I couldn't resist. I sent in a puppy reservation and bought my first one without ever having actually seen a Telomian."

"I first heard about the plight of the Chinook in 1980 or 1981, when there were only about 40 living dogs," says Bobi Martin. "The idea of being able to save a species from extinction was irresistable." Jody Nathan agrees. "It feels good to know that you are helping to save a breed from becoming extinct."

In 1973, an article about the Chinese Shar-Pei, or Chinese Fighting Dog as he was then called, appeared in an American dog magazine. The article made an appeal to dog lovers to help save this endangered breed. Many current Shar-Pei breeders were attracted to this unusual dog and couldn't bear to think that such an interesting and ancient breed might cease to exist. However, who among us could possibly have predicted the incredible popularity of the Shar-Pei today? There are many other dog breeds that are faced with the danger of extinction. It is a long, arduous task to pull a breed back from the edge of oblivion, but it would be hard to imagine more satisfying work. Americans have proved highly successful in helping to save breeds. Without the support of Americans, it is virtually assured that the Portuguese Water Dog would have disappeared entirely. There are many other breeds that need our help. In these days of mounting environmental and animal awareness, there are still many more challenges to be met. In our own small way, we have a unique opportunity to give something back to the dogs that have brought us such pleasure.

I hope you will enjoy this exploration of some of the rare breeds currently being promoted in this country. Their histories are fascinating, their traits admirable, and their owners wonderfully dedicated Many of the breeds contained in this book are still in their infancy in this country. It will fall to the breeders to wisely and faithfully guide them into popularity. I have been fascinated and inspired by rare breed owners' enthusiasm and devotion to their dogs. May we love, cherish and protect them in the coming years. These fantastic breeds are certainly worth celebrating!

A stunning head study of a Dogue de Bordeaux owned by Jacque Dive, of France.

The impressive Simsek White Bird, a one-year-old male imported from Turkey. Owned by Orysia Dawydiak and David Sims, of Odessa Farms, Charlottetown, Prince Edward Island, Canada.

Aba Pamuk Odessa with her eight-week-old daughter, Kuchuk. Owned by Orysia Dawydiak and David Sims.

Chapter 2

The Akbash Dog

The Akbash Dog has a an etherial beauty. One can picture him on the crest of a hill, surveying his domain. The sun glints off his white coat. His piercing eyes scan the horizon. Suddenly he sees something and his stare becomes remarkably intense. When he moves, with lightening fast strides, awesome power and a cat-like grace, we come to appreciate him for the beautiful and magnificent animal that he is.

Owners of the Abash Dog have delved meticulously into the history of dogs in Turkey. They are hampered by the lack of written documentation and the fact that there are no kennel clubs or studbook registries in all of Turkey. Written accounts of encounters with Turkish dogs are scant and were penned by visitors to the country who had no background in cynology. They believe, nevertheless, that there is a long undocumented tradition of purebred dog breeding in this remote country. It is their opinion that the Akbash Dog is a recently discovered member of the family of white livestock guarding breeds that exists throughout Europe. These include the Great Pyrenees (from France and Spain), the Kuvasz and Komondor (from Hungary), the Maremma- Abruzzese (from Italy), the Slovak Tchouvatch (from Czechoslovakia) and the Tatra Sheepdog (from Poland). Indeed, they theorize that the more primitive Akbash Dog may actually be the progenitor of these better known breeds.

Anatolian Shepherd owners respect this extensive research, but disagree with the conclusions drawn from the studies. They hold that while some colors are most prevalent in certain regions, all fall under the banner of a single breed. Sadly, we may never know the truth about the origins or separate breed status of the dogs from Turkey. In future years, this issue will likely be arbitrated by kennel clubs around the world. England just had the dilemma of trying to shed light on this issue. I wish these organizations luck. Those who share their homes with these magnificent Turkish dogs hold strongly and passionately to their beliefs. We may never know if these Akbash Dog historians are correct in their conclusions, but their research makes for fascinating reading.

Archaeological finds indicate that dogs have made their homes in Asia Minor since 7,000 B.C. The record clearly shows that both mastiff-type dogs and coursing hounds have lived in the region for centuries. The large and fiercely aggressive mastiff-like dogs were superb guard dogs and were probably used in times of war. They have been described as being lion-like and "the size of asses." Akbash Dog historians believe that these same dogs may also have been used to guard livestock in times of peace.

There are numerous references to coursing hounds in this area. Indeed, they were often referred to as Turkish Greyhounds. Passages written in the 1800's describe these dogs as being less speedy than the Greyhound and somewhat coarser in appearance, but wonderfully strong and powerful. An English visitor to Turkey described a scene in 1813, when the son of a lord prepared to leave on a hunting expedition, "...on a white courser magnificently caparisoned in housing of crimson velvet embossed with gold. His lance was borne by a page, and in the right hand he held a hawk, being followed by several couples of greyhounds." This should come as no surprise, for the hunting of gazehounds has enjoyed a long tradition in Moslem countries.

Akbash Dog supporters belive that these gazehounds interbred with the mastiff-type dogs, to form the basis of the Akbash Dog. A look at the decidedly racey features and elegant sighthound-type angulation of many Akbash Dog imports would seem to confirm this theory. Other gazehound characteristics (such as low tolerance to anesthesia) have also been noticed in these Turkish natives.

Akbash Dog supporters believe that there is more than one sheepguarding breed found in Turkey. They hold that the *akkus* (meaning white bird) or the *akbas* (white head) is a distinct and separate breed. Those who have scoured Turkey, in search of outstanding imports, have found these white dogs in western Turkey, principally in the provinces of Afyon, Ankara, Bilicek, Bolu, Eskisehir, Isparta, Konya and Kutahya.

They believe that the other Turkish sheep guarding breed is the *Kangal* or *Karabash* (meaning black head). The breed is most often found in the Kangal region of eastern Turkey, named for the Aga of Kangal. These dogs are noted for their massive size and black masked faces.

Akbash Dog supporters believe that all piebald or spotted dogs are mutts and should not be confused with purebreds. It should be noted that this is not a universally held opinion, and that other experienced dog authorities vehemently disagree with this assertion. They believe that the Akbash Dog is simply a white version of the sheep guardian long known in Turkey. Whatever the case, the Akbash Dog has attracted much attention in this country and is well on his way to carving a niche for himself in American dogdom.

The Akbash Dog came the attention of dog lovers through the dedicated efforts of David and Judith Nelson. They first observed the breed when they rented a country home, while staying in Turkey. There they saw the large impressive dogs that accompanied the shepherds and their flocks. The more the couple saw of these beautiful dogs, the more fascinated they became. Soon a small puppy joined their home, much to the consternation of native residents. It is generally conceded, in Turkey, that these dogs are unsuitable as pets. Many natives warned the Nelsons that the dog would turn on them. What the Nelsons discovered, however, was that their puppy was a loving and devoted companion. They had the rare experience of breeding the Akbash Dog in his native Turkey, and they learned all they could of the breed in its homeland. On their return to the United States, they were accompanied by their Akbash Dog, and they have returned to Turkey several times to select additional breeding stock.

Whatever his origin or breed status, the Akbash Dog remains a most respected livestock guardian

breed in Turkey. These dogs have never been herders. They live side by side with the sheep and bond closely with them. The Turkish sheep industry is much larger that its American counterpart. Flocks are still attacked by wolves, wild dogs, jackals and bears, although the predator threat seems to be diminishing. The livestock guardian is essential to the safety of the flock. Breeding has continued, mostly, according to the age old tenet of survival of the fittest, with the strongest, most dominant males servicing the bitches. Breeders fear that, with the diminishing predator threat, the Akbash Dog may become more scarce in his homeland. The lack of routine vaccinations, and the dearth of information about proper diet and care, could also have repercussions on the Turkish Akbash Dog population.

Akbash Dogs are very impressive and beautiful. They have a wonderful combination of long legged elegance and massive power, and must always be capable of great speed and superb agility. These large dogs take a long time to mature and may not achieve their full size until they are three years of age. Dogs generally measure 30-34 inches at the shoulder and weigh approximately 120 pounds, while bitches stand 28-32 inches and weigh about 90 pounds. They have deep chests and a level back, although there should be a slight arch over the loin. Often, these dogs give the appearance of being rather long in body. The Akbash Dog frequently has hind dewclaws, and some dogs are born with double dewclaws on their rear feet. Most breeders prefer to remove these. The Akbash Dog has a double coat that is white in color, although pale cream colored markings on the ears are permitted. The skin (not the coat) may well be pigmented. Akbash Dog coats may be either short or long. The long coat is quite profuse and very beautiful. Some longhaired Akbash have slightly wavey coats, but the coat is flat lying rather than stand-off. The mane, or ruff, on the neck, is also more pronounced in long haired dogs. Longhaired specimens have profuse feathering on their tails, which are carried low when the dog is at rest. When he moves or becomes excited, the beautiful tail is carried high. Smooth coated Akbash Dogs have a medium length coat, which is much less impressive in appearance than their heavily coated counterparts. As would be expected, they look racier in appearance and one would, at first glance, assume that these dogs are smaller and have less substantial bone. The Akbash Dog has beautiful almond shaped eyes that may vary from a light to a deep brown. In motion, the Akbash Dog is truly lovely with his springy gait.

David Sims and Orysia Dawydiak, of Charlottetown, Prince Edward Island, Canada, are enthusiastic supporters of the working Akbash Dog. David has a PhD in veterinary sciences and Orysia holds a degree in animal science. "We were looking for a working breed that had not been bred for show. We saw an ad in a sheep trade magazine and wrote for information. We did not have much experience with other breeds prior to becoming involved with the Akbash Dog. We looked long and carefully before jumping in at the first good opportunity." The couple has learned a great deal from their dogs and they hope that the Akbash Dog will remain valued as a livestock guardian. Several of the breed make their home at David and Orysia's Odessa Farms.

"We have trained several Akbash Dogs as livestock guardians for sheep and goats, and several for obedience work," the couple says. "These dogs are natural guardians. They will guard whatever they are raised with, be it sheep, goats, horses, people or cats. Some are versatile and will guard several things. If given a chance, most will gravitate toward humans. After all, they know where the good times are! We find that they tend to prefer goats to sheep. Goats are more interesting and they reciprocate with play, while sheep are relatively boring. Occasionally, you will find individuals that show more interest in livestock than people and vice versa. For this reason, we temperament test all of our pups and try to place them in appropriate homes. We feel this makes for more successful placements.

"We've seen several instances where young guard dogs have 'stolen' newborn lambs from their mothers and tried to play mother themselves. This behavior is discouraged and doesn't usually recur. Even our indoor pet Akbash male has adopted lambs that we brought into the house to revive after a tough or cold delivery. He cuddles them, licks them and cleans them and he will growl at any dog or cat that approaches 'his' lamb. Our pet bitch has allowed orphaned lambs to suckle her when she was nursing her own pups. Most recently we heard that one of our four month old male pups had tried to take over a Whippet bitch's litter when she left them momentarily. The owner had to intercede to prevent a dispute.

"Akbash Dogs are creatures of habit. Anything that deviates from the routine puts them into the alert mode. That is how they function as guardians. This is why we suggest to pet owners that they expose their puppy to any stimuli that the dog may encounter later in life. This way he can accept it all and accomodate it as routine. They do resist change.

"Akbash Dogs tend to be gentle, passive, yet protective of what they consider theirs. Certain individuals can be quite dominant and would not be suitable for families that had little or no experience with dogs, or who were too 'soft.'" They are more independent than some breeds, but they are also intelligent and will figure things out quickly. This combination of loyalty, independence and intelligence is what appeals most to us.

"The owner of an Akbash Dog must be firm and consistent. Prior experience with other dogs is helpful. We strongly recommend pubic obedience sessions. Those interested in the breed must understand that this breed needs either space or exercise. These are large, athletic dogs with racing sighthound ancestry. Their coats suit them ideally for hot or cold weather, although they do shed seasonally. Generally, these are calm dogs that do not bark unless they perceive a real problem. They are very easy to keep in the house, for such a large dog.

"Akbash Dogs are highly trainable, if the owner employs the correct techniques and the right attitude. They are very independent, yet at the same time, quite sensitive to correction. Because of this they are not the easiest breed to train, especially for someone who is impatient. They are good with children IF they have been raised with them or exposed to them in puppyhood. They make excellent watchdogs. They are aggressive when the owner is not at home or if they are threatened directly." Those with other breeds should be aware that the Akbash Dog may be aggressive with other dogs. This may well derive from their innate perception that another dog poses a threat to their charges. The standard states, "The mature Akbash Dog is usually aloof with strangers and often hostile towards strange dogs."

Akbash Dog enthusiasts have been an active force in the rare breed movement. Attempts have been made to ensure that the Akbash Dog will be placed in both working and companion homes. The breed has successfully competed in conformation shows and has achieved notable success, including at least one Best in Show. Akbash Dogs are now actively competing in obedience and their number is sure to grow. Breeders have taken great care to demonstrate the versatile nature of the breed. At least one Akbash Dog has been protection trained, and another has participated in coursing events. Recently, an Akbash Dog became a certified Independence Dog and aids her handicapped, wheelchair bound owner. Certainly, this is a breed we will hear much more from in the future. Turkish residents must clearly be astounded that this breed, thought to be unsuitable as a pet, has come so far.

The great Johnson's King Kong, owned by John D. and Mildred Johnson, Johnson's American Bulldogs, Summerville, Georgia.

Johnson's Mean Machine, one of the studs owned by John D. and Mildred Johnson.

A lovely American Bulldog bitch and her puppies, from the Johnson's Kennels, in Georgia.

An adorable pair of American Bulldog puppies bred by John D. and Mildred Johnson.

This bitch, owned by the Johnsons, demonstrates the shorter, stockier type of American Bulldog.

The hero, Johnson's Dick the Bruiser. Tiny's cropped ears and docked tail are nor typical of the breed.

Chapter 3

The American Bulldog

"My Dad got his first American Bulldog when he was 14 years old. That was 75 years ago," says John D. Johnson. "Our family has been associated with this breed for a very long time." John D., as he prefers to be called, acquired his first puppy when only three years of age. His father took him to visit a man who lived nearby. Beside the chimney was a litter of puppies. "I can still see those puppies as if it were yesterday. My father said, 'Come on, John D, pick out one for yourself'". The young boy reached down and selected a fat male puppy. "I should have selected a female," Mr. Johnson smiled, "that was the first mistake I ever made."

John D.'s little puppy turned out to be an ideal companion. The boy and dog were inseparable. This dog was such a terrific friend that the boy longed to breed these animals. He pestered his father to allow him to acquire a bitch. "Dad didn't mind a stud dog, but he knew that if I ever had a litter of puppies, I'd never part with them. I was fourteen when I finally got my first bitch."

Mr. Johnson's love and enthusiasm for the American Bulldog is readily apparent to those who are fortunate enough to visit his Summerville, Georgia home. John D. and his wife, Mildred, share their beautiful 60-acre home, in the north Georgia mountains, with two dozen of these rare dogs. "When Millie and I were first married, she couldn't stand dogs. She didn't even want one to touch her. But I loved the breed so much that, I guess, she had to love them or leave me." One has only to watch the Johnsons' rapport with their dogs to realize that they are full partners in their efforts to preserve the American Bulldog.

"We have spent untold thousands of dollars preserving this breed of dog. When I was a boy, there were many of these dogs around. But, by the time I was a grown man, they had started to disappear. There were many people like my Dad who wanted only one or two, but they didn't really care about breeding them. Someone had to spend the time and money, and I love this breed. Whenever we heard of a good dog that was available, we bought it to add to our breeding program. We have advertised far and wide, and others are becoming interested. The American Bulldog is making a comeback."

The history of the Bulldog is well documented. Early Bulldogs were the helpmates of medieval butchers. There was even a prevalent theory that the meat of a bull which had been baited was more tender. From this start, the "sport" of bullbaiting gained popularity in England. Bulls were tethered with ropes, amidst the wild cheering of the crowds, and dogs were turned loose to confront them. Ideally, the dog was to grasp the bull by the nose and force him to his knees. Many a dog was thrown in the air or gouged by the huge horns. "They should have been shot for the things they did with those dogs," Mr. Johnson said. Certainly, most dog lovers today would fully agree.

In 1730, England purchased a large tract of land, in what is now southern Georgia, from the Creek Indians. Settlers brought their dogs with them, and the Bulldog proved admirably suited to his new home. These pioneers needed a multi-purpose farm dog that could protect their property. There were no fences in the vast wilderness and raids by hostile Indians, outlaws, and the many predators native to the area were a common occurrence. The Bulldog became a

11

valuable addition on these isolated homesteads.

In England, with the demise of bullbaiting, the Bulldog was bred down in size and eventually took on the shape of the dog now exhibited in our modern shows. His counterpart in the United States, however, retained the size and character of the original Bulldog. In fact, many of today's American Bulldogs show a marked resemblance to early depictions of the English Bulldog. "In this country, we never bred them down in size," Mr. Johnson says. "The American Bulldog is still a large animal."

The American Bulldog has, indeed, found use as a multi- purpose dog. They have been used to hunt bears, wild hogs, squirrels, and even to tree racoons. In addition to protection of the home, the Johnsons' Bulldogs have aided in their cattle raising activities. The Johnsons were, at one time, breeders of top-winning Angus, and Millie trained one of their dogs, Blackjack, to help drive the large cattle. "His natural inclination was to go to the head of the bulls," says Millie, "but I trained him to walk behind them. Blackjack and I could move the cattle into the barn in a fraction of the time it would have taken me alone."

Packs of wild dogs pose a real threat to livestock raisers in many parts of the country today, and the South is no exception. Feral dogs have even been known to challenge man. The American Bulldog has proven a worthy deterrent. For all their large size, they are incredibly swift and agile. "Dick the Bruiser", affectionately nicknamed Tiny by his owners, was one of the couple's most able dogs. The Johnsons credit him with saving their lives and their livestock on several occasions. In one of his most notable confrontations, Dick saved the life of a neighbor. The Johnsons were away from home when a neighbor saw a pack of wild dogs approaching their pasture. He grabbed his gun and loosed Dick. The wild dogs disappeared over a small rise, with the man and Dick in hot pursuit. Suddenly, the duo found themselves surrounded by the pack. In a one-on-one fight, the Bulldog will go for his opponent's throat, but in a fight with a pack, he will resort to slashing tactics. The American Bulldog has an innate ability to think for himself in such situations and he generally singles out the leader for his first assault. Dick, using his great weight and speed, crashed into the pack's leader, knocking him to the ground and stunning him. Then he quickly turned to attack the remaining dogs. The man shot one dog while Dick managed to keep three others at bay. Suddenly, Dick broke away and attacked a fourth dog that was sneaking up on the man. Out of ammunition now, the man ran for his house to reload. Dick was left to fend off the other dogs. As the neighbor passed the Johnson home, he released Tuffie, a bitch. When he returned with his now loaded gun, he found only one remaining live wild dog, and

Dick had him in a stranglehold. The 95 pound Dick was missed by all when he died at nine years of age.

The Johnsons stress that the American Bulldog is very trainable. Contrary to the information contained in one recent book, the breed is not used as a fighting dog. "They will fight, but you can train them not to," Mr. Johnson says. "I start with mine, individually, as puppies. They should be trained to turn loose of any dog on command. The dogs obey both me and my wife. They're very smart and they want to please." Mr. Johnson is this country's leading breeder of the rare American Bulldog. The dogs in his kennel are well cared for and show a great love for people. They are wonderfully affectionate and loyal, and will give their all to those they love. There is a considerable size variation in the breed. "Some people prefer the slightly shorter legged, stocky dog, while others want a leggier, more massive animal," John D. states. The couple has both in their kennel. Many of the Johnsons' most successful stud dogs have been in the 95-130 pound range. Bitches are, of course, proportionally smaller. All of the Johnson dogs have the look of sound, well-muscled athletes. Particularly impressive, to the author, were several of the young adults and older puppies, who teemed with quality. For the time being, with John D. and Mildred Johnson's careful program of line breeding, the continuation of the impressive American Bulldog seems assured. But, "we're not young anymore," the Johnsons warn, "and we pray that other people will become as dedicated to this breed as we are. That's the only way that the future of these wonderful dogs can be guaranteed."

Chapter 4

The American Eskimo

"With all his wonderful qualities, I don't know why God even bothered making another breed," jokes Pat Cotton of Austin, Texas. Owners of other breeds might strongly disagree, but such enthusiasm is typical of American Eskimo owners. The "Eskie," as he is commonly called, is often referred to as the "dog beautiful." Indeed, with his snowy white coat, patent leather nose and sparkling dark eyes, he attracts a great deal of attention. What captivates his owners and wins their devotion, however, is his wonderful personality.

The American Eskimo is a member of the large Spitz family. Numerous Spitz breeds, varying somewhat in color and appearance, have made their homes in countries all around the world. The Spitz breeds have a long history, extending back thousands of years. All are characterized by their wedge-shaped heads, prick ears and double coats. Most have tails that curl over the back. Several of the world's Spitz breeds are all white in color. Those familiar with A.K.C. breeds are sure to note the American Eskimo's resemblance to the Samoyed. Indeed, heavily boned Eskies often look like miniature Sammys.

While it is difficult to pinpoint the Eskie's precise origin, it is believed that he came to this country with early German immigrants. The "Great Spitz" is a breed recognized, to this day, in Germany. This breed's standard allows for size variations and color differences, including black, grey, brown and white. The *Weisser Grosspitz* is pure white in color, and measures a little over 15 inches at the shoulder. In Germany, the Great Spitz was bred down in size to produce the very popular *Kleinspitz*, known in this country as the Pomeranian.

Breeds remarkably similiar in appearance to the American Eskimo have made their way around the world. The Volpino, or *Volpino Italiano*, is also known as the Italian Spitz. We know that this breed has existed in Italy since the days when records on dogs were first kept. It is said that dogs of this type are pictured on old Roman carvings and in drawings. The Volpino is quite small, with a longer, silkier coat than would be acceptable for an American Eskimo.

One of Japan's most popular breeds in Japan is the Japanese Spitz. A recent visitor to the island stated that he saw these small white dogs playing with children along the seashore. A Japanese breeder recently visited this country and remarked on the amazing similiarity of the American Eskimo to his Japanese counterpart. A few Japanese Spitz have been imported to Great Britain, where they have attracted much attention. Descriptions of their temperament and personality are identical to that of the American Eskimo.

In the early 1900's, several "White Spitz" accompanied their German owners to this country. Mr. and Mrs. F. M. Hall were prominent early breeders. They had a fine kennel with lovely specimens which ranged from 24 to 40 pounds. The couple kept careful records of their breeding activities and worked to establish the breed in this country. The United Kennel Club first recognized these dogs as a distinctive breed in 1913, but it was not until 1917 that the name, American Eskimo, was adopted. For many years the breed remained quite rare. Today, there are thousands of American Eskimos, and the breed is prospering.

The Eskimo has much to recommend him as a

Grand Champion "PR" Shamroc's Daybrk Starbuck and his daughter, Champion "PR" Shamroc's Nordic Scandal, owned by Brenda O'Sullivan, of Reno, Nev.

Grand Champion "PR" Hofman's Lil' Bit Country, owned by Nancy J. Hofman, of Norwalk, California.

fine companion for the home. The breed is hardy and fun loving. Eskies are noted for their high intelligence, willingness to please, and easy trainability. They housebreak easily at a very early age. These are entertaining dogs who demonstrate great devotion to their families. The Eskie is naturally wary of strangers and makes an ideal watchdog. The United Kennel Club recognizes two varieties in this breed, so owners can select the size that most suits their lifestyle. "Standard" size Eskies range from 15 inches to 19 inches, and can weigh 18-35 pounds. "Miniatures" tip the scales at 10-20 pounds, and measure in at 11 inches to 14 inches. Recently, some breeders have worked to produce "Toys," but this variety is still rare and has not been recognized by the U.K.C.

The American Eskimo is quite striking in appearance and resembles the larger sledding breeds. He is well-balanced, with a square body shape. He has the look of a smart, alert dog, is quite agile, and very strong for his size. His coat is, generally, pure white with black points, although the standard permits some cream markings. The coat is heavily furred on the neck, giving the appearance of a ruff or mane, which is particularly pronounced on males. The coat is very profuse on the hindquarters, and fanciers refer to this as "trousers." His heavily plumed tail is carried jauntily over the back.

At first glance, those unfamiliar with the breed would assume that the American Eskimo requires long hours of grooming. Not so. Often a weekly brushing will suffice, although show dogs are sometimes brushed daily. You may find occasional mats behind the ears or on the trousers but, in general, the Eskie coat is not prone to matting. The

coat is self-cleansing and, for a white dog, this breed stays remarkably clean. Baths are seldom necessary. "My Eskies sometimes get out and tromp in the mud," says Brenda O'Sullivan of Reno, Nevada, "and they look positively black. However, the mud dries and flakes out of the coat, and my Eskies turn white again." The American Eskimo does shed its coat periodically. Males generally shed once a year. Females are apt to shed following their seasons, and will always lose coat after they deliver puppies. This shedding period, if left unchecked, will extend over a two-to-three week period, and your home will be

"PR" Cotton's Frosti Playboy, a Miniature, pictured with his owner, Pat Cotton, of Austin, Texas.

A nine-week-old American Eskimo puppy, owned by Brenda O'Sullivan, of Reno, Nevada.

filled with great tufts of snowy hair. The nuisance of shedding can be eliminated, if the owner will comb out the loose hair when he first notices that the dog is beginning to blow coat. Your Eskie will feel and look better, and your vaccuum cleaner won't have to work overtime.

The American Eskimo is a fun loving breed that enjoys romping and playing. They often delight in thinking up antics to entertain their owners. Eskies

want to be a part of the family, and do not do well when they are deprived of this contact. They are always alert and eager to please, although they do tend, at times, to be headstrong. New owners should be consistent, and handle this breed gently, but firmly. The dog should know that you are the boss, and not be permitted to take over and dictate to the household. The Eskie is naturally wary of strangers, and the new owner should make every effort to socialize his puppy. Exposure to strange people, unfamiliar circumstances and other dogs will ensure a well adjusted, self-confident dog that is able to take any new situation in stride. The Eskie adjusts well to life in the city or the country. The breed does love to bark, so if you live in an apartment or on a city lot, where neighbors are likely to object, it is best to reprimand the dog for excessive barking.

With his natural protectiveness, the American Eskimo is a superb watchdog. "No stranger can enter our home until we've told our Eskies that it's okay," says LaVerne Williams, of Amarillo, Texas. The American Eskimo forms a strong bond with his family, and quickly recognizes his home and its boundaries. He seems to feel that it is his responsibility and obligation to protect both his owners and their property.

Eskies enjoy the company of children. Without question, all breeders agree that this is an ideal child's playmate. "Children seem to be special to these dogs," says Brenda O'Sullivan. "My dogs are very attentive, and follow my seven year old daughter and her friends around the yard, joining them in games of fetch and keep away." La Verne Williams would certainly agree. The 55-year old Mrs. Williams has owned American Eskimos since she was a child. Mr.

Grand Champion U-UD "PR" Northern Lights Nokomis clearing the high jump.

Grand Champion U-UD "PR" Northern Lights Nokomis demonstrates the broad jump. Owned by Donna J. Blews, West Springfield, Massachusetts.

and Mrs. Williams' children are now grown, and their grandchildren are older. Recently, a friend with a rambunctious and mischievous two year old came to visit. Mrs. Williams wasn't sure how her dog would react. "The mother shook her finger at the child and rather harshly corrected him," LaVerne said. "Our Eskie became very protective. When she displayed anger, our Eskie got between the mother and child and, in no uncertain terms, let the mother know that she was not to hurt that child." Mrs. Williams was surprised by the dog's reaction, and tried him with several other children. "Each time he steps in to protect them."

The American Eskimo is bright, intelligent and easily trained. They are often among the top scorers in obedience competition. Donna Blews, of West Springfield, Massachusetts, has been very successful in obedience competition. "The American Eskimo excels in obedience, and they very much enjoy the work," says Mrs. Blews, who owns both obedience titled dogs and champions. "They are a working breed,

and this is a trait that they share with other working breeds. They are always tops in their classes. They train very easily, although some individuals have a stubborn streak. Often, this is because the owner doesn't want to hurt the poor puppy. You have to take the upper hand and show the Eskie that you're the boss. When I am putting one of my Eskies through a routine, my other dogs become very excited and even jealous. They can't wait for their turn to work."

With his loving personality and long list of outstanding attributes, it is no wonder that the American Eskimo is attracting a host of loyal fans wherever he goes. The dogs are hardy and suffer from few health problems. They adjust well to any climate and endear themselves to their owners. "If I could think of the kindest thing I could do for a dear friend," says LaVerne Williams, "I'd probably give them an American Eskimo." Other Eskie owners would certainly agree.

Grand Champion U-UD, U-CDX, U-CD "PR" King Arthur Pendragon, owned by Donna J. Blews.

Chapter 5

The American Hairless Terrier

What happens when two dedicated dog lovers share a dream that everyone else describes as hopeless and a waste of time? Most of us would listen to the experts and abandon our goal. Edwin and Willie Scott, of Trout, Louisiana, do not accept "no" easily though, and this couple, with no previous breeding experience, managed to achieve what all the experts considered an impossibility. They developed the first new hairless breed of dog to come our way in several thousand years. In addition, their newly evolved breed was different from all the other hairless dog types found in the entire world.

The American Hairless Terrier, as they dubbed the breed, is quite unique and distinctive. While all other hairless breeds suffer from incomplete and faulty dentition, their little dogs have a full set of healthy teeth. Absolutely no skin problems have occurred in the American Hairless. Many other hairless breeds possess a tuft of hair on the skull, the feet or the tail, but the Scotts' little terriers carry only a few stray and crinkly hairs on their eyebrows and whiskers.

This unusual story began in 1972, when friends gave the Scotts a little Rat Terrier puppy. Born in a normal litter of Rat Terriers, this tiny baby was completely hairless. The Scotts dubbed her Josephine, and she quickly captured the hearts of the two adults and their sons, Jeff and John. The Scotts soon discovered that Jo, as she was nicknamed, was an ideal house dog. She was always very clean and never had fleas, a distinct advantage in the heat and humidity of Louisiana life. There were no telltale hairs to be left on furniture, and the Scotts never had to brush dog hairs from their clothes. So fully did she captivate the household, that this bright little dog developed an amazing vocabulary of words. Ice cream became one of her favorite foods, and when the word was mentioned, Jo would lick her lips in anticipation. When Jo accompanied one of the Scotts on their frequent trips into town, she would bark when the ice cream stand came into sight.

The Scotts enjoy traveling, and Jo became a seasoned rider. The little dog was a familiar sight in the Scotts' motor home, where she would perch near the window to keep an eye on everything. So fond was the little dog of traveling, that at the very mention of the word "go," she would spring into action. With joyous barks, she would leap off the ground and run, often in circles, to the door. So convincing was her performance, that Jo was seldom left at home. No wonder she was fond of traveling, for wherever the unusual Josephine went, she attracted much attention. Few people had ever seen a hairless dog, and Jo was, after all, unique. Only the most hardened soul could resist petting her smooth, silky skin, and Jo loved it all.

As Jo matured, the Scotts became intrigued with the idea of breeding her and producing more hairless pups. After all, they were ideal house dogs, and the Scotts couldn't imagine owning another breed after Josephine. While they had owned dogs in the past, they had no experience with breeding and little knowledge of genetics. They began to discuss their dream with anyone and everyone, including university scientists. The reply was always the same. You will be wasting your time. It's impossible, they were told time and time again. Experts tried to convince the Scotts that Josephine was just a "freak of nature," and would never reproduce the hairless trait. It was difficult, though, for the Scotts to accept these negative reports, and what did they have to lose? They had already decided that they would breed Josephine.

When Josephine was one year old, she was bred to a Rat Terrier. Three little females were born, followed by a male. To the Scotts delight, one was hairless. They named their new female puppy Gypsy, and even Josephine seemed to realize that this baby

Trout Creek's Dusty Hill, owned by Willie and Edwin Scott, Trout, Louisiana. (Dick Scott photo)

was different. She handled her gently and tenderly, and watched over her with special care. The Scotts were ecstatic, for they now believed that it would be possible for them to create a wholly new and distinct breed.

The next few years were replete with disappointments. Although bred several times, Jo produced only coated pups. The Scotts placed these in good homes and continued to try. They bred Josephine once more, but vowed that this would be her last litter. At nine years of age, she was still in good health, and the Scotts wanted to keep it that way. Josephine was too special to take chances with. However, on December 31, 1981, Josephine presented the Scotts with her last litter. Two coated females, Petunia and Queenie, and a hairless female, Jemima, were born. The Scotts held their breath. As in the past, Jo produced a male, and the Scotts saw that he was hairless. They named him Snoopy. All were hardy, happy and healthy.

When this final litter from Josephine turned one year of age, the Scotts embarked on a full scale breeding program. Snoopy was bred to all of his sisters. Jemima whelped a litter of all hairless pups and, most encouraging to the Scotts, both Petunia and Queenie's litters contained hairless and coated puppies. They were on their way. The Scotts kept all of the puppies, and their house quickly became crowded. They built a kennel adjoining the house and christened it Trout Creek Kennels.

The Scotts have kept meticulous records to document all their breeding efforts. They retained all the puppies from their breedings, and over 80 dogs now make their home at Trout Creek Kennels. Each new litter is still anxiously anticipated. The Scotts' successful breeding program has even attracted attention from the scientific community. D.P. Sponenberg, affiliated with the Department of Pathobiology at the Virginia-Maryland Regional School of Veterinary Medicine, wrote a paper detailing the Scotts' accomplishments. He concluded that, in this new breed, the hairless trait was due to a recessive gene.

American Hairless Terriers are born with a little hair, but the Scotts say that it is noticeably different from coated Rat Terrier pups. The sparse hair is very short and fuzzy. Soon after birth they start to shed, beginning with any hair on the head. The rest of the hair falls out, and by the time the American Hairless is six weeks old he will be completely naked. These little dogs often have a mottled or splotched pattern on their pink skins. Large black spots are apparent at birth, but additional small spots may appear as the dog matures. Brown spots are often added as the dog ages.

The American Hairless is a small, well balanced and muscular dog. He has a sleek and elegant look, and weighs from 7 to 10 pounds. The breed always has upstanding ears. Tail length may vary greatly. Anything from a naturally bobbed tail to a full length appendage is permissible. Every puppy is very much an individual. The skin of the American Hairless is smooth and soft. Some precautions must be taken, however, for the skin is sensitive to the sun and has a tendency to burn.

The Scotts are a good example to all dog lovers. Their perseverance and persistance, even in the face of seemingly insurmountable odds, is a testament to their love for Josephine and their dream. Too often we tend to rely on the experts and assume they know everything. One stubborn couple, following a vision which everyone deemed impossible, taught us all something. The odds against the Scotts were incredible. Even the experts have had to shake their heads in wonder. Yet, they did do it, and dog lovers the world over owe them a debt of gratitude for their initiative.

Hisar Kafur, better known as Bubba, was the winner of the 1985 National Specialty. Owned by Robert C. Ballard, of Alpine, California.

Chapter 6

The Anatolian Shepherd Dog

For more than 6,000 years, the *Coban Kopegi* has patrolled the Anatolian Plateau of Asia Minor. In this rugged and primitive land, he has served as the shepherd's sole defense against predatory wolves. The Central Anatolian Plateau is a harsh and unforgiving land. From the valleys, at elevations of 3,000 feet above sea level, rise mountain peaks 5,000-10,000 feet in height. Summers are dry and forbidding, with scarce water and temperatures reaching 120 degrees. The winters are equally demanding, with deep snow covering the ground and thermometers plunging to 60 degrees below zero. Here, the *Coban Kopegi*, or "Shepherd's Dog," evolved into the hardy, independent and impressive working dog necessary to perform his duties and withstand the rigors of his homeland. Dog lovers are finding that the opportunity to share their homes with this ancient breed is, indeed, a "Turkish delight."

As in many Moslem countries, in Turkey, dogs are often viewed as "unclean" and accorded little consideration. Anatolians are never housed as pets, and their sole worth lies in their value as livestock guardians. They are functional tools in the Turkish shepherd's struggle for survival. The Anatolian is a livestock guarding breed, not a herder. He lives his life in constant association with his sheep or goat charges, and is accepted as a member of the flock. Often, he will be seen lying quietly or scouting the perimeters of his domain, occasionally standing alone on high ground, searching for any potential threat. When he encounters an interloper, the Anatolian becomes ferocious in appearance, attacks ruthlessly and rarely is he bested. His extraordinary speed and agility enable him to dispatch a full grown wolf in a one-on-one confrontation. Turkish shepherds

sometimes equip their dogs with wrought iron collars, festooned with wicked spikes, to better protect them in the battle. This practice may stem from the days when the Anatolian was a valuable adjutant in times of war. It was said that one of these massive dogs was capable of pulling a man from astride a horse. The iron collar is often seen as a "badge of honor," accorded to dogs who have successfully killed a wolf.

In 1966, Lt. Robert C. Ballard, USN, began a two-year tour of duty in Turkey. As they drove from Naples, Italy, to their new home in Ankara, the Ballards saw the dogs which accompanied the flocks, but they took little notice. Two months later, the Ballards' vehicle, parked on the street, was ransacked. Arrangements were promptly made for a closer parking place and a fenced yard. Friends also suggested that the Ballards purchase a dog. However, purebred dogs are not easily found in Turkey, where there are no kennel clubs. Friends suggested that Bob try the Ankara zoo, which included a dog section. "I went there with the intention of buying the best quality German Shepherd available," Mr. Ballard said. The only German Shepherds were of very poor quality, and the zookeeper gazed quizzically at Mr. Ballard when he asked about pedigree. As he strolled through the dog section, composed of some fifteen or so runs containing various breeds, Mr. Ballard's attention was drawn to several large cream colored dogs. He recognized them as the dogs that he'd seen on his initial drive into the country. The sign on their kennel run read "Coban Kopek." With no interpreter along to help, communication was difficult, but Bob Ballard was determined to learn about this breed.

On New Year's Day, in 1967, Mr. Ballard

Duman of Arkadas, a truly versatile Anatolian owned by Wallace and Maureen Austin, of Alpine, Calif. This winner of the 1984 National Specialty is a working livestock guardian. (Austin photo)

invited one of his Turkish friends to accompany him on a drive in the countryside, to search for a puppy. "After only three months in the country, my Turkish was miserably inadequate. I appealed to my friend's sense of duty and adventure, since I made it clear that I was going with or without him. In his mind, I was eccentric, if not unbalanced, and he decided that he would come along if only to protect me." To Mr. Ballard's delight, he found that the Turkish townspeople and villagers were eager to learn about these outsiders, and they were treated to the finest in old-world hospitality. An hour's drive from Ankara, in the village of Karapinar, they found their puppy. They named the six-week old brown and white pup, Zorba (Turkish for tyrant).

Zorba more than met the Ballard's expectations. Most Turks were familiar with the farm dogs, and knew that they were capable of dealing effectively with intruders. Even as a three-month old puppy, no one dared to trespass on Zorba's property. "Mission accomplished," Mr. Ballard says. But, unlike his semi-wild parents, Zorba was given abundant love and affection. With an improved diet, he grew into a large impressive animal, and the family was won over by his loving disposition and vigilant protectiveness. He quickly became a full-fledged member of the Ballard family.

Mr. Ballard tried to locate other Anatolian owners in the United States, but without success. As the end of his tour of duty approached, he began to scout the countryside for a mate for Zorba. Vehicles are not common in the Turkish countryside, and the roads are not designed for them. On one trip, it was necessary to stop the vehicle, on four separate occasions, to break rocks with a sledge hammer and make the road passable. In fact, motor vehicles of any kind were so uncommon that the dogs viewed them as very large predators and didn't hesitate to confront them. In one village, Mr. Ballard was told that the last motor vehicle to enter the area was in 1945! Little wonder that the dogs were on alert. The Ballards finally located a female pup in a farming settlement west of the village of Turk Taciri. They named the little puppy Peki (Turkish for OK). Zorba and Peki accompanied the family when they returned to the United States.

Zorba and Peki's first litter was born in 1970, after Bob Ballard returned from a stint in Vietnam. Bob and Dorothy Ballard maintained close contact with the owners of puppies from this litter. The couple organized a picnic for the new Anatolian owners, and it was unanimously decided to form a Club. It was a sound decision, for today there are over 1,000 Anatolians listed in the Club's registry.

Anatolian Shepherd Dogs are territorial and intelligent. "They are affectionate and sensitive to those they know and accept," says Bob Ballard. "Love given is returned many times over." Anatolians are much more independent than other breeds. "You're unlikely to see an Anatolian catching a frisbee or fetching a ball. My dogs seem to think that if you threw it away, you must not want it," Mr. Ballard smiles. Maureen Austin, of Alpine, California, fully agrees. "The Anatolian is smart, quick to learn, but a very independent thinker. This is an asset for a livestock guardian, but can be frustrating when you call him to you, and he decides to think for himself and do something else first!" Anatolians become very attached to their families. When they pause and lean heavily against your leg, you will know that you have been fully accepted.

There is no doubt that the Anatolian makes a superb watchdog. From early puppyhood, he should understand clearly that his human master is the "leader of the pack." "A basic rule in my home," says Bob Ballard, "is that any family person outranks any dog. Even the top dog must subordinate to children as well as adults." But, Anatolian owners caution, this breed is highly suspicious of strangers, and new owners must realize this and act responsibly. "Our dogs are all socialized and well behaved in public," says Maureen Austin. "However, when arriving at our home, neither long time friends nor strangers would be foolish enough to get out of their cars. Our dogs recognize that when we appear, we have taken control. They sit back and watch to make sure that everything is all right." Anatolians require a formal introduction to all strangers. "Anatolians are unquestionably good guard dogs, without being hyperactive," says Bob Ballard. "Even the bluffers are too impressive for the average bad guy to challenge." The Ballards' Zorba was a very good natured dog, who tipped the scales at 136 pounds. At ten years of age, he successfully removed the padding from a professional guard dog agitator. "As a breeder, I strive to produce well-balanced dogs, who are courageous without undue aggressiveness. When confronting a trespasser, I want the dog to give some warning and afford the intruder a chance to retreat."

Anatolian Shepherds are best socialized and trained as young puppies. It is wise to remember that it is much easier to handle and discipline a twenty pound puppy than a massive adult. When properly socialized and trained, Anatolians are very adaptable, as Mary Ewald, of Jacksonville, Florida, discovered. "I am a traveling salesman for a veterinary insecticide manufacturer," Mary says. "I'm on the road for five days and four nights, each and every week. During my first year on the job, I was given an eight week old puppy by my long time friend, Louise Emmanuel, of Birinci Anatolians, in Clinton, Maryland. I was single, loved dogs and stayed in some less than safe hotels.

"B.A. Beyaz Kiz Kalesi, better known as Kizzy, became my best buddy and copilot for the next three years. She would sit in the front seat and keep an eye on her surroundings. Not once did she complain when we drove for six straight hours. Every morning we would split an Egg McMuffin at McDonald's. Every day she had at least one hamburger. I swear she would wag her tail when the Golden Arches came in sight," Mary laughs.

"Kizzy grew from a cute twenty-pound puppy to a very impressive 100 plus pound Anatolian, with about 100,000 miles on her odometer. Hotels weren't usually a problem. Kiz housebroke herself at an early age, so most establishments accepted her. She would often be left by herself for eight hours while I worked the area. I would leave the television on to keep her company and hang a 'Do Not Disturb' sign on the door. When I returned, Kizzy would be sitting on 'her' bed, watching the evening news.

"Because her first three years were so unpredicatable, Kiz is very hard to rattle. She takes everything in stride and believes most people like her as much as she likes them. Not once in our travels did she show unwarranted aggression towards anyone. Yet, I felt safe no matter where I stayed.

"Kizzy gave up her jet set life for motherhood when I married. She now stays home and guards her horses, ducks and cats. Most of the time, I think she is content, but I don't leave car doors open around her. She always ends up in the passenger seat, ready to hit the road again!"

It is, however, as a livestock guardian that the Anatolian excels. While this breed makes a fine pet, most breeders like to place their dogs in working homes. Maureen Austin, a member of the Anatolian Shepherd Dog Club of America's Board of Directors,

Hisar Kafur, an impressive and powerful Anatolian, owned by Robert C. Ballard, of Alpine, California.

wholeheartedly agrees. Maureen and her husband, Wallace, raise both Anatolians and Nubian goats, in what they call the Arkadas Project. Arkadas means "good friend" in Turkish. The Austins offer discounts to working homes, and Arkadas bred dogs are currently at work guarding goats, sheep, llamas and chickens. Maureen first became acquainted with the Anatolian when she wrote an article for the local paper. "I had heard about a new breed that had its headquarters in Alpine." Maureen became fascinated, and soon an Anatolian joined the Austin household. In an effort to preserve the breed's working traits, the Austins purchased a herd of goats for their dogs! "Where we live, our biggest predator problems are coyotes, domestic dogs and undocumented farm workers from neighboring Mexico. A goat kid is considered a delicacy by all.

"The Anatolian Shepherd's desire to work is instinctive," Maureen says. "It hasn't been obliterated by generations of pet only breedings. This breed has a very adoptive nature. We have a two year old female which has displayed excellent guarding abilities since we acquired her at twelve weeks. She assists me at all goat kiddings and her help is invaluable. When a doe is giving birth to her second or third kid and doesn't have time to attend to the firstborns, my bitch takes over. She mothers the goat kids, loving and licking them into the world. As soon as the doe has time for these duties, the dog backs off and lets her care for her own babies. It is beautiful to observe.

"Last spring, we had two premature doe kids. They were born three weeks early and their sucking reflexes were undeveloped. I tried to get them to nurse their mother, but to no avail. I placed them on my patio and had to force feed them. Imagine my surprise when I glanced out one day and found my two doelings nursing on my bitch!"

The Austins introduce their young puppies to the goats. They feel that the animals will form a better bond when this is done. Puppies may occasionally try to play with the goats, but such behavior should be stopped immediately. Even as puppies, Anatolians are strong, and their sharp baby teeth can inflict damage. "We take our puppies along with us when we do chores," Maureen says. "This way we are able to correct bad behavior the instant it

B. A. Beyaz Kiz Kalesi, the travelling Anatolian, and Maranda's Mihnet, owned by Randall and Mary Ewald, of Jacksonville, Florida.

happens and praise good behavior as well."

Even when they are not introduced to livestock as puppies, Anatolians often take, immediately, to their animal charges. One of the Austin dogs was first exposed to goats at seven years of age. "One day she uprooted a manzanita bush, to which she was tied, to protect her grazing goats from a pack of domestic dogs." Such devotion is common among working Anatolians. One dog adopted a dead lamb. All day, the dog stood vigil beside the lifeless body, occasionally licking the lamb in an effort to revive it. The Anatolian would not allow anyone to remove the body, and the owners found it necessary to divert the dog's attention, before they were able to bury the little lamb. "We can rest easier," Maureen Austin says, "knowing that our goats have their own 24 hour-a-day guardians in our Anatolian Shepherd Dogs.

"The owner of a 'pet' Anatolian may not appreciate this breed's desire to 'work'," Mrs. Austin says. "The Anatolian Shepherd will bark, particularly at night, at any and all strange noises. To the owner and neighbors, the barking may be considered a nuisance. Puppies seem to be the worst barkers, but that's because they are still sorting out what is a threat and what's acceptable." Mary Ewald agrees. "My dogs tend to sleep during the hot part of the day, but they're very alert at night. Any unusual occurance causes them to bark, be it strange cats, cars, or wild animals."

Anatolians are large, slow maturing dogs. Adult bitches measure 27 inches at the shoulder and weigh over 80 pounds. Males often exceed 100 pounds and stand an impressive 29 inches tall. When at work, they have a decidedly slinky, lion-like grace. Their muscular bodies demonstrate a perfect blend of speed, agility and strength. The Anatolian Shepherd Dog Club of America permits a wide range of colors. While some color variations seem to be more prevalent in various areas of Turkey, the Club contends that they are all one and the same breed. Anatolians can be all tan or all white or any variation of the two. In Turkey, tan dogs with a black nose and ears are referred to as *karabas* (karabash), which translates to "black head", while all white specimens are often characterized as *akbas* (akbash) or "white head."

Color differences have led to confusion in the proper categorization of this Turkish breed. Advocates of the all white dogs believe that they are a separate and distinct breed. Bob Ballard disagrees. He has owned Turkish imports that were all white, as well as those featuring karabash coloration. "I find nothing wrong with the color variations, and contend that they are color specialties of the same breed. I predicted, in the early 1970's, that some breeders would favor one color and would eventually try to isolate certain color schemes. However, to regard the different color patterns as separate breeds is, if not dishonest, at least misleading."

Eventually, the American Kennel Club will have to sort out the dilemma if the Anatolian is to take his rightful place on the A.K.C.'s list of recognized breeds. A recent ruling by the English Kennel Club may have an impact on the decision. After years of hearings, and thousands of pages of testimony, the Kennel Club adopted an all-embracing policy with regard to color and affirmed the breed as the Anatolian Shepherd Dog. A Kennel Club appointed geneticist testified that he considered the introduction of the terms "karabash" and "akbash" unfortunate and regrettable, and he advised that the terms be forever dropped.

Anatolian owners in this country applaud the ruling by the Kennel Club of England. They feel that their all-encompassing policy will serve to further the breed by increasing the available gene pool outside of Turkey. "I have had fawn puppies born to two registered all-white Akbash parents," says Mary Ewald, of Maranda Anatolians.

Regardless of the color dispute, the Anatolian is attracting great attention. Representatives of the breed now make their home in over forty-five states, and Anatolians now reside in England, Canada, Mexico, Japan and other countries. A continuing stream of imports has strengthened the gene pool available to breeders, and there are now more than twenty distinct bloodlines.

Little did Robert Ballard realize, in 1966, that the ransacking of his car would alter his life. A very private person, his only interest was in obtaining a superior watchdog that was not hyperactive and would be suitable as a family pet. Considering that Zorba was the Ballards' first dog, it seems somewhat ironic that Bob would become the initial advocate for this impressive Turkish breed. Dog lovers owe him a debt of gratitude for introducing us to the extraordinary Anatolian Shepherd Dog.

Maranda's Mihnet, owned by Randall and Mary Ewald, Maranda Kennels, Jacksonville, Florida.

The Argentine Dogo is a gentle and loving children's companion. Graciela Hoff's son poses with his best friend.
(Ramos photo)

Chapter 7

The Argentine Dogo

"I love this breed. They are great dogs," says Graciela Hoff, of Rio Grande, Puerto Rico. "The Argentine Dogo makes a wonderful pet who shows an incredible loyalty toward his family. He is multifunctional and can hunt, protect you and be your best friend. They are very smart dogs. In Argentina, they are even used as guide dogs for the blind. They have a unique blend of courage and calmness. These dogs think for themselves, and their innate intelligence allows them to size up a situation and react appropriately," Graciela says.

Mrs. Hoff is a native of Buenos Aires, Argentina. She first saw the breed in her homeland, but was somewhat frightened by their aggressive protectiveness. She moved to Puerto Rico eight years ago, and it was there that she became acquainted with the breed first hand. "I immediately fell in love with the breed, and the more time I spent with them the more I realized how truly special they were," Graciela enthuses. This bubbly, energetic and enthusiastic woman has launched a crusade for the Argentine Dogo. Indeed, puppies born at her Borinquen Kennels, in Rio Grande, Puerto Rico, now make their homes in several of the United States and throughout the Caribbean. She has scored some notable wins with her lovely Dogo bitch, Ayentina de la Jota. "My dream is that the Argentine Dogo will become better known in the United States, and that one day it will be recognized by the American Kennel Club," the dedicated Graciela says. "This is my dream and I believe it will happen. I know it will take hard work for many years, and I may be an old lady by then, but the day will come."

The Argentine Dogo's story goes back to 1917.

Hunting has always been popular in Argentina, but most exciting of all is the thrill of pursuing big game. In the Colonial period, many aristocratic Spanish families settled in the vicinity of Cordova. Dog fighting was a favorite pastime, and huge amounts were wagered on these bouts. The residents tried many experimental crosses to produce the ideal fighting dog. Finally, by crossing the Bull Terrier, the Bulldog and the Mastiff, they perfected a breed that was savage and insensitive to pain. This dog became known as the Fighting Dog of Cordova. Actually, it's a wonder this fighting dog survived, for he was reputed to be so ferocious that stud dogs would even attack bitches in season.

Dr. Antonio Nores Martinez was a respected surgeon and an avid hunter. He admired the courage of the Cordova and tried to use it for big game hunting. However, the breed was just too aggressive. Big game dogs are generally hunted in packs, and the Cordova had little interest in anything but fighting with the other dogs. Further, he lacked the scenting ability that Dr. Martinez so wanted. It soon became apparant that if Dr. Martinez was to have the kind of hunter he desired, he would have to create the dog himself. Aided by his brother, Agustin, he embarked on a breeding adventure. Fortunately, the Doctor had a thorough knowledge of genetics.

The Fighting Dog of Cordova was used as the basis for their new breeding program. They crossed the Cordova with the Great Dane, and succeeded in toning down the aggressiveness and adding height. Next, they added Pointer blood to improve nose and give the ability to air scent. Next, Dr. Martinez bred to the Boxer for self assurance and quietness.

The impressive Argentine Dogo Champion Tilcara.

This important cross also contributed to the newly emerging breed's intelligence, and made the dogs easier to work with and train. In an effort to increase the power of the jaws and lend overall strength, he turned to the Dogue de Bordeaux. A cross to the Irish Wolfhound added speed and enhanced his new breed's hunting instinct. By doubling up on the Cordova's Bulldog and Bull Terrier background, he retained the tenacity, courage and insenstivity to pain so essential in the hunt. In his hunting trips, Dr. Martinez had discovered that a white coat was a distinct advantage in the heavy underbrush, and for this trait he turned to the Great Pyrenees. He had long admired the breed's rugged beauty and ability to thrive in all climates. Finally, he bred to the Spanish Mastiff to ensure the breed a strong and solid exterior. Thus, the Argentine Dogo is a masterful blending of ten different breeds. What Dr. Martinez and his brother succeeded in producing was a dog uniquely fashioned to meet the demands of the Argentine hunt. He named his creation in honor of his beloved homeland.

The Argentine Dogo may be the world's most unique hound. He certainly bears little resemblance to other members of the hound group. In order to appreciate this breed, it is necessary to understand the Argentine style of hunting. By American standards, Argentine big game hunting is primitive. No firearms are used, and the hunter faces the prey with only his dogs and a large knife. Wild boar and big cats still abound in the wilderness areas of Argentina, and these are the animals that the hunter pursues.

The Argentine hunter usually employs a local guide, with his own small tracking dogs. This individual and his dogs are thoroughly familiar with the area and save time in pinpointing the location of game. Dogos are hunted in packs of four or five dogs. Hunts are conducted in complete silence, and no smoking is allowed. Only the pad of the dogs' feet and the cry of an occasional bird pierces the quiet. The hunters and their dogs may have to walk for many miles before they encounter game, and all the participants must be in excellent physical condition.

When game is located, the Dogos spring into action. The excitement mounts and the men's hearts begin to race, as they struggle through the dense, spiny underbrush to reach the dogs. The Argentine Dogo is expected to attack and hold the wild boar or the cougar until the hunter can arrive. This phase of the hunt is called the *monteria*. It is extremely dangerous work, for the wild boar may exceed 400 pounds and is equipped with fearsome tusks that can slash and kill a dog. The cougar is exceptionally cunning and wily, and relies on the strength of his forelegs to battle the dogs. It takes a dog of unusual strength, agility and tenacity to hold one of these animals, and if the Dogo shrinks in fear he will probably be killed or seriously injured. He must show restraint, though. While he will probably injure the game, he cannot kill it. After all, it wouldn't be much of a hunt if the animal was dead before the hunter arrived. While the Dogos keep the animal's tusks or claws away from the humans, the hunter ends the prey's life immediately, with a quick knife thrust to the heart.

The day is still not over, though. A boar's carcass must be butchered and carried to the campsite. While a cougar need only be skinned, his pelt is still a heavy burden. If any Dogo is injured, the hunter will heft him over his shoulders and carry him to camp. This is no easy feat at the end of a long hunt, where the man may have been hiking for six hours. When they arrive at the camp, the Dogos are always cared for first. They will be toweled down, have their wounds dressed and be given food and water. Dogs who seem overcome with exhaustion will be given an injection of glucose.

Big game hunting is much more than a sport in Argentina. It is a tradition. Inappropriate behavior on the part of a hunter's Dogos would mean a loss of his personal prestige. The Argentine hunter has a saying that it is he who takes his dogs to the hunt and not his dogs who bring the hunt to him. Therefore, much time is spent in training the future hunter. All signs of aggression are reprimanded sternly, in puppyhood, for the Dogo must be able to hunt in a pack. Great emphasis is placed on obedience, for the Dogo must respond instantly to commands from his master or any member of the hunting party. It is illegal to hunt on certain areas

The Argentine Dogo is a superb guard dog. (Ramos photo)

29

of the pampas because of possible destruction to grain fields or livestock. Further, Argentina has its share of endangered species, and these are strictly off limits for hunting. The Argentine Dogo's intelligence, fortified by proper training, allows him to adapt to these requirements, as one prominent hunter can attest. He succeeded in capturing and taming a cougar, and it shared his home for many years. Even after a day spent battling big cats, the Dogo's wounds would be licked by his feline friend. Never did the Argentine Dogo show the slightest aggressiveness toward the tame cougar.

Big game hunting is still popular in many parts of the United States, and it will be exciting to see if the Dogo can serve hunters here. Certainly he should be able to compete successfully with the large hounds used in big game hunting. It would be expected that American hunters would adapt this breed to suit American styles. It is not realistic to expect that the American hunter would trade in his rifle for a knife.

"The Argentine Dogo is an excellent pet," says Graciela Hoff. "They are very loving dogs who become an invaluable member of the family. They are quiet dogs around the house. A Dogo is never hyperactive. They don't bark unless something is going on. This breed develops a very special relationship with children. In Argentina, they are often used as babysitters. I have two young sons, and the dogs have become their favorite playmates. Sometimes they even ride my Dogos as if they were horses. The kids can pull their ears and tails, and the dogs don't even react. I think this may be because they are so insensitive to pain. They never hold a grudge, either. The Argentine Dogo is so very patient with the children. Often, my dogs are far more patient than I am," she laughs.

"They make wonderful guard dogs. No one would dare come into my home when one of my Argentine Dogos is in the front yard. They become very aggressive and they look positively ferocious. They will bark, snarl and show their teeth. My dogs give me a great sense of security. I never have to feel afraid, with one of my dogs in the house. And yet, if I allow a stranger into the house, the dogs accept it and realize that it is all right. You couldn't ask for a better protection dog. They are smart and can be easily trained in obedience. They are even suitable for advanced forms of training, like schutzhund."

The Argentine Dogo is an impressive dog that turns heads wherever he goes. With his sleek, satiny white coat, he commands attention. The standard says, "The Argentine Dogo should give the appearance of an elegant, smooth, well balanced dog capable of stepping out of the show ring and

participating in the hunt." He has a massive head and a broad chest. His dark or hazel eyes have a rare intensity and convey intelligence. The breed should have a black nose, although some pink spotting is permissable (the majority of the nose should always be black). His ears are cropped short to prevent injury in the hunt. The skin on his neck is also quite thick and somewhat loose. Again this helps to prevent serious injury when he is battling game. The Dogo is a large dog standing 24 to 27 inches at the shoulder and weighing in at 80 to 100 pounds. His coat is very short, with no hint of an undercoat. This is certainly understandable in a dog that hails from the tropics. His color should be pure white, although the standard allows for small markings on the head. Still, Dogo breeders strive for the pure white coat. As with many white breeds, the Argentine Dogo may suffer from deafness. Conscientious breeders watch for this defect and cull affected puppies. Anyone interested in purchasing a Dogo puppy should ask about a guarantee in the event of deafness.

"I am a native of Argentina," Graciela Hoff says, "but I love the United States, and I want to share this breed from my homeland with Americans. I have devoted myself to introducing this breed to the United States. I am sure that Americans will find this breed as fantastic as I do." Mrs. Hoff is the president of the International Argentine Dogo Club, which has done much to promote the breed in this country. "My dream is to have this breed recognized by the American Kennel Club. One day I want to sit in the stands at Westminster and watch a beautiful and elegant Argentine Dogo gait around the ring."

The lovely Dogo bitch, Ayentina de la Jota, owned by Graciela Hoff, Borinquen Kennels, Rio Grande, Puerto Rico, is close to her International Champion title.

Chapter 8

The Australian Kelpie

"A good working dog is worth as much as a good working man," says Mrs. Jennifer M. Barr, of Hamley Bridge, South Australia. There are those that contend that the Australian Kelpie can take the place of several working men on a sheep ranch. Indeed, stockmen from Australia have perfected a breed that has an unquenchable appetite for work, and a wonderfully loving and stable temperament. This dog from "down under" has captured the attention of stockmen and dog lovers in this country, too. And rightly so, for the Kelpie is a wonderful companion. Whether he makes his home on a range or in the suburbs, the irrepressable Kelpie offers a great deal to those who love dogs.

"Very intelligent, loyal, eager, bubbly, excitable, keen, alert, friendly. These all fit the Kelpie's personality and temperament," says Ms. Gill Rogers, of Carey Gulley, in South Australia. "He is very loyal toward all his family, not just one member. He is friendly toward others and will often use them to his own advantage by instigating a game of fetch. However, he would never consider bestowing too much affection on them. That he reserves for his family and other very special friends. He loves to be near his family and will follow them like a shadow, watching and waiting to be asked to do something. His enthusiasm for life and work is unsurpassable.

"They are very intelligent. One of my dogs, Kimba (the aboriginal word for 'fire'), loves his game of fetch, and he delights in finding new ways to encourage people to join him in his game. When the farrier (one who shoes horses) is visiting, he becomes the center of his attention. Kimba knows he can always convince Bill to throw his ball, merely by placing it on top of the tool Bill will use next. He is rarely wrong in his selection.

"The Kelpie is exceptionally good with children. Kids can dish out some pretty rough treatment, but the Kelpie will endure this with equanimity. Kelpies make good watchdogs. They are very alert and so pick up the slightest noise. They will respond with a lot of noise and bluff, but chances are when the intruder offers a hand the Kelpie will lick it in friendship. Temperament is of the utmost importance, and the Kelpie should never be aggressive toward people or other dogs. They are often required to work with a number of strange dogs, and they should be able to cooperate and work harmoniously with them.

"The Kelpie adapts well to city life, if he is given regular exercise. Above all, he needs mental stimulation, and lots of love and affection. His personality and intelligence, coupled with his need for affection, make him a first class obedience dog. He has untiring enthusiasm and, at times, a telepathic ability that may result in his responding to commands before they can be given.

"Because Kelpies are so athletic and intelligent, they naturally become bored and destructive when too often left to their own devices. When this happens, it can be very hard to contain a Kelpie, even with the highest of fences. However, when given sufficient love and attention, it would be difficult to find a better pet. A Kelpie that does not work will often adopt a substitute form of stimulation. The game of fetch is often the chosen substitute, and he can become quite obsessed with this game." Those interested in sharing their non-working home with an Australian Kelpie should heed

Ms. Rogers' words. A Kelpie that is bored may have a tendency to wander away from home in his search for excitement and challenge.

Despite fanciful tales that attribute the Kelpie's background to the Dingo, or hold that he is half fox and half Collie, this sheepdog had his roots in Scotland. The breed began in the 1860's in Australia. Most authorities believe that the breed carries Border Collie blood. Whatever his pedigree, the Australians succeeded in molding a working dog that was perfectly suited to the rigors of his new homeland.

Mr. Allan and Mr. Elliot, the owners of Geraldra Station (station is the Aussie term for ranch), imported two sheepdogs from Scotland. When their new black and tan dogs, named Brutus and Jenny, arrived at Geraldra, the partners discovered that they had mated aboard ship. From this litter came some notable working dogs, including an impressive male named Caesar.

Nearby, at North Bolero Station, lived an overseer named John Gleeson. Mr. Gleeson had purchased a black and tan Collie from a Scottish cabinet maker in Victoria. He named the little pup Kelpie, after a Scottish water spirit, and trained her for work on sheep. She proved to be an exemplary worker, and Mr. Gleeson bred her to a black male named Moss. Their litter included a number of excellent working dogs.

For Kelpie's second litter, Mr. Gleeson bred her to Caesar. A bitch puppy was given to Mr. King, the manager of Wollongough Station, near Condobolin. He named the little female, Kelpie, in honor of her dam. In about 1874, this second Kelpie was entered at the Forbes Society Sheepdog Trial, in New South Wales. The judge was the very knowledgeable Mr. Clive Mylecharam. Kelpie's performance electrified the crowd. She easily won the trial and gained a widespread reputation for her superb and diligent work. Everyone wanted one of

Australian Champion Happyvalley Ocker, winner of three Royal Show Challenge Certificates. Owned by Ms. Gill Rogers, of Australia. (Harrison photo)

Elfinvale Bruno, backing and forcing sheep in the drafting yard. Owned by Drew Barr.

Elfinvale Bruno, backing sheep in Australia. Owned by Drew Barr, of South Australia.

her pups, and they began to call them "Kelpie's pups." Soon, the offspring of all these foundation dogs gained great popularity among stockmen and, eventually, they would come to be known as, simply, "Kelpies." Although there were other outcrosses, the resultant progeny were always bred back to the original line and, over the years, a breed evolved that was known for its extraordinary enthusiasm and ability.

The Kelpie has endless enthusiasm for his work. The breed has a keen nose, which comes in handy when he is asked to separate his own sheep from those of another owner. He seems to thrive in any climate and will work tirelessly, even when the temperature exceeds 100 degrees. The Kelpie uses what stockmen call "eye" in managing his charges. When the sheep dare to break ranks, the dog crouches and fixes them with an unwavering and very intense stare that seems almost to hypnotize them. Seldom will they challenge his authority.

While the Kelpie may be cast out to bring back the sheep from far reaches on the farm, it is in paddock work that he excels. Photographs of a Kelpie astride the backs of sheep often catch the attention of novices. Sheep have a natural reluctance to go through a gate. Often the leaders of the "mob" (or flock) will stop in their tracks, and the close packed flock cannot move. This is when the Kelpie springs into action. He will leap on their backs and make his way to the front of the pack. When he reaches the reluctant leaders, he squeezes to the ground and prods them forward. This is extremely hazardous work, and the dog must have a large measure of courage, for he could be trampled or injured.

"The Kelpie loves to work and will endure

great hardships when working," says Gill Rogers. "At the local abatoirs (slaughterhouses), the yards are cobbled. This is very rough on a dog's feet, and it is necessary to spell them frequently. One Kelpie I know loved to work so much that he refused to stop for his rest. Instead, he jumped into the next yard and worked for another stockman. By the time he was taken home, the pads on all four of his feet were torn and bleeding, but it hadn't stopped that gutsy little dog from doing what he loved."

A very close bond forms between the shepherd and his Kelpie, for the dog is a real working partner in day to day duties. Australian history is replete with stories of the Kelpie's extraordinary devotion and unflinching courage. A drover and his large red Kelpie were rounding up livestock in the outback. The man's horse threw him, and the fall broke his leg in several places. For three days, he lay on the ground unable to move. His Kelpie kept him warm during the nights. During the day, the Kelpie made his way to a creek and immersed his head in the water. The drover then licked the water from his Kelpie's neck and head. After three days, the drover's horse was found at a farmstead. Neighbors, realizing that something was amiss, organized a search party. They finally found the drover, with his Kelpie at his side.

"The Kelpie will show his strong working abilities at a very young age," Ms. Rogers says. "Puppies of five and six weeks will start to herd sheep and other animals. They will often adopt the crouched position and show 'eye.' It is at this stage that a working dog's training is usually started, by allowing him to familiarize himself with the sheep." The Kelpie is controlled by means of

The beautiful Australian Champion Happyvalley Ocker, owned by Ms. Gill Rogers, of Australia.

verbal commands or hand signals. Experienced stockmen say that the Kelpie can see signals at an extraordinary distance that no other breed can equal. The Kelpie may also be cast out blind to gather stock on the vast sheep ranches. Here, he must rely on his own instincts, his experience and his innate common sense.

The Australian Kelpie is a medium size dog who should always be in hard muscular condition. His backskull is broad and his prick ears are very mobile. His almond-shaped eyes radiate warmth and friendliness, and one always has the impression that the Kelpie is thinking. He has a short to medium length outercoat, with a dense undercoat. This enables him to endure extremes in temperature and protects him from the rain. The coat is longer on the hind legs and around the neck, where it forms a ruff. The Kelpie comes in a wonderful array of colors. He may be solid black, solid red, fawn, chocolate, red and tan, black and tan or a smokey blue. Male Kelpies stand 18-20 inches tall, and bitches measure 17-19 inches. Movement is of paramount importance, for the Kelpie must be able to endure an entire day on the trail, and he must

have the agility to be able to turn suddenly, even at high speeds. The Australian breed standard says, "To produce the almost limitless stamina demanded of a working sheepdog in the wide open spaces, the Kelpie must be perfectly sound, both in construction and movement."

The Kelpie is a hardy dog, and health problems are a rarity. Hip dysplasia, until recently, was virtually unheard of in the breed, but there have been cases reported in the last few years. Those seeking breeding or working stock, should question breeders about the prevalence of this trait in their lines.

For those seeking a good working dog and an outstanding companion, you need look no further than the Australian Kelpie. The other breeds imported to this country from Australia have had great success. They have found a host of loyal and dedicated enthusiasts. who are impressed with their abilities and superb temperaments. Indeed, the Aussies seem to have a talent for providing us with versatile breeds that are stable and loving. Visit the home of a Kelpie if you have the chance. You are sure to be impressed with this cheerful and loyal friend.

Elfinvale Bruno, backing and forcing sheep in the drenching race. Owned by Drew Barr.

Chapter 9

The Australian Shepherd

The one word that best describes the Australian Shepherd is "versatile." The Aussie, as he is commonly called, has excelled as a devoted companion, a superb obedience dog, a diligent worker, a vigilant home protector and a top-winning show dog. "With proper training and socialization, the Aussie is capable of performing any task," says Patricia Headley, of Long Eddy, New York. Certainly many owners agree, and there are now more than 28,000 Aussies registered with the Australian Shepherd Club of America. With his medium size, his smart good looks, and his wonderful devotion to family, the Aussie is sure to attract more attention.

Despite his name, it is believed that the Aussie did not originate in Australia. Many Australian Shepherd enthusiasts have delved meticulously into the breed's background, and it would be a disservice to them to try to summarize their extensive research in this brief chapter. One thing is known, however. The Aussie has long been the partner of Basque sheepherders, and it was these industrious people who brought the breed to the United States, from Australia, in the latter part of the 1800's. Some evidence exists that other Aussies came to this country at an earlier date. Stockmen in the western U.S. were impressed with the working abilities of the little merle colored dogs. They identified the dogs with the Australian sheep that had been imported to augment the American sheep industry, and began calling these hardy workers Australian Shepherds.

To fully appreciate the breed's importance to the Basque shepherds, it is necessary to understand something of their lifestyle. The Basque homeland straddles the border between France and Spain. The Basque region is small, occupying only 100 miles in any direction. The small farms of the area have been in existence for many generations. Elonzo LaBorde still has vivid memories of his homeland, although he has been in this country for some seventy years. The Florida resident, now in his late eighties, sat beside the swimming pool in his modern home, recalling his Basque past. "We lived on a small farm," he said. "There was my parents and my eight brothers and sisters. It was a hard life, but it was all we knew. I can remember sharing a bed with four of my brothers. It seems so long ago, now," he said, glancing around at his spacious home and yard. "We always had sheep. In April or May, the men would take them to the mountain grazing areas, the *olhak*, that's what it was called. The women stayed in the village to work and to tend the gardens. We produced everything we ate. My mother was a fantastic cook, even when she had little to work with, and I still miss Basque cooking.

"It was a difficult life that held little promise for many of us youngsters," Mr. LaBorde continued. "When a father died, the family's entire holdings would be inherited by only one of his children, generally the oldest son. Perhaps this is why so many holdings have remained in family hands for centuries, rather than being split up. For me, in a family with many boys, there seemed little hope for the future. My only choices were to leave or go into the priesthood, and I just couldn't see myself in that kind of life. There were a few Basques who had emigrated to other countries, some to the United States. A few returned home when they had 'made

1500 reasons why movement really counts. Champion Just Jake of Las Rocosa CD, STD-CS, OTD-D, owned by Jeanne Joy Hartnagle, of Boulder, Colorado.

Champion Las Rocosa Little Wolf STD-CD, owned by Jeanne Joy Hartnagle, deemonstrates low heeling on a steer.

good'. My brothers and I talked about leaving and striking it rich, and then coming back home."

Although elderly now, Elonzo has the look of a robust man who has lived his life in the sun. His face is wrinkled, tanned and hardened from the harsh elements. "I already had an uncle in Nevada and, when I was seventeen, I joined him in America. I had great dreams, but I was unprepared for the life here. It was so different than my homeland. All you could see, for mile after mile, was scrubby sagebrush and rocks. I couldn't imagine that it was possible to raise sheep on such land. The first thing my uncle did, before I went out on the range, was to give me a blue and white sheepdog. Without him, I could never have made it. He was a terrific worker, and I would have gone crazy if it weren't for his companionship. Some men did go crazy from the sheer loneliness. We would say that they had been 'sagebrushed.' I've never admitted this before, but there were many nights when I cried myself to sleep. If there was any way that I could have gone home, I would have.

"It was hard work, but it was possible to make money in those days," Mr. LaBorde said. Indeed, many Basques developed a keen pride in their work, and they were successful. They were competitive and industrious, and they believed that, with hard work,they could accomplish anything. They gained a reputation as extraordinary sheepmen, and their lambs often achieved the highest weights. Every penny was scrupulously saved, for they were eager for the opportunity to own their own land. Their working dogs were of the highest calibre, too, and this did not escape the notice of other ranchers. However, such success was not always appreciated by the Americans of the west. "There was a great deal of prejudice," Elonzo recalled. "We were called 'Bascos' and a whole lot worse," he smiles. "There were always problems with the cattlemen who resented us, and I don't think anybody was too fond of us. We stayed close to our own when we weren't alone on the range. I always felt sort of alone because I didn't love the sheep raising life as much as the others did."

The Basques did have notable success and they were recognized, however grudgingly, for their prowess. "We out- Americanized the Americans," Elonzo said. "We outworked many of them, and we didn't blame bad luck for our failures. It was frustrating. You would lose some of your stock to coyotes, but we just worked harder." One poem, published in the early 1900's, captured the spirit of the Basque initiative.

Champion Gefion's All That Glitters CDX, STD-S clearing the high jump. Owned by Gefion Kennels, Moretown, Vermont.

> *Five years the Basque will follow the sheep,*
> *And every cent he gets he'll keep.*
> *Except what little goes for clothes.*
> *And then the first thing someone knows*
> *He's jumped his job and bought a band*
> *And taken up some vacant land;*
> *And then the fellows who still prate,*
> *About hard luck and unkind fate,*
> *And wail because they have no pull,*
> *May help the "Basquo" clip his wool.*

"I left Nevada many, many years ago," Mr. LaBorde said. "A man came through and he was going to Florida. He told me that there was a lot of work for a man that was hard working and good with his hands. I left with him and got a job in construction here. I really never regretted leaving. My sister comes to visit sometimes, but she doesn't like it. She calls me an *errikuak*, a town person, and thinks that I am miserable.

"I have very fond memories of our dogs," Elonzo says. "I can't imagine why they would call them Australian Shepherds, though. They should be named Basque Shepherds. We've known these dogs for a long time. You know, I never thought I would see another one after I left the West. Several

Hawk Hill Chilla Cella, a red merle, owned by Alice Ward, of Felton, Pennsylvania.

years ago, I was at a gas station and this woman pulled up, with three dogs in her car. I couldn't believe my eyes. I spent over an hour there, at the pumps, talking to her, and she came to visit me a week later and we talked some more. A couple of months after that, she brought a little puppy with a big bow on his neck. She moved away and I haven't been able to find her. I owe her much. Just looking at my dog makes me feel young again." Somehow, it seems appropriate that this man, so fiercely proud of his Basque heritage, should once again own one of these dogs.

"The Australian Shepherd is a sensitive dog that becomes a very devoted friend," says Alice Ward, of Felton, Pennsylvannia. "This breed thrives on attention and praise. They form a very close bond with their owners. I describe it as a 'sixth sense.' The Aussie will often be able to determine what you want by the tone of your voice, your mannerisms or even the look on your face. Properly raised, Aussies are extremely happy and outgoing dogs. They are generally somewhat reserved with strangers, but this does not mean that they are timid." Indeed, breeders strongly urge puppy buyers to socialize their Aussies. While the breed is somewhat stand-offish with strangers, Aussies who are not introduced to other people, or exposed to a variety of stimuli, can become quite shy. "They need lots of love," Mrs. Ward says, "and if they get it the results are wonderful."

Obedience classes may be one of the best ways to socialize a youngster. The Aussie clearly excels at this task, and many dogs have garnered High in Trial awards. Some breeders say that Aussies have a distinctive "willing" attitude that is characterized by their extreme desire to please. Their natural agility makes them ideal jumpers in the advanced obedience exercises. In the obedience ring, their eyes never seem to leave their owner, and dog and man function as a team. If training is kept a fun exercise, the Aussie demonstrates an exuberant, happy attitude that catches the eye of spectators and judges alike. "They are highly trainable," says Mrs. Ward, "and they love the attention that goes with training."

The Aussie makes a very capable watchdog. He has a naturally protective nature, and will not allow a stranger into his yard without the owner's approval. "They generally make good watchdogs because of their close bond with their family," Alice Ward says. Patricia Headley agrees. "Aussies will naturally protect, but are not aggressive. However, don't expect an Aussie to stand idly by if you or your loved ones are being attacked! They will naturally protect their own. I find this a desirable quality in the breed. Remember, proper socialization, at a young age, prevents unwanted accidental aggression."

With their easy going nature, Aussies can get along well with other dogs. This breed also seems to have a special affinity toward children. "They tend to remain perpetual puppies, and they love lots and lots of play. Because of this quality, they make excellent children's dogs. They love romps, fetching balls, and they are excellent frisbee dogs," Patricia Headley says.

Temperaments among Aussies vary somewhat, and the prospective purchaser should take the time to discuss personality with the breeder. Some Aussies are much more docile and quiet than others, and may be more appropriate for the suburban home. Other Australian Shepherd breeders select for what are called "hot blooded" individuals. These dogs are much more active and alert, and seem always on the go. This quality is especially appealing in a working environment, or for very active families, but may be too much for a home with retired people.

There is no denying the fact that the Australian Shepherd is a very attractive breed. At 18 to 23 inches, the Aussie is a medium size dog, with a totally balanced appearance that is evident whether standing or in motion. He should always appear to have the strength and stamina necessary for a long day on the open range, where he may be following the livestock for many miles. His true manner of moving has attracted the attention of many judges in rare breed shows. Some Aussies are born with a natural bobtail, and the standard allows this to be up to four inches in length. Aussies who do not exhibit this natural feature, are docked soon after birth. The Aussie's medium length coat adequately protects him from the elements. It requires minimal care, with once a week brushing usually sufficient. Like most double-coated breeds, they do periodically shed their downy undercoats. If the owner will take comb in hand and strip out the remaining undercoat, shedding will be minimized and the house will stay clean and neat.

New owners are often captivated by the wide array of Aussie colors. No matter the hue, coat color should be clear and rich. The attractive and unusual coat patterns are sometimes trimmed in white. The merle colorations in this breed are particularly attractive and eye-catching. Color patterns may be beautifully blended or startlingly contrasted, and this adds to the fun of breeding

Australian Shepherds. The merle colors may be lightly flecked, mottled, marbled or splotched. All add to the unique individuality of the breed and make every Aussie distinctive. The blue merle, one of the most popular colorations, can range from an almost blue-black to a steel grey, or from a powder blue to a silver blue. The red Aussie can range from a deep liver to a coppery rust color, and the red merle may also exhibit these variations. Pigmentation of the nose, lips, and eye rims corresponds to coat color, with red and red merles having liver pigmentation, while blue merles feature black coloration. Eye color is also influenced by coat color and pigmentation, and the standard allows for any combination of blue, brown and/or amber. Some Aussies will have one blue eye and one brown, giving them a rather startling appearance to those unfamiliar with the breed. It should be noted that the gene which controls merling, in the Aussie, also carries a blind/deaf factor. This serious condition

The impressive and beautiful Champion Las Rocosa Little Wolf STD-CD, owned by Jeanne Joy Hartnagle, of Boulder, Colorado.

Gefion's On Your Toes, owned by Gefion Kennels, of Moretown, Vermont. (Gray photo)

only springs from merle to merle breedings, and all responsible Aussie breeders are well aware of the condition. Knowledgeable breeders can detect this defect by its accompanying color pattern at birth and they euthanize affected puppies.

As a herding dog, the Australian Shepherd is hard to beat. The successful working dog can take the place of several men in a livestock operation. Anyone who has tried to round up a scattered herd of cattle, or load a flock of skittish sheep, without the help of a good herding dog, can tell you that it's an all day task.

"I've owned several breeds of herding dogs, but the Aussie is tops," says Vicky Ganns. "I don't show my dogs and I don't even breed, so I'm certainly no expert on the breed," the Alabama resident says, "but I can tell you something about these dogs, as workers, and that's where they shine. An Aussie can do anything on a farm. Mine has even brought me eggs and never was one broken. Some people have dogs that specialize on one type of stock, but we have several different kinds of stock here, and our Aussies can handle them all. It's fascinating to watch them change their working style, depending on the stock they're handling. They have a very special power that oldtimers call 'presence, which allows them to handle their charges. Koala, here, is very smart and canny. He will expend only as much energy as the job requires. While he's always eager to work, he never dashes about madly. I think he has common sense. I swear, by using his common sense, he could last all day long. This is invaluable when we are trying to load

the stock. We never have to worry that he's going to run weight off the animals before they get to the auction barn. Since we get paid by weight, that's real important."

It takes a great deal of courage for a medium sized dog to face a recalcitrant 2,000 pound bull, but the Aussie is up to the task. Some Aussies work silently, while others find that barking is quite effective. In working with cattle, the Aussie must, sometimes, back up his bark with a bite, commonly called the "grip." He may rake the back of the hock with his teeth, or use a well placed nip to insure that the animals keep moving. If he is working with a herd of cows who have calves at their sides, or a flock of sheep with little lambs, he will generally refrain from barking and upsetting the mothers. Through experience, the Aussie will have learned that such actions make the mothers nervous, and they are much more likely to turn on the dog and challenge him. With cattle, the Aussie may be much more bold and hard, while he may take a more gentle, although assertive, stance with sheep. When herding ducks, the Aussie must remain calm during the excitement of the flapping wings. He must be agile and constantly alert, and dog and owner must work as a team. While the working Aussie is wonderfully responsive to his master's commands, he also has the ability to think for himself and act accordingly.

"Aussie's have a very strong herding instinct. I've only seen one dog that didn't turn on to the stock. I think that, because of this natural instinct, even the first time farmer can get a good working dog. He may not know anything about training a stock dog, but the Australian Shepherd is so smart that he will pick up on what the owner wants. If you have patience and take the Aussie out with you when you go about your chores on the farm, the dog will figure out what you want. I think it's a good idea to teach them some basic commands, but I've seen people who've never owned a dog come up with some acceptable workers. It helps a lot if you get a dog from working bloodlines," Mrs. Ganns says.

Australian Shepherd owners have an amazing enthusiasm for their breed. Who can blame them? They have a terrifically versatile breed, which responds so well to his owner's every wish that he can be trained for anything. What's more, he excels at every task. "There's nothing like an Aussie," one owner says. "Once you've shared your life with one of these dogs and let them into your heart, you'll never own another breed." Other Aussie owners would certainly agree.

Chapter 10

The Beauceron

The Beauceron is a newcomer to this country. He has attracted much attention for his appearance, which, to the untrained eye, is reminiscent of a cross between a Doberman Pinscher and a German Shepherd. Those who are familiar with the breed say that the Beauceron has a kind heart, and the uncanny ability to sense his owners moods and desires. A loyal and unselfish breed, the Beauceron makes an ideal pet.

The Beauceron is a distinctly French breed, said to have been developed solely in that country, with no crosses to foreign breeds. Indeed, it is a very old working dog. Sheepherding breeds have long been known in France and are depicted in tapestries from the eighth century. Writings from the twelfth, fourteenth and sixteenth centuries mention herding dogs. It is thought that a passage in a manuscript, written in 1587, is the first specific mention of a dog of the Beauceron's description.

In France, the breed is called *Berger de la Beauce* (Shepherd of the Beauce). La Beauce is a plains region surrounding Paris, and is generally acknowledged as the cradle of the breed. The Beauceron shares a common heritage with his cousin the *Berger de la Brie*, recognized in this country as the Briard. While the two breeds appear quite different in appearance, both serve the same working functions. In the early days, the French farmer was not at all concerned with type. He cared only about practical working qualities, and the shepherd dogs were of an extremely diverse type. All fell under the general category of *chien de la plaine* or "dog of the plain." They could be found in all coat colors and coat lengths. While hunting dogs

were highly esteemed in those days, the French accorded little consideration to these rough and rugged working dogs. In those very early years, the Beauceron and the Briard served more as livestock guardians, defending the animals from predators, such as wolves and human poachers. With the advent of the French Revolution, their function changed. The land was no longer strictly in the hands of the nobility, but was divided among the people, resulting in more farmers on smaller holdings. The Beauceron and the Briard became herding dogs whose work was essential, for those early French farms were not fenced. Undoubtedly, they also doubled as watchdogs for their masters' homes.

In 1809, a priest, Abbé Rozier, wrote an article on these French herding dogs. It was he who first described the differences and used the terms *Berger de la Brie* and *Berger de la Beauce*. He described the Beauce as a shorthaired, mastiff-like dog, and said that the Brie was a longhaired dog of different type. According to French writings, during the late years of the 19th century, there was a meeting of cattle and sheep breeders. It was there that the decision was made to name the longhaired dogs after the area of Brie and the shorthaired types after the Beauce region. Both breeds still varied greatly in type. In 1900. the Beauceron was first exhibited at a show. The first Beauceron champion, a bitch named Bergere, bears little resemblance to the breed known today. She was said to have been semi-longhaired. Indeed, we are told that the coats were often longer than today's standard allows, the muzzles were thinner and the size was significantly smaller. The tan markings on the feet may also have extended higher up on the leg, and this may have given rise to the early breed nickname of "Red Stockings."

In the 1900's, more attention has been paid to Beauceron breeding. A club, The Friends of the Beauceron, was established in 1911. In 1927, the first book devoted exclusively to the Beauceron, was written by Monsieur A. Siraudin. This book is still held in such esteem that it is considered, by many, to be the "Beauceron Bible." During both World Wars, Beaucerons earned respect as military dogs. They were applauded for their strength, and machine gun ammunition belts were often wrapped around their sturdy bodies, to be carried to gun emplacements. With their intelligence, they were often used as messenger and sentry dogs. Incredible stories have been told about their powers of observation and perception.

The Beauceron is still best known in his native France. In 1984, approximately 3,200 Beaucerons were born. Although still used for herding, the breed is most often used in police work, and serves in the canine units of both the French army and police. The breed has spread to other European countries, although it has not yet achieved the popularity enjoyed in France. There is growing interest in the Beauceron in Belgium, where approximately 20 litters are registered annually. Holland is home to about 350 Beaucerons, and there are about 30 more in Germany. The Beauceron is a newcomer to the United States, where many Americans caught their first glimpse of the breed in the James Bond film, "Moonraker."

The Beauceron is a large, powerful dog that bears some resemblance to the Doberman Pinscher. Males stand 25-27 1/2 inches at the shoulder, while females measure 24-26 3/4 inches. They have broad, deep chests and straight backs, and should always be robust and well muscled. The coat is short and dense, and along the back bone should measure about 1-1 1/2 inches in length. Beaucerons have longer feathering on their tails and the backs of their thighs. The Beauceron comes in two color patterns: the common black and tan, and the rare harlequin. While the nose is always black, eye color corresponds to coat color. A small spot of white is permitted on the chest, but even this is considered a fault. The standard allows for both cropped and uncropped ears, although there is a decided preference for clipped ears. One of the essential breed characteristics, and a topic of endless debate in Beauceron circles, is the standard's call for rear double dewclaws. The standard states, "Dogs otherwise well qualified as to type but lacking

Prepwash Decidedly, a three month old Australian Shepherd puppy, relaxes with the Beauceron, Altesse de la Beauté Rustique. Both are owned by Truus Manders, of Holland.

A quartet of outstanding Beaucerons, from left to right, Champion Quiche de la Beauté Rustique, Champion Taquine de la Beauté Rustique, Champion Myra de la Sylvade, Champion Quito de la Beauté Rustique. All are owned by Mrs. Truus Manders, of Holland.

double dewclaws can take only a mention." There is a curious, somewhat superstitious, tradition attached to the presence of double dewclaws. Old time ranchers believed that you could select a good working pup from a litter by picking the one with these double appendages. Indeed, this contention may have led to the establishment of this trait in the first place. Some old timers believe that the double dewclaws allow the Beauceron to more easily climb onto the backs of the sheep. Others point out that there is little muscular control in the dewclaws, and that other breeds, such as the Australian Kelpie, are very adept without benefit of double dewclaws. There was, in the past, a heated debate on this subject, when the Federacion Cynologique Internationale proposed eliminating this requirement. The parent club, in France, firmly held that without double dewclaws the dog could not be considered a Beauceron.

The lovely harlequin Beauceron almost became extinct, but French breeders, most notably, Mme. L. Delaire, of *Kennel de la Horde Noire,* have dedicated themselves to reviving the harlequin. The coat color most closely resembles that of a dappled Dachshund or a merle Great Dane. The harlequin is required to have the rich tan or red markings found on the black and tan Beauceron, and these are said to be difficult to achieve. It is generally conceded that it is much more difficult to breed a superior harlequin. To help the situation, the French Kennel Club decided to allow harlequins to compete as a separate variety. However, in all other countries black and tans and harlequins are shown together.

"The intelligence, the obedience, and the activity of the Beauce are proverbial," wrote Boulet d'Elbouef. "He is also a faithful guard and a brave defender, and his herding instinct seems to be inborn, transmitted from his ancestors through the centuries." Enthusiastic Beauceron owners would certainly agree. Indeed, the Beauceron makes a wonderful family companion. The breed is intelligent and loyal, and enjoys pleasing his master. He takes his guarding duties seriously and is not prone to wandering away from home. The breed is naturally somewhat wary of strangers, and it is important to thoroughly socialize your new Beauceron puppy.

The Beauceron is an eager and willing worker, but he performs best when he is trained by his owner. While professional trainers can achieve adequate results, it is with the guidance and encouragement of his loving owner that the

Champion Myra de la Sylvade, obedience champion of all breeds, in 1980 and 1981. Owned by Mrs Truus Manders, of Holland.

Beauceron becomes a superior working dog. Be prepared to vary your training procedure and keep the work fun. The Beauceron is eager to learn, but does not respond well to harsh discipline. Praise or a disapproving word are more effective. This breed has an excellent memory and training is not likely to be forgotten. The Beauceron is very independent in temperament and does not have a "slave's soul." He is more likely to view himself as your partner and your friend, than merely as a dog to be ordered around.

Mrs. Truus Manders, of Holland, believes in keeping Beauceron training fun. "A well trained dog should have a lot of fun in his work," Mrs. Manders says. She has owned Beaucerons for the last thirteen years and was instrumental in the formation of the Netherlands Beauceron Club. Recently an Australian Shepherd joined the Manders household. "I take my dogs everywhere," Truus says, "even to the city and on holiday. They are very used to this. In Holland, many Beaucerons live in cities." Mrs. Manders is concerned by some of the advertisements she has seen for the breed, in American dog magazines. "I saw an advertisement for aggressive Beauceron. These people should hang their heads in shame. A good Beauceron is not aggressive. He is fearless, but very sociable with people and dogs. In Holland, we have a nature test. Before any Beauceron is allowed to be bred he must pass this

test. Aggressive or timid dogs are never bred." Mrs. Manders advises that, if at all possible, you should see the parents of a puppy before you make your purchase. Steer clear of any puppies whose parents are shy or aggressive.

The Beauceron, with his sharp looks and wonderful working abilities, is sure to attract more attention in this country. While this is not the breed for everyone, those who have the time to devote to this French native will be amply rewarded with a wonderful and loyal companion. With the close companionship of those he loves, the Beauceron becomes a devoted and loyal friend. He wants only to be by your side. We will certainly be seeing more of this outstanding dog at upcoming rare breed events.

Champion Quiche de la Beauté Rustique was Holland's obedience champion in 1982, 1983 and 1984. Owned by Mrs. Truus Manders, of Holland.

Chapter 11

The Boykin Spaniel

A very long time ago, there was a man with a small spaniel that was an excellent retriever. The man trained his little dog to fetch a silver dollar, and that dog would pursue the coin wherever it was thrown. No matter how dense the brush, how high the cornfield or thick the pasture grass, that little fellow would find and retrieve the coin. Well, one day the man was showing off for a stranger, and he flung that coin as far as he could into the woods. A young boy happened to be walking through the woods, and he picked up the shiny silver dollar and tucked it into his pocket. But, that didn't deter the little dog. In his zeal to obey his master, he brought the coin home, boy and all. And that, my friends, is how the Boykin Spaniel got his name.

Not really. While some folks delight in telling this tall tale, the Boykin is a product of South Carolina and the hunting conditions that prevailed there. He is a cocky, enthusiastic and energetic all-rounder, who has won the admiration of hunting enthusiasts who've had the opportunity to observe him at work. He is a combination spaniel and retriever. His small size makes him ideal for duck hunting in lightweight, easily transported boats. Indeed, he has been described as "the dog that doesn't rock the boat." The dove is a favorite game bird in the South, and the Boykin is commonly acknowledged as the premier dove dog by those fortunate enough to shoot over him. In addition, his winning personality and love of family have made him a welcome addition to households all over this country. The Boykin Spaniel was recently accepted for registration by the United Kennel Club, and we will, undoubtedly, be hearing more from this perky little dog.

At 14 to 18 inches tall, the Boykin is leggier and rangier than the Cocker Spaniel. Dog fanciers will note the resemblance to the American Water Spaniel, which is most apparent in the breed's rich, solid liver coat. The Boykin, however, lacks the mass of curls that American Water Spaniels display. His coat can be either moderately curly or flat and is of medium length. His 25 to 40 pounds makes him an ideal size for a housedog. He has floppy spaniel ears, an alert and intelligent expression, and dark yellow or brown eyes.

The very beginning of Boykin Spaniel history was hardly auspicious. On a Sunday morning, sometime between 1905 and 1910, a man in Spartenburg, South Carolina, took a leisurely walk to church. Alec White noticed that a small puppy was trailing him. He reached down to pet and talk to the pup, and then resumed walking. After church services had concluded, he noticed that the pup was waiting for him. The little male, named "Dumpy," joined the White household. Alec White soon discovered that the little fellow was a particularly adept retriever. When Dumpy accompanied the avid duck hunter on his frequent forays, the dog's performance often surpassed the larger retrievers. Mr. White sent Dumpy to his friend and hunting partner, Whit Boykin.

For generations, the Boykin family had hunted the land near the Wateree River Swamp. Small boats were the norm on the waters of the Wateree and, on many occasions, big retrievers capsized the small craft. The lands around the Wateree were a nesting area for the wild turkey, and these large birds were abundant. Wild turkeys were hunted, in those days, by two distinct methods. When there was a large hunting party, the birds were "driven," much in the way that early hunters conducted "deer drives." A line

Two generations of Boykin Spaniels, Greywood Woody and Greywood Poppy. Both are owned by Tom Lord, Greywood Kennels, Columbia, South Carolina. (Lee West photo)

of men would spread out and begin walking. The dogs, working the ground just ahead of the men, would become excited when they scented the birds. Quickly, the dogs flushed the birds and barked as they took to wing. The hunters were ready, and many birds were shot. Meanwhile, the dogs busied themselves trailing crippled birds. There were also solitary hunts, engaged in by one man and one dog. In such circumstances, the dog located and flushed a flock, and the hunter constructed a blind close by. The man and dog then settled into the blind and began calling in the wild turkeys, generally using a hand-carved turkey call. It is said that the decision was made to dock the dogs' tails because they rustled the leaves too much when secreted in a turkey blind.

Whit Boykin and his hunting companions were impressed with Dumpy's performance, not only on turkey, but also on ducks. For years they had wanted a breed convenient enough to fit in a small boat and, yet, rugged enough to suit their hunting requirements. They let it be known that they were searching for a mate for Dumpy, and they acquired a small reddish

brown part-Spaniel bitch that they named Singo. We are indebted to James Sweet for researching and accumulating records on early Boykin breeding. While his notes are far from complete, we do at least have a rudimentary picture of the dogs that contributed to the Boykin Spaniel of today. One Boykin family member owned a Springer Spaniel, and it was this dog that he bred to his Boykin. Bolivar Boykin had a registered American Water Spaniel that he used for an outcross in the 1940's. On at least two separate occasions, small Pointers were known to have been mated to Boykins. Cheasapeake Bay Retriever blood was also introduced to improve retrieving ability and provide added bone. The Boykin was, and still is, a hunting dog, and so it can be assumed that the dogs interbred with the early Boykins had already proven their abilities in the field.

Today's Boykin is primarily used to hunt dove and to retrieve ducks. Some owners have also used them on such upland game birds as grouse, quail and pheasant. Those interested in the breed should be apprised that the little Boykin cannot generally handle geese, and may have difficulty in swift moving water. Some owners report that their dogs do not like retrieving in frigid waters. The Boykin has attracted a great deal of attention from dove hunters. They have much more stamina in the hot Southern summer sun than larger dogs. They are easily trained and have abundant common sense. In the field, they are extremely enthusiastic and will dash madly to retrieve downed birds.

The Boykin is an ideal family dog, and The Boykin Spaniel Society strongly encourages those interested in the breed to recognize this. "He thrives on attention from the entire family and is good with children, which makes him an ideal house dog. It has been found that the closer the relationship between a Boykin and his master, the better hunter he is. The blending of the Boykin's intelligence and retrieving ability, together with their characteristic desire to please, and the speed, agility and endurance with which they do so, is probably the combination that makes this breed so unique. Because of these characteristics, if you are looking for a hunting dog to be trained by a professional and kept in a kennel until you are ready to go hunting, find yourself another dog. The Boykin is NOT for you," the Society says. The Society also informs those interested in the breed that the Boykin cannot tolerate the harsh training methods applied to some other hunting breeds.

Lee West, of Wisacky, South Carolina, is enthusiastic about the Boykin. "Boykins have a gentle and tender disposition. They can be trained easily. You have to explain what you want, and then they are most willing. They love affection, and it is part of training." Mr. West actively hunts with his Boykins. "They are natural retrievers for doves and ducks. But, I must admit that I just can't put them in water below 45 degrees. They are great swimmers and take to the water naturally. They are eager to work and to please," Mr. West stresses. "I have had one dog completely trained by four months, and I think that the earlier you start with them, the better it is. The Boykin Spaniel is an easy dog to manage at home and in the field. They are great family dogs and love children."

There were several attempts to form a Boykin club, but it was not until 1977 that the Boykin Spaniel Society was officially established. A Camden, South Carolina, veterinarian, Peter B. McKoy, became alarmed at the increased incidence of indiscriminate breeding. Along with members of the Boykin clan, and other enthusiasts, he succeeded in forming the Society. A breed registry was established in 1979. "We have 4,359 Boykins registered with the Society," says Ellie Hurlburt, the Society's Executive Secretary. Annual retriever trials are well attended, but the aura is more that of a family outing. The Society promotes the responsible breeding of Boykins. There is some incidence of hip dysplasia in the breed, and Boykin Spaniel owners are encouraged to x-ray all breeding stock.

Word of this hardy and happy little dog is spreading, and there are now Boykins in most of the states in this country. Their recognition by the United Kennel Club should do much to further the popularity of this deserving breed. As Lee West says, "Boykins will take only a short time to win your heart."

The impressive Terramara's Achad, a multi-Best of Breed winner, bred and owned by Terry Bagley, Terramara Kennels, Grand Centre, Canada.

Chapter 12

The Canaan Dog

"The Canaan Dog is your 'partner,' your friend. He senses your moods. He communicates with his eyes, his nearness and his voice. You know that he cares for you," says Lorraine Stephens, the Secretary of the Canaan Club of America. "This breed is so very distinctive from any other dog, that it is sometimes difficult to explain the Canaan's unique character to those unfamiliar with the breed." People who have had the opportunity to know the Canaan would agree wholeheartedly with Mrs. Stephens. While the characteristics of many of the newly introduced rare breeds have been molded largely by "survival of the fittest," the Canaan is the only breed that has thrived totally without the influence or intervention of man. His extraordinary intelligence and amazing adaptability allowed him to prosper as a feral animal. But, perhaps most incredible, after over 40 years of domestication and selective breeding, his spirit retains the characteristics that served him so well in the wild and ensured his survival. The Canaan offers purebred dog enthusiasts the opportunity to share their homes with a unique animal, whose soul remains unchanged by man's meddling.

The Canaan has existed in a small area of the Middle East for more than 3,000 years. Rock carvings and drawings from pre- Biblical times attest to the presence of the *Kelef Kanani*. It is even thought that a Canaan, adorned with a golden collar, was tethered to the throne of Queen Jezebel. Indeed, several references in the Bible appear to apply to this native dog of the region.

The Canaan might have remained a wild "pariah" (ownerless) dog, were it not for the work of an extraordinary woman. The story of this dedicated dog lover began in Europe in the 1920's and 1930's. Drs.

Rudolph and Rudolphina Menzel were well known Boxer breeders and cynological authorities. They were dog training pioneers, and the publication of their innovative book on the use of dogs in scent discrimination led them to employment with the German Reichswehr and the Austrian Police. When Hitler came to power, the couple made a hasty escape to Palestine.

It was in her new country that Dr. Menzel was presented with an extraordinary challenge. The newly formed *Haganah* (Israeli Defense Force) saw the need for a dog that could serve in the coming struggle for independence. Rudolphina seemed the perfect candidate to spearhead such a search. Dr. Menzel first endeavored to work with the European breeds with which she was so familiar, but it didn't take long to realize that they couldn't adapt to the rigors of climate in her new homeland. She had, however, observed a race of dogs that, despite the lack of water and available food, thrived in the wild. During her travels, she saw these dogs in and around Bedouin camps and Druse settlements. The Arabs had long been familiar with these wild animals, and often stole male puppies from litters, to be kept as guards and protectors of livestock. These factors led Dr. Menzel to believe that the "Canaan" Dog, as she christened the breed, might well provide the solution to her problem.

Dr. Menzel's redomestication of the Canaan is certainly one of the most interesting stories in the annals of dog literature. Her first success came in 1935, when she captured "Dugma" ("model" or "example" in Hebrew) on the Sebulon Coastal Plain. This striking male evaded capture, despite diligent efforts, for over six months. With the breed's uncanny knack for avoiding danger and sensing the presence of man, Dugma effectively eluded his captors. Playing on Dugma's interest in a female, Dr. Menzel finally lured him into range. Armed with a ready supply of fresh meat, she finally captured Dugma in her yard.

One of Dr. Menzel's most interesting captures concerned a bitch named "Pera" (the Hebrew word for "flourishing"). Pera was first observed on her daily hunting trips and, when followed, it was discovered that she had a litter of puppies secreted in a cave. While she was away on one of her forays, the puppies were hand fed, and the strongest were removed and taken to Dr. Menzel's kennel. Several hours later, Pera appeared with her remaining puppies in tow. Frantically, she began digging a hole under the fence. When the gate was opened, she promptly marched through and happily accepted her new domesticated life.

International, Mexican, World, Champion of the Americas and American Champion Beth Din Sorcerer's Apprentice, owned by Hinda Bergman, of Beth Din Kennels, Raleigh, North Carolina.

The Canaans served their new masters admirably. They were alert and quick and, due to their tremendous sense of territoriality, they proved able guards. Some assisted in locating the dead and wounded. The dogs displayed a real forte for locating mines. In 1948, at the conclusion of the War For Independence, Dr. Menzel continued her training experiments with the Canaan. She established the country's first center for the blind, and the Canaan became the nation's first seeing-eye dog. It should be

noted here that, in most countries around the world, protectiveness is not discouraged in leader dogs. In the United States, formulaters of guide dog programs discard any animal that demonstrates a willingness to protect his owner. The theory is that, in the event his unseeing owner is injured or should need assistance, a "good Samaritan" should not be deterred by a protective dog.

The Canaan was first brought to North America by Mrs. Ursula Berkowitz. A long time dog lover who was very proud of her cultural heritage, Mrs. Berkowitz wondered if there was any breed of dog from Israel. She dashed off a letter and soon began an active correspondence with Rudolphina Menzel. Two years later, in 1965, the first four Canaans arrived in California. After an 8,000 mile voyage, which took six weeks to complete, Mrs. Berkowitz was finally able to see her new dogs. Dr. Menzel had hand picked the four. Two came from her institue for the blind, one was purchased from the Druse and another from Bedouin tribesmen. Mrs. Berkowitz had made a committment to Dr. Menzel that she would do everything in her power to establish the breed in the United States. Jay and Bertha Sheaffer, successful Dalmatian breeders, bought a puppy from Ursula Berkowitz's first litter. In 1972, Mrs. Berkowitz died of cancer, and the Sheaffer's took over as the primary public relations advocates for the breed. Without their dedication and support, the Canaan's promising start might have fizzled completely. In 1975, Mrs. Marguerite Lachs took over as the Canaan stud book guardian. Today there are about 600 registered Canaans in North America, and both the United States and Canada have thriving national clubs. One can only imagine that Mrs. Berkowitz would have been very pleased.

A medium size, attractive and totally natural dog, the Canaan (a member of the Spitz family) is easily cared for. His medium length coat comes in a variety of lovely colors and needs only an occasional brushing. The breed sheds seasonally. A very clean dog, the Canaan rarely needs to be bathed. The food and water requirements of these dogs are minimal. Tests conducted in Israel have proven conclusively that the Canaan requires less water than any other breed. They also dissipate their body heat very efficiently, an adaptation which, doubtless, contributed to their survival in the harsh desert. The Canaan requires less food than other breeds and, when fed diets that cause other breeds to suffer, this amazing animal continues to maintain peak condition. Survival of the fittest has molded a healthy, hardy animal. One of the few disadvantages of this breed is the Canaan's penchant for digging holes.

The key to gaining an appreciation of the Canaan's unique temperament lies in understanding his inherent territoriality. While other breeds ably guard their master's home and property out of love and respect for their owners, the Canaan's approach is quite different. This breed believes that the home, yard (no matter if it's a small city lot or vast acreage), and everything included therein is **his**. This trait makes the Canaan invaluable in bomb and mine detection, as he will readily sound an alert when a strange object is placed on his property. Testing in Israel suggests that a Canaan can sense an intruder at a very great distance. They have been known to spot strangers that are one and a quarter miles away. "The Canaan circles an intruder, staying just out of reach. All the while he continues to bark very loudly. They will not shut up until the person leaves," states Lorraine Stephens. "This breed is an extremely effective guard dog. Because they circle, rather than rushing in to bite, like many other breeds, they are not easily neutralized by mace, and they aren't likely to be struck by a club. Most potential burglars find it simpler to go elsewhere. I do not want to give the impression that the Canaan is an indiscriminate barker. When all the dogs in my neighborhood bark, my Canaans are on the alert, but when they bark it's for real." It was these qualities that led Mrs. Stephens to acquire her first Canaan. When their small town began to grow, and the crime rate rose, Mrs. Stephens became concerned. When the house next door was burglarized, her concern turned to alarm. "My husband was working the four p.m. to midnight shift, and I was alone at home with two small boys." Lorraine contacted a guard dog kennel and told them that she wished to buy a trained German Shepherd or Doberman. The trainer refused to sell her such a dog because of her young children. He told Mrs. Stephens that what she needed was a good watchdog. When she asked for his recommendation, the man said, "You won't find a better watchdog than the Canaan." The next day, the Stephens family purchased their first Canaan. Little did Lorraine Stephens realize that this small puppy would win her heart and lead to the establishment of her Geva Kennels, in Newcastle, Oklahoma.

The Canaan is not aggressive with people, but the dogs are naturally suspicious. They do not appreciate being touched by strangers. Canaans are extremely loyal and devoted to their families. Often they will select one family member as their favorite. "They have an uncanny ability to sense my moods and they are extremely loving and caring," Mrs. Stephens says. The Canaan is never a fawning type of dog. They rarely follow their owners about the house, but they are keenly aware of every family member's location at all times. The breed thrives on love and attention, and responds with tremendous loyalty. Canaans seem to have a special affinity with children and they do quite well when raised with other dogs. "When living together in a group, they become very attached to all members of the pack," says Marguerite Lachs, of Los Angeles, California. "Dozens of times a day you will

Geva's Gilana me Padre, a Canaan bitch. Gilana is owned by Lorraine Stephens, Geva Kennels, Newcastle, Oklahoma.

see them 'kiss' or give a lick on the muzzle to another of their group." The Canaan, however, can be quite fearsome to strange dogs. He is not a wanderer and rarely strays from his territory.

Owners frequently are charmed by the Canaan's ability to vocalize. "Of the many Canaans I've owned," Lorraine Stephens says, "each has made his own distinctive vocal sounds. I speak in English and my dogs answer in 'Canaani.' Our guests are amazed at the range of sounds my dogs are capable of making."

Breeders strongly suggest that the Canaan puppy be adequately socialized. Exposure to a multitude of new experiences prepares them for anything they may encounter. Obedience training is very desirable and the Canaan is an apt pupil. They frequently learn an exercise by observing another dog being trained. Due to their extreme intelligence, the trainer should diversify the routine to prevent the Canaan from becoming bored.

Dog lovers frequently complain that their animals don't live long enough. The Canaan is certainly an exception. At 11 and 12 years of age, it is quite common to find the Canaan performing his working duties. In Israel, there have been reports of Canaans that were 18 and 20 years of age and still fully alert and healthy. For dog show enthusiasts, the Canaan's

this point. Dreidle, one of the breed's most influential sires, won his first National Specialty in 1977, at eight years of age. But, this was just the beginning for the flashy dog. He repeated this win in 1978, 1979, and 1980. Dreidle came out of retirement, at twelve years of age, to earn his Tracking Dog degree. By conventional dog standards, the Canaan's lifespan is quite remarkable.

Canaans still exist in the wild. Packs are generally composed of five to twenty animals. Curiously, in the wild, males are not always dominant, as we have been led to believe. Generally nocturnal, they will feed at dawn and/or after twilight. They catch native game and scavenge in refuse pits.

Spatterdash Dreidle (left), winner of the National Specialties in 1977, '78, '79 and '80. Spatterdash Limor (right), Best of Opposite Sex at the 1976, '82 and '83 National Specialties. Both these outstanding Canaans are owned by Bryna Comsky, Ha'Aretz Kennels, Hoffman Estates, Illinois. '

While the Canaan is an able livestock guard, in the wild he will resort to stealing domestic stock. Pregnant bitches remove themselves from the pack and raise their puppies on their own. Occasionally they will be found in the company of an adult male. The litter is sometimes born in a cave, but often the Canaan bitch digs an elaborate den for her charges. These are kept scrupulously clean. At about seven months, the bitch and her puppies generally return to the pack.

For centuries, the Bedouins have stolen pups from wild bitches to use as livestock herders and guardians. The lot of the Bedouin-owned Canaan is not pleasant, by our standards. Only males are captured, and the Bedouin has little regard for the bitch, except to provide a source of additional puppies. Male pups are tied until they reach maturity and become semi-domesticated. The line between the wild dog and his semi-domesticated brethern is a very fine one. In the aftermath of the Six Day War, in 1967, Syrians

longevity has significant advantages. The breed seems to stay in excellent condition and act quite spry to a ripe old age. Many Canaans have first begun their show careers when breeds of a similiar size would be considered over the hill. Lorraine Stephens characterizes Canaans as "late bloomers." The remarkable career of Spatterdash Dreidle, owned by Bryna Comsky, of Illinois, clearly demonstrates

fled the Golan region. Their Canaans effectively assimilated into the wild. While the Bedouin cherishes and shares his tent with his Saluki, the Canaan is hardly esteemed. The approach of a human may mean a swift kick or he may be thrown a scrap of food. He does not bond with his Bedouin owner as he does with his devoted domestic family. While he rarely strays from the encampment, he does not seem enamored of his masters. Only Bedouin children seem to be able to handle the Canaan. The dogs seem to trust them.

The Canaan is becoming endangered in his native land, and lovers of these rare dogs have become quite concerned. The Israeli government has launched a rabies eradication program. Dogs must either be vaccinated or shot, and breeders fear that the Canaan will eventually disappear from the wild. Rabies control officers acknowledge that the Canaan is most difficult to eliminate. With their uncanny intelligence, they are more difficult to shoot than most wild animals. Further, they are incredibly adept at avoiding poisoned meat and discerning traps.

Israeli breeders continue to capture wild Canaans. The animals, and their resulting progeny, undergo a judging process before being admitted into the stud book. While Israeli breeders place great importance on incorporating wild stock into their breeding programs, American breeders, with an eye to A.K.C. recognition, do not allow the registration of wild born stock. Israeli imports are registered with the Canaan Club of America, but only if they are accompanied with a full five-generation pedigree.

Dog lovers, who wish to share their homes with a unique and distinctive animal would be wise to consider the Canaan Dog. It would be a shame if Israel's "Dog of Distinction" were allowed to lapse into obscurity. The hard working members of the Canaan Clubs, in both the United States and Canada, have made remarkable strides. Canaan Dog owners think their breed is "special." Those fortunate enough to observe the breed first-hand will certainly concur.

Aleph of Star Pine, the first Canaan Dog born in the United States, owned by Mrs. Jay C. Sheaffer, of Lehigh Acres, Florida.

Chuva, owned by Arthur Yanoff, always stays close to her sheep. (John Knapp photo)

Chuva places herself between her sheep and any perceived threat, in this case the photographer. (Knapp photo)

Chapter 13

The Castro Laboreiro

In northern Portugal there is a small, remote village. Castro Laboreiro, literally "village of laborers," is located north of the River Douro, between Mounts Peneda and Suajo. In this mountainous area, flocks of sheep tend to be small. The residents have developed a very unique breed that is distinct from the other livestock guarding breeds. While most sheep guardians are large and carry heavy coats, this Portuguese breed is medium sized and short coated. The dog of these mountain shepherds bears the name of their Portuguese village.

The Castro Laboreiro has served Portuguese flock owners for more than 1,000 years. He is often seen leading or following the flocks to their pastures. Since his native home is so remote, it is believed that the breed has remained pure and virtually unchanged to the present day. Only in the past few years, has the Castro attracted the attention of dog fanciers. He is a newcomer to show rings, and only recently has a standard been formulated.

Upon first seeing a Castro Laboreiro, most people think that it resembles a nondescript Labrador Retriever. Indeed, there are some authorities who believe the breed may be one of the Labrador's progenitors. The Castro is a medium size, sturdily built dog with strong musculature. Castros are agile and quick. Their short coats most often come in black, which is brindled with reddish or brown tones. Dogs are from 22-24 inches tall and range between 66-88 pounds. The smaller bitches measure in at 20-22 inches and tip the scales at 44-66 pounds. With his medium size and easily cared for waterproof coat, the Castro would be a valuable aid to small scale homesteaders in this country.

Arthur Yanoff, an acclaimed abstract artist, makes his home on a small farm in Concord, New Hampshire. Mr. Yanoff has long employed terriers to control rodents and small predators around his poultry pens. When he decided to add a small flock of Southdown sheep to his menagerie, Mr. Yanoff began to research livestock guarding breeds. As elsewhere in the country, wild dogs endanger sheep flocks throughout New England. Arthur felt, however, that the large livestock guardians were unsuitable for his mini-farm. When he read of the Castro Laboreiro, he contacted Ray and Lorna Coppinger at Hampshire College, in Amherst, Massachussets. The Coppingers have an ongoing research program that evaluates the suitability of various foreign breeds for American livestock operations. They have imported several breeds and placed them with ranchers, who are required to keep a journal detailing the work the dogs perform. The Coppingers were interested, and three dogs were imported from Portugal. Arthur Yanoff owns a bitch from the first Castro Laboreiro litter born in this country.

Chuva has proven a valuable addition to the Yanoff farm. "She lives with the sheep and is totally attuned to them. She is very protective of them, yet appropriately restrained in her defensive posture." Chuva takes her duties so seriously that she will ignore butterflies and birds, until they get too near the sheep. Then, she will leap at them to frighten them away from her charges. "She respects her boundaries and does not jump the pasture fence. This is particularly important on small farms in populated areas," says Yanoff.

"Chuva is excellent with our other dogs, except when she doesn't want them to get too close to the sheep or newborn lambs," Arthur says. Normally,

Chuva, a lovely Castro Laboreiro bitch, owned by Arthur Yanoff, of Concord, New Hampshire. (John Knapp photo)

challenged. She is excellent with children," says Yanoff who has a young daughter, "and while she is protective, she is not unduly aggressive."

Arthur Yanoff is particularly impressed with the Castro's intelligence. "I consider my Castro the fastest learner of any breed that I have worked with." But, Mr. Yanoff cautions, the Castro Laboreiro has been bred for centuries to think independently and size up situations for himself. "While more handler sensitive and responsive than many of the other livestock guarding breeds, she doesn't perform obedience commands with consistency," he says.

With his short coat, medium size, and minimal grooming requirements, the Castro Laboreiro may have a great future in this country. Arthur Yanoff hopes that one day the Castro will be more widely known around the world.

Chuva will be found lying quietly in the pasture, or curled in a corner of the barn. But, as soon as she senses the presence of another dog, Chuva will place herself at the side of the sheep. "She is one of the flock," Mr. Yanoff says. If a dog gets too close to the fence, Chuva protectively herds the sheep into the barn. The Castro has a very distinctive bark when disturbed. It starts out as a deep bark, and rapidly rises to a high-pitched crescendo. "That alone is enough to scare Frankenstein," Arthur Yanoff remarks. "She is very powerful and agile, and could be a formidable fighter if she were seriously

Chapter 14

The Catahoula Leopard Dog

Those interested in owning a dog who shares a unique place in American history, should consider the Catahoula Leopard Dog. This breed may, in fact, be the only native American breed from the lower forty-eight states. I first saw a Catahoula many years ago, while visiting relatives in Louisiana. It was hog butchering time, and the huge beasts ranged free in the backwaters of my uncle's vast property. We mounted our horses and, accompanied by two Catahoulas, headed for the swamp. The sun can be unbearably hot in Louisiana, and the swampy areas have their share of mosquitoes and flying insects. It felt oppressive, but the dogs didn't seem to mind. The hogs were rooting in the heavy brush, which we found impossible to penetrate. Suddenly, we heard the dogs barking, and before long they emerged from the swamp with the charging hogs in pursuit. They stopped occasionally to worry and annoy the huge beasts into following them and they agilely avoided the animals' vicious charges. My uncle and I galloped to the corral, it's gates wide open in invitation. Before we knew it, the dogs had arrived with the hogs close on their heels. They ran swiftly into the enclosure and, while my uncle closed the gate, I watched as the dogs leaped over the fence. Although out of breath, they seemed to smile with pride at their accomplishment.

This is just one of the many talents of the Louisiana Catahoula Leopard Dog. He is one of the most amazingly versatile dogs known to man. It's hard to believe that there is anything a good "Cat," as they are affectionately called, can't do. This breed, which holds the distinction of being proclaimed Louisiana's Official State Dog, is a multi-purpose breed *par excellence*. They have an amazing inherent desire to herd livestock, and have been used, with great success, for hunting a diverse array of both small and large game. Further, the Catahoula is a superb home guardian, with a strong protective instinct. A great family or child's companion, the breed has also been successfully trained in obedience. Some owners have taught their Cats to perform a wide array of tricks. It is little wonder that Catahoula owners are so proud of their dogs, and so anxious to protect the traits of the versatile Cat.

Due to the lack of written records, it is difficult to definitively pinpoint the ancestry of the Catahoula. The ancestors of the present day Catahoula were thought to be the companions of native American Indians, who made their home in Louisiana. The breed takes it's name from the Catahoula Lakes in Louisiana. The word "Catahoula" means "beautiful clear water" in Indian parlance. When Hernando de Soto first visited this country in the 1500's, we know that powerful dogs accompanied him on his extended journey through the South. When we study the logs of de Soto's trip, we learn that, in some parts of the South, dogs were bred by the Indians as a food source. The brutal and barbaric de Soto often loosed his dogs on the unsuspecting Indians. Hardly known for any shred of humanity, de Soto and his men abandoned any injured or wounded dogs, and these were accepted and cared for by the Indians. When white settlers came to the area, they adopted the striking Indian dogs. The animals were used for a variety of purposes and seemed ideally suited to the homesteaders' early way of life. Strong enough to herd livestock (traditionally left to survive and fatten

The impressive Riverside Fraidy, owned by W. Bernard Ellis, of Indianola, Mississippi.

in the wilderness), canny enough to track and hunt game, loyal enough to defend the isolated homesteads, the Catahoula was also aggressive enough to protect his master from wanderers and vagabonds who were up to no good.

It is possible that, at a later date, French settlers brought Beaucerons to the Louisiana area, and that the Catahoula may owe part of his heritage to this breed, but that cannot be adequately verified. Eventually, Catahoulas made their way to Texas, where the cowboys found them ideal on tough, often half-wild livestock. The cowboys began to refer to the breed as "Leopard Dogs," due to their distinctive coloration. Whatever combination produced the Catahoula we know today, they have retained the strength and versatility that enabled them to serve the native and early Americans so well.

The Catahoula Leopard Dog is striking and unusual in appearance. This is a medium to large breed. Females measure 20 to 24 inches at the shoulder, while males typically measure 22 to 26 inches. A Catahoula's weight may vary between 50 and 95 pounds. The breed's most distinctive feature is it's white, or "glass," eyes. While the breed is not required to have the "glass" eye, most breeder's prefer it as an essential part of breed type, and it is a must in successful show dogs. While Catahoulas come in a wide range of colors, the distinctive leopard spotting is the most desired. These will often be blue or blue-gray, with white trim, or black with a gray leopard marking. The standard allows for this diversity: "Leopards are to be preferred, and may come in blue/gray/black/liver/red/white/ and patched. Trim may be black/white/tan/red/buff. Solid colors acceptable are black, brindle, red, chocolate and yellow." Their sleek coats are, generally, short and

easy to care for. The Cat has a broad chest, wide backskull, and muscular body. Coonhunters and cattlemen often prefer a slightly leggier and rangier dog, while hogmen and squirrel hunters like a shorter, stockier dog.

Catahoulas are very intelligent, uncommonly devoted and affectionate. They are eager to please and quick to learn, although some owners report that their dogs are not particularly fond of coming when called. They often develop into one man or one family dogs. This trait contributes to their reputation as watchdogs. "The Catahoula is usually shy, and doesn't like strangers. They can become extremely aggressive with age. They are very possessive, and this makes them excellent guard dogs," says Emma Ellis, of Indianola, Mississippi. Dr. Bernard and Emma Ellis first learned of the Catahoula when they moved to Mississippi. They were very impressed with the breed. "We took trips into the backwoods of Louisiana to contact people who had Catahoula dogs. Most of them were still breeding the same dogs owned by their grand and great grandparents." Mrs. Ellis believes firmly in early training. "The Catahoula must be trained so that you can control your dog no matter how big he gets." Patricia Headley, of Long Eddy, New York, agrees. She is a new Cat owner who is more widely known for her fine Australian Shepherds. Ms. Headley lives alone on 115 acres, and her "Siouxie" provides protection. "The Catahoula is not a breed for everyone. They are extremely protective unless they are very well socialized, and this is continually done." The dogs seem to be quite individualistic in their tolerance for strangers. Some will accept frequent visitors to the home, while others keep their distance and avoid friendly gestures.

This nine month old puppy bitch is already herding horses on a 200 acre ranch. Owned by Bobby Weems, of Bessemer, Alabama.

The Catahoula is an ideal children's companion. They become extremely devoted to children in the family. One owner stated that he believed that a kidnapper would have to kill his dog before he could carry away his small charges. The dogs seem to tolerate a great deal of ear and tail pulling with equanimity. Owners should be aware that, while the Cat may be devoted to his own children, he may not extend this attitude to strange children. "Visiting children are still viewed as strangers, just short ones," says Emma Ellis.

The breed is healthy and hardy, and requires little care. Cats are not fussy in their feeding requirements and thrive on any good dog food. "The Catahoula needs space to run, even if it is just a big backyard or a city park," Mrs. Ellis says. This breed may surprise you with a few tricks and abilities all his own. "My father's dog," says Emma Ellis, "was afraid of power tools. He would edge between my father and his work area, trying to push him away from the saws. This dog also picked up after my father. He would sometimes leave tools laying around the yard. When he went back to search for them, he would discover that his Catahoula had gathered them and arranged them on the shop floor."

Hunting enthusiasts give high praise to the Catahoula's talents. Catahoulas have proven their abilities, time and again, on a variety of game. The Cat is an able coon dog and is often run with more traditional raccoon hunting breeds. Hunters report that the breed seems to gain a special enjoyment from hunting coon, and that Cats possess excellent night vision. The wily raccoon is a real challenge when it takes to the water. Coons are excellent swimmers, and when they lure a dog to the water, they will often turn and jump on his back. The dog, in this vulnerable position, is then set upon by the coon, with his claws and teeth. The Catahoula seems

This Catahoula puppy shows the distinctive leopard markings. Bred by Bobby Weems, of Bessemer, Ala.

This older Catahoula puppy, owned by Bobby Weems, is in the truck and ready to go.

particularly adept at defeating the coon in water. The National Association of Louisiana Catahoulas, Inc. (NALC) says, "Down here, they stopped putting Catahoulas in the 'Coon on a Log' trials because it just wasn't fair for the coon to lose all the time."

Squirrel hunters have reported equal success with the Cat. They say the dogs are quickly and easily trained. The breed's excellent eyesight is a distinct advantage when working squirrel. Dogs are generally started out by being exposed to a freshly killed squirrel. Little other training is necessary.

As a deer hunter, the Cat is a winner. Unlike the other hounds generally used on deer, he works closer to the hunter, and will not disappear for days at a time. They are silent trailers and, unlike the more traditional hound breeds, they air scent their prey. One will occasionally find a Cat that ground trails and gives tongue, but this is rare. "We have an older female who will blood trail wounded deer, which is legal in our state," Emma Ellis says. "One day she was trying to locate a 'down' buck. There wasn't much blood, but the hunter was sure it was a killing shot. When she finally found the buck, he wasn't hurt at all. He had only been nicked and he was very angry. He didn't run, and she worked him just like a cow, constantly darting in and snapping at his head. By doing this, she brought him right up to, and in among, the hunters. Catahoulas consider this type of action, whether with a deer, hog or cow, to be play. They do it automatically. Occasionally, you will find one that doesn't have the instinct, and there's no way you can teach it to them. Your training should center around controlling the dog at this 'play,' with voice instructions or hand signals."

Hog hunters often use the Catahoula, and prefer to run their dogs in pairs or trios. Some people have referred to the Cats as "coward" dogs, because of their unusual working style. Facing a large Southern razorack, though, requires tenacity and an abundance of courage. The Catahoula aggravates or worries the hog by running, snapping and barking. They will continue such action, whether working domestic or wild hogs, until the animals bunch together, and they will hold them in this position until their master arrives. Often one dog will concentrate on the head, another will handle the side, and the third will bring up the rear.

As a stockdog, the Catahoula's working style is truly unique. While he can handle gentle stock, it is in work with tough, nasty and dangerous stock that he excells. The NALC advises stockmen to stay out of the way and let the Cat take over. "Sit back and let your Catahoula do what comes naturally." The Cat uses the same method that he employs when hunting. He will circle the herd, teasing and barking until they begin to bunch. Dogs are often introduced to herding activities by working with experienced herders, and most stockmen report that they learn quickly. Still, it is best to work young dogs on calves. Cats have gained an enviable reputation for their work with Brahma bulls. Often, the Cat will bite the large bull on the nose, knowing full well that he will get a fight. But that's the desired response, and it enables the dog to annoy and anger the animal into following him. In Texas, there are freelance cowboys who can be hired to round up particularly nasty and difficult stock. Many of these freelancers have found the Catahoula an invaluable partner. The Catahoula will grab a cow or steer by the nose, and then jump free allowing the cowboy to rope the recalcitrant animal. It's a hard way to earn a living, and it requires a robust and hard dog. The Cat fits the bill. Owners are fond of saying that the Catahoula "can out work and out last any other breed."

The Catahoula was once threatened with extinction through crossbreeding, but the breed has made a solid comeback. Mr. Kline Rushing, a dedicated breeder and an avid Catahoula devotee, compiled a great deal of material on the breed, some of it written down for the first time. He passed away in 1977 and, as a tribute to his memory, his daughter, Mrs. Betty Eaves, established the National Association of Louisiana Catahoulas in that same year. The NALC sponsors working cow trials as well as conformation shows. One 1984 gathering featured a record 168 Catahoulas. The bill declaring the breed Louisiana's official state dog also designated the NALC the official registry for the breed. The members declare that this is "a uniqueness we aim to keep with honor and pride."

The Catahoula Leopard Dog is truly unique and distinctive. This native American breed will continue to prosper in the South. Word of these versatile dogs has now spread across the country and, while his roots may remain in Louisiana, it appears that the Catahoula is destined for wider popularity.

Chapter 15

The Cavalier King Charles Spaniel

It's difficult to imagine a more exquisitely beautiful breed than the Cavalier King Charles Spaniel. With their convenient size, eagerness to please, smart good looks and loving, stable personality, this small spaniel is attracting much attention. Once the companion of royalty, the Cavalier has now joined the President's family. Indeed, the Cavalier, with his many wonderful qualities, is growing in popularity. Fortunately, Cavalier breeders are a dedicated group who are devoted to ensuring that their breed will grow slowly and wisely. They have seen that sudden popularity can be devastating to a breed and are determined to save the Cavalier from such a fate.

We have difficulty documenting the history of most breeds, but the charming Cavalier has been well known for centuries. The predecessors of the modern Cavalier King Charles Spaniel have long been the companions of royalty. Writings dating back to 1486 speak of small spaniels. The esteemed dog writer, Dr. Johannes Caius, discusses the "Spaniell gentle or comforter" in one of the earliest texts on dogs. These small spaniels take their name from the days when they were closely associated with King Charles I of England. The King's love for and devotion to his dogs certainly did much to promote popularity. The famous diarist, Samuel Pepys, frequently complained about the King's affinity for his dogs. He cited one meeting of the Privy Coucil at which the King was far more interested in playing with his dogs than attending to the business at hand. Clearly, the dogs were equally devoted to the King. A story is told of a subject who approached the royal coach. The King warned him not to place his hands on the door as he spoke, but the man did not heed his advice. Sure enough, he was bitten by one of the royal spaniels and is reported to have cried, "God Bless your Majesty, but God damn your dogs." So fond did the owners become of their little companions that many unscrupulous people took to kidnapping the small spaniels. They could be assured that a substantial reward would be offered for their return.

The family tradition for owning the diminutive spaniels was carried on by James II, brother to Charles II, after the later's death. His spaniels accompanied him everywhere. On one ocean voyage, the King and the crew encountered a particularly rough sea and it was decided that they would have to abandon ship. The King's concern was clear as he bellowed, "Save the dogs and the Duke of Monmouth!"

It was during the days of William and Mary that the Pug attracted attention and became the companion of English nobility. While there is no concrete evidence, it may have been during this period that the Pug was interbred with the small spaniels. We do know that the conformation of the breed changed. The backskulls became domed, the eyes were rounder and much more prominent, and the muzzles were shortened significantly and had an accentuated stop. The coats became more profuse and show dogs had masses of silky hair.

These were the dogs that Mr. Roswell Eldridge found when he visited England to acquire a small spaniel in the 1920's. He had longed for a dog such as those pictured in the paintings of Van Dyke, Landseer, Watteau, Gainesborough and others. Instead, he was upset to find only the tiny and delicate Toy Spaniels. In this country, this breed is now classified as the English Toy Spaniel, although in

England the breed is known as the King Charles Spaniel. It must have greatly distressed Mr. Eldridge for he took a bold step. In 1926, he placed an announcement in the catalog for England's most prestigious dog show, Crufts. It featured a reproduction of Landseer's famous painting, "Cavalier's Pets." Beneath this a notice stated:

"Blenheim Spaniels of the Old Type, as shown in pictures of Charles II's time, long face, no stop, flat skull, not inclined to be domed with spot in centre of skull. The first prize of £25 in Class 947 and 948 are given by Roswell Eldridge, Esq., of New York, USA. Prizes go to the nearest to type required."

The beautiful Champion Maxholt Special Secret of Chadwick, owned by C. Anne Robins, of Cos Cob, Connecticut, is a top winner.

Twenty-five pounds was a significant and generous sum in those days, and the notice created a furor among King Charles Spaniel breeders. Many were appalled at the notion that such a considerable sum should be awarded to dogs that they carefully culled from their breeding programs. King Charles Spaniels that possessed the nose that Mr. Eldridge called for stood no chance in the British show ring, and the prospect that these inferior specimens would not only be exhibited, but also rewarded, was contemptible. There were a few breeders, however, who saw Mr. Eldridge's offering as a challenge. It might have been that they wished to have a place for

puppies that would have otherwise been useless to them. Although many of these dogs had lovely conformation their longer noses made them useless for competition. Many otherwise good dogs reproduced this trait and had to be eliminated from conscientious breeding programs. Mr. Eldridge's offer continued for five years, and entries, in the beginning, were quite low. Still, English breeders endured and several became intrigued with the task of producing the "Old Type" spaniels. At the Crufts show in 1928, a small group of fanciers banded together to form a club and they christened their new breed "The Cavalier King Charles Spaniel." It was some years before the Kennel Club of England would allow a separate registry for the old type spaniels, and breeders were left to register their dogs as "Cavalier type." Unfortunately, Mr. Roswell died just a month before that 1928 Cruft's show and never lived to see his dream.

Early breeders faced many problems in stabilizing true Cavalier breed type. Since it was necessary to focus initially on the desired head type, some other points suffered. Markings on early breeding stock were often disappointing. Breeders were also hampered by the availability of breeding stock. In order to avoid excessive inbreeding, the new Cavalier enthusiasts could only look once again to the short faced King Charles Spaniel. Naturally, this made breed progress difficult, but the Cavalier devotees persevered. Eventually, the breed was accorded separate recognition status by England's Kennel Club. The breed has continued to thrive in Great Britain. In 1973, an impressive Cavalier scored Best in Show at Crufts. Unfortunately, there were disappointing consequences to this triumph. Breed popularity soared and the demand for Cavaliers was extraordinary. Many breeders were besieged with requests for puppies and breeding stock, and concerned breeders became alarmed. Entries at shows were tremendously high. The Cavalier craze in England has diminished somewhat, but the breed remains a popular choice among pet owners.

Mrs. W.L. Lyons Brown is credited with establishing the breed in the United States. The Kentucky resident received a trio of Cavaliers from an

Kilspindie Ferdinand, the sire of champions, like all Cavaliers, enjoys the outdoors. This impressive dog is owned by Elizabeth Spalding, Kilspindie Cavaliers, Falmouth, Maine.

English friend. She became fascinated with this cheerful breed and searched for other American owners. These dedicated owners banded together in 1956 to form the Cavalier King Charles Spaniel Club,U.S.A. (CKCSC). They held their first specialty show in 1962 at the lovely home of the George Garvin Browns, in Kentucky. The breed has substantially progressed since those early days, and more than 5,000 Cavaliers now make their homes in this country. There are now well supported regional clubs and national specialty entries often number in the hundreds. A code of ethics helps to ensure the welfare of the breed.

The Cavalier King Charles Spaniel is a beautiful dog by anyone's standard. Their dark expressive eyes have an almost human quality and they are naturally photogenic. Indeed, while owners of other breeds have difficulty getting good photographs, Cavalier owners generally have several scrapbooks full of photos. Most breeders say that their dogs love nothing better than to pose for a camera. The Cavalier is a small well balanced dog. He comes by his beautiful looks naturally and is never trimmed for the show ring. His backskull is very flat without a hint of a dome. Unlike his relative the English Toy Spaniel, the Cavalier has a very shallow stop. The Cavalier standard permits the docking of tails, but specifies that no more than one-third of the appendage may be removed. Since the amount to be removed is so slight, most owners don't bother to dock. The silky coat of the Cavalier is glorious. While it should never

curl, a slight wave is permitted. Their spaniel ears are long and heavily feathered.

The Cavalier comes in four distinct and very beautiful colors. All the colors are brilliant and rich. Ruby colored dogs are a solid red. Black and tans have a jet black base coat, with clearly defined tan markings on the chest, the legs, beneath the tail, on the cheeks and over the eyes. The tricolor pattern is quite striking. It features well placed black and white markings, with tan trim on the inside of the legs and ears, on the underside of the tail and over the eyes. Blenheims are very popular, as well they should be, for they have a long history. The standard describes the Blenheim colorations as "rich chestnut marking well broken up on a pearly white ground. The markings should be evenly divided on the head, leaving room between the ears for the much valued lozenge mark or spot (a unique characteristic of the breed)." This color pattern, once also known as the Marlborough Spaniel, takes his name from Blenheim Palace, the home of the Dukes of Marlborough. It is said that Sarah, Duchess of Blenheim, waited anxiously in the Palace for any word of her husband's success or defeat at the Battle of Blenheim. Her constant companion was a small spaniel and, in her worried state, she continually pressed her thumb on his forehead. This spot, sometimes called the Blenheim thumbprint, is a distinctive characteristic of this color pattern. The Cavalier stands 12-13 inches tall and weighs from 13-18 pounds. This convenient size suits him well to both city and country living.

With his long history as a "comforter", the Cavalier enjoys and needs a close association with people. It would be difficult to find a better housedog than the jaunty Cavalier. Conscientious breeders take

Erin Cochran holds two precious Cavalier puppies bred by her parents, Susan and William Cochran, of Rome, Georgia.

great care in preserving the breed's wonderful temperament. A true Cavalier should never be wild, wilfull, bad tempered, or an uncontrollable barker. These beautiful dogs are happy, friendly and affectionate. They seem to greet everything in life with enthusiasm and a wag of the tail. They are intelligent and always willing to please, a quality that makes them ideal obedience dogs. With their gentle and sweet personality, Cavaliers do not respond well to harsh treatment.

"They are great little dogs," Susan Cochran says. "They love people and are the type that will lick them and greet them with enthusiasm. They are not barkers. I have sold puppies to people who've called me back to tell me that their dog was mute," Susan laughs. "I've explained that their dog was just happy and quiet. They still seemed skeptical. I suggested that they shut the dog in the bathroom for a minute or two, where he was away from humans. Sure enough, their Cavalier barked. They love people and they need human contact."

The people-loving Cavaliers do not do well when they are deprived of human contact. The Cavalier King Charles Spaniel Club, U.S.A. stresses this point. "Cavaliers are not kennel dogs. Because of their history of 400 years of close contact with their owners and their development as lap dogs, they become neurotic and morose when deprived of full family membership. They do not thrive when left alone all day. They are highly intelligent and require the same consistent and loving discipline as does a child."

In fact, it is very difficult to say anything unflattering about the Cavalier. Breeders have done a superb job of maintaining superior temperament. "Cavaliers do shed, occasionally chew things, sometimes forget their manners-bark, make a puddle, etc.," says the CKCSC. "In other words, they really are first and always DOGS, in spite of their ethereal faces!"

Although the Cavalier is a small companion, they are not mere lap dogs. While they enjoy creature comforts and will willingly curl up beside you on the sofa, they are still active dogs. They are descended from sporting spaniels, and some Cavaliers show an aptitude for hunting. Your Cavalier will benefit from exercise, both mental and physical, and will enjoy accompanying you on a walk in the country. A sturdy little dog, many owners are suprised to discover that the Cavalier has amazing stamina. Most Cavaliers love nothing better than a romp in the woods.

William and Susan Cochran say that their Cavaliers are active little dogs. The couple raised American Cockers for years. "I got very tired of the long hours spent trimming, and the Cocker's pervasive doggy odor," Susan says. William purchased a Cavalier puppy as a Christmas present for his wife. "But Mary is really William's dog," Susan says. "She can always be found sitting next to him. We have a spring fed creek behind our house, and Mary quickly became an avid swimmer. It was her concern for William that first led her into the water. When he dived in, she became very anxious and was soon accompanying him. She really loves the water and will fetch a thrown stick all day long."

"They are active and sporting little dogs which require a great deal of exercise," the CKCSC explains. "They have an instinct to give chase, and they must be enclosed in a fenced yard or they will surely come to grief under the wheels of cars. They cannot be turned loose to run in a neighborhood, and most breeders will require a fenced yard as a prerequisite to Cavalier ownership."

Most breeders consider the Cavalier a suitable companion for children, although, as with any small breed, they generally look for a home with well behaved children. "I find them ideal with children," Susan Cochran says. "I love the way this breed deals with them. If a child is in a grumpy mood or becomes too rough, the Cavalier will just leave. When they see that the child has calmed down and is acting properly, they will return for more play. Our Cavaliers are ideal playmates for my daughter, Erin. Several of them sleep with her. Mary, our first Cavalier, will get under the covers, lie on her back and place her head on Erin's pillow. When it's story reading time, I find Erin and several of the Cavaliers waiting for me. I think they enjoy it as much as Erin does," Susan laughs.

The Cavalier is also very even tempered with other dogs. Those used to other breeds, where there is jealousy or where stud dogs can seldom be trusted together, find the Cavalier's attitude delightful and refreshing. Even strange dogs are often welcomed by the gay Cavalier. Indeed, an aggressive Cavalier would be entirely untypical and such temperament would be a major fault.

The Cavalier is to easy to groom and care for. The standard specifically forbids any trimming other than clipping the hair from between the pads on the underside of the feet. Their silky coats require only occasional baths and even when they have gotten themselves good and muddy, the dirt will dry and flake off. They do shed, but this problem will be minimized by brushing. Three or four times a week, the Cavalier should be brushed and combed. This should take only about five or ten minutes, and your Cavalier will always appear in peak condition. Special care should be paid to the ears. The ears need to be cleaned, and tangles are more prone to develop on ear feathering. Tangles may also develop on the longer hair on the back legs, tail and under the armpits.

Your Cavalier will thrive on a sensible diet and

breeders will be glad to advise you as to choice of food. Breeders caution that the Cavalier is a hearty eater and owners should never allow him to become overweight. With their winsome faces, Cavaliers can become superb con artists where food is concerned. With a sensible diet, sufficient exercise, routine veterinary care and lots of love, your Cavalier should thrive. This breed is hardy and healthy, and can be expected to live for 13-15 years.

Those devoted to the breed are very protective of the Cavalier. "Especially at this time, with the increased visibility of our breed, "the CKCSC says, "we are determined not to allow a surge of popularity to sweep away the lovely qualities...which we have worked...to develop and maintain...The emotional and physical quality of the life being considered for each Cavalier is the primary concern of his/her breeder and of the Club."

American and Canadian Champion Only of Kenstaff, Am./Can. CDX and Champion Maxholt Special Secret of Chadwick, two lovely Cavaliers owned by C. Anne Robins, of Cos Cob, Connecticut.

The exquisite Champion Lejo's Halo of Phaedrean,winner of eight Bests In Show, owned by Lee and John Bakuckas, Lejo's Kennels, Hollywood, Philadelphia, Pennsylvania.

Chapter 16

The Chinese Crested

The Chinese Crested is the most popular of the hairless breeds in this country. He has attracted great attention for his unusual and distinctive appearance. Indeed, the growing popularity of the Chinese Crested may well have contributed to the proliferating interest in other hairless breeds. Those who see a Chinese Crested for the first time usually think they are either beautiful or ugly. However, anyone fortunate enough to spend time with these delightful dogs are quickly won over by their charm. Their gay antics and exceptionally bright personality soon win your heart and capture your affections.

The hairless breeds have long been known to dog fanciers and are believed to be thousands of years old. Some early writers greeted them with scorn, categorizing the dogs as "freaks." Indeed, hairless dogs were considered as such unusual novelties that several British dog lovers housed collections of them in their kennels. In the 1830's the Zoological Society's Gardens, in London, featured an exhibit of hairless dogs. There was a great deal of speculation about the cause of the hairlessness, and post mortems were performed on dogs in an attempt to explain this deviation. All proved fruitless.

The exact origin of all the hairless breeds has often puzzled scholars, for they have been found in many diverse and widely scattered parts of the world. Most authorities agree with the esteemed German naturalist, Dr. A. E. Brehm. "The hairless dog *(Canis Africanus)* has its origin in the African Continent, from where he emigrated to Guinea, Manila, China and then to America." Indeed, many hairless dogs have been cited in various countries. The Abyssinian or African Sand Dog, Turkish Hairless Dogs, Guatamalan Hairless Dogs, the African Elephant Dog, the Small African Greyhound, Nubian Dogs, the Indian Rampur Dog and the Buenos Aires Hairless Dog have all been mentioned by writers over the years.

It's difficult to pinpoint the exact history of the Chinese Crested, but it has been said that they were selectively bred by the famous Han family and the Mandarins. Indeed, the breed may have made its home in China for hundreds of years. The noble families of China have always had a preference for small toy breeds, and surely the distinctive Chinese Crested would have been honored. Chinese breeders developed two different breed types. One type of Crested was called the "Hunting Dog." These dogs had cobby bodies and more substantial bone. Their whole appearance was one of a larger, less refined and heavier animal, and this type is no longer preferred by modern breed fanciers. The other type was called the "Treasure House Guardians," and these small, elegant and very refined dogs were wonderfully slender in appearance. It is this "deer type" that is seen in show rings in this country.

The 14th century was an exciting time in China, for there was much trade with distant countries. The Chinese Crested made his way to foreign lands with the precious Chinese tea. It is doubtful that any examples of the breed remain in China today. The Communist Revolution condemned the raising of dogs as a bourgeois luxury. A few do appear to have left with refugees fleeing to Hong Kong and other countries surrounding the South China Sea.

We do not know precisely when the Chinese Crested first made an appearance on American soil. It is said that a pair of the dogs made a dramatic appearance at Westminster, in 1885. Certainly, the flamboyant Gypsy Rose Lee, the famed stripper, brought much attention to the breed. She owned several Cresteds and was utterly devoted to them. Her little dogs accompanied her on her travels and she delighted in showing them off. Still, the breed was not popular, and Deborah Woods, of Homestead, Florida is often credited with preserving the breed. In 1967, she and other fanciers organized a club for the Crested. Since then, popularity has increased dramatically, and Cresteds now make their home in all of the United States and several foreign countries.

The Chinese Crested is a fine boned, small dog who is wonderfully graceful. His ears are erect and rather large. His almond shaped eyes are dark and radiate warmth. The Crested may come in any color or combination of colors. His nose is black or self-colored in liver dogs, but may be lighter in lighter colored dogs. The Chinese Crested has long and amazingly dexterous toes. Owners say that they can curl their toes around your finger. Males measure less than 13 inches at the shoulder, while females may not exceed 12 inches. The breed comes in two varieties: the hairless and the powderpuff.

Hairless dogs are not completely naked. In fact, the breed takes its name from the "crest" on its head. This silky topknot is often long and flowing. Cresteds generally have hair on their feet, which breeders refer to as "socks." Furthermore, they have an attractive plume on their tails. Hairless Chinese Cresteds always have the typical missing premolars, and there may be other absent teeth. Their skin is wonderfully smooth to the touch. Some owners say that it feels just like satin and is uniquely warm. Because of this quality, history is replete with stories of the hairless dogs' curative powers. Claims have been made for their ability to cure arthritis, and many owners have used them as living heating pads. Since he has no fur to harbor fleas or dandruff, the Crested is a very tidy dog, and the logical choice for the scrupulously clean homemaker. Owners report that the hairless breeds are very fastidious and will frequently clean themselves. Their lack of doggy odor is a welcome bonus. Some precautions are, however, necessary. "You must not keep a hairless dog directly in the sun because of sun poisoning," say Lee and John Bakuckas, of Philadelphia, Pennsylvannia. "In freezing weather, you must also provide them with a warm coat." Most Chinese Crested owners bathe their companions frequently, to prevent the eruption of blackheads. They also advocate the use of a sunscreen or a moisturizer to keep the skin smooth and supple and protect it from the sun. It is advisable to steer clear of oils which contain lanolin. New owners should also be apprised that the Chinese Crested may have an adverse reaction to wool. Because his teeth are somewhat fragile, most owners refrain from giving bones to their hairless dogs. Moistening and softening their food will also help to eliminate potential dental problems.

Many people are surprised to learn that a fully haired puppy is often found in hairless litters. Crested breeders refer to these as "powderpuffs" because their hair is very downy and soft. It is claimed that these tiny puppies keep their hairless littermates warm, until they are able to generate sufficient body heat on their own. Powderpuffs also have a full compliment of teeth. They have a short undercoat and a longer thin outercoat. The Chinese Crested standard says that this creates "a veil-like effect." Powderpuffs are shown as a separate variety in this country. Powderpuffs are often produced in litters from two hairless parents, and powderpuff Cresteds will produce both Hairless and powderpuff puppies.

The Chinese Crested is friendly and full of fun. These dogs become strongly attached to their owners and are very loyal. They make excellent house pets with their gay and enchanting personalities. Chinese Cresteds are quite bright and have been successfully trained in obedience. They are quick to make friends and have a very happy go lucky temperament. Despite their somewhat fragile appearance, most owners report that the Chinese Crested is a hardy and healthy dog. "They are great for older people and those who live in apartments," Lee and John Bakuckas say. They are enthusiastic supporters of the Chinese Crested, and were first attracted by the breed's unusual appearance. Several dogs make their home at their Lejo's Chinese Cresteds. While the breed is very good with children, they must not be handled roughly. "If placed with children, we make certain it's a family that will give a toy breed the correct handling," the couple explains. For his size, the Chinese Crested makes a wonderful burglar alarm. "They will bark like a large watchdog," the Bakuckases say.

With his unique appearance and marvelous character, the Chinese Crested is sure to continue to attract attention. Currently, there are more than 2,000 Chinese Cresteds registered in this country. The breed has been granted Miscellaneous Class status by the American Kennel Club and, with official recognition, their numbers are certain to increase. This delightful pet of the Chinese should continue to gain a following. With his distinctive looks, he will be a wonderful addition to American show rings. Already, he has made his presence felt in rare breed shows, where there have been several Best in Show winners. These little dogs have an elegance and a graceful quality that is quite captivating.

Chapter 17

The Chinese Shar-Pei

The story of the Chinese Shar-Pei, and its dramatic rescue from the very edge of extinction, is one of the most stunning success stories in the dog world. Indeed, this tale of triumph may well have contributed to the increasing interest in other rare breeds. From his status as dogdom's rarest breed (according to the Guinness Book of World Records), the Chinese Shar-Pei became the world's most sought after breed. Where once he had been totally unknown, within a few short years, the distinctive wrinkled puppies were offered for sale by the elite Neiman Marcus stores. Responsible breeders were besieged with pet store requests for entire litters. Prices for the unique puppies skyrocketed, and those with dollar signs in their eyes saw the Chinese Shar-Pei as an easy way to turn a quick profit. Unscrupulous profiteers touted the breed as a worthwhile and lucrative investment. But, along the way, this most unusual dog found a host of loyal owners, who repaid the breed's devotion with their own. Where once the future of this breed lay in the hands of only a few, there are now many people who have come to treasure his unique features and outstanding temperament. To them will fall the task of properly educating the public and preserving the qualities that make this breed so endearing. The story of the Chinese Shar-Pei is also a testament to the warm generosity of American dog lovers, who refused to allow an ancient dog to lapse into obscurity.

It seems ironic, considering his present superstar status and the high cost of a Shar-Pei puppy, that this dog was once the companion of the peasant people. Not for him the royal palace of the Emperors and Empresses. He was the dog of the common man...the poor family struggling to feed and clothe themselves. There is no doubt that the Chinese Shar-Pei is a very ancient dog. The breed is believed to have originated in the area surrounding the South China Sea, most likely, Dah Let in Kwan Tung Province. He served his peasant masters as a multi-purpose breed to herd whatever livestock they might be fortunate enough to own, to help them secure food by hunting, and to protect his family and their property from wild predators. But, it was as a home and property guardian that he was most esteemed. Life for the peasant farmer was not an easy one and he was often at the mercy of barbarian thieves. Indeed, this may well have been when the breed's menacing "warrior scowl" was selectively bred. A strong, devoted and fierce looking dog would, most certainly, have been a deterrent. Clay statues from the Han Dynasty (202 B.C. to A.D. 220) show us a dog that closely resembles the modern Shar-Pei (albeit, without his excessive wrinkles) and, even in these ancient art objects, his facial characteristics are clearly visible.

In later years, Dah Let (located not far from Canton) would enjoy a reputation as a gambling center. There wasn't much in the way of formal entertainment and dog fighting became one of the popular diversions. It is to this period that the Chinese Shar- Pei owes the development of his unique and distinctive physical traits. Certainly the peasant farmer must have seen the fighting pits as a way to increase his income and his personal stature. Any edge that would make his dogs more competitive would certainly have been tried and, it is reasonable to assume, that there was selective breeding. These dog fighters developed the Shar-Pei's distinctive coat,

Loong Ch'ai Ho-Gee Poon, a very impressive Shar-Pei male. Ho-Geee is owned by Betsy Davison, Loong Ch'ai Kennels, Sarasota, Florida.

which is bristly and would have been unpleasant in the mouth of an adversary. His tiny ears are characteristic of many fighting breeds and helped to avoid painful wounds in bouts. His small, deep-set eyes were less prone to injury. His recurved canine teeth made it almost impossible for an opponent to slip from his strangleholds. His excessively wrinkled coat, which has attracted more attention than any of his other attributes, enabled him to twist and attack his opponent even while being held. The excessive skin also made it more difficult for an adversary to inflict injury on vital organs. The Shar-Pei, or Chinese Fighting Dog, as he became known during this era, enjoyed great popularity. It is now believed, by those most thoroughly familiar with the Chinese Shar-Pei's characteristics and temperament, that he was not a willing fighter. Noted authorities conjecture that the breed was tormented or induced with alcohol or drugs (possibly even fed gunpowder) in an attempt to make him into a fighting machine. Gradually, China and the area around Canton was opened to the West. With them, foreigners brought their Western fighting dogs and the Shar-Pei was no match. The breed began to decline.

Once again, this noble dog became the companion of the lowly peasant. His lot in life was to provide protection for his master, his family, and his property. It may have been during these hard times that the Shar-Pei was bred primarily for

intelligence. Those animals that were incapable of serving their masters' needs adequately, were slaughtered and used for food. Their skins provided clothing for the family. Only those dogs displaying high intelligence and superb companion dog qualities were allowed to reproduce.

Perhaps the breed would have continued to exist in small pockets throughout southern China and the surrounding areas, were it not for the Communist takeover. Dogs were considered a bourgeois luxury and had no place in the newly forming classless society. Food should be reserved for humans, not used to feed unnecessary canines. In order to enact its programs, the Communist government imposed a tax on those owning dogs, and very few owners were able to retain their pets. In 1947, the tax was once again increased, and the breed's existence was threatened still further. By 1950, only a few scattered specimens remained and the Chinese Shar-Pei seemed doomed.

Fortunately, a few Shar-Pei had made their way into the hands of Hong Kong dog fanciers and breeders. Many people in this country, still recall seeing the photo of a rare "Chinese Fighting Dog" in a magazine which featured an article on endangered breeds. And indeed, this ancient breed probably would have been lost in the near future, except for a remarkably fortunate twist of fate. A young breeder from Hong Kong happened to see the article. Matgo Law owned several Chinese Fighting Dogs and was concerned for the breed's future. Foremost in his mind was the thought that Hong Kong might be returned to

This beautiful black ten-week-old puppy, grew up to become Champion Gold's Lotus of Noah's Ark. Owned by Gayle Gold, House of Gold Kennels, Charlotte, North Carolina.

China, and that canines there might suffer from the same fate that befell Chinese dogs. Was there interest in the breed in the United States, he wondered? Would Americans be interested in helping to save this breed? The chances for success seemed remote, but it was worth a try.

Mr. Law penned a poignant letter to the editor of the magazine. It was a plea for Americans to help save a breed. He included scant details on the breed's history, a few notes on their temperament, and a standard. He offered to sell puppies to anyone that might be interested. Most importantly, he included several photos of adult and puppy Shar-Pei. Many of us will always recall our first glance at these strange looking dogs. So different, so totally unlike any breed known in the United States at that time, the article aroused great interest. Mr. Law received over 200 requests for additional information and puppies. One can only imagine that he must have been totally unprepared for such an outpouring of interest. Certainly, he did not have sufficient breeding stock to meet all the requests. But slowly, a few Shar-Pei began to make their way to this country and they found a very receptive and intrigued public.

One of the earliest recipients of Mr. Law's dogs was a California couple, Ernest W. and Madeline Albright. The Albrights, who were approaching retirement, had been looking into dog breeds. They thought dog breeding would provide them with an

A group of four-week-old Chinese Shar-Pei puppies fromTommie Sue Mason's GilSu Kennels, Inc., in Pensacola, Florida.

ideal hobby, and they wanted a medium sized dog that would be a good home protector. It was, again, one of those fortunate quirks of fate that Mr. and Mrs. Albright saw the photos of Mr. Law's dogs and were intrigued with the Shar-Pei. Ernest Albright began a public relations blitz that, perhaps more than any other occurrence, was responsible for the tremendous public interest and enthusiasm for the Shar-Pei. At every opportunity, he submitted articles and photos of his dogs for publication. His dogs were photographed and appeared in countless newspapers and magazines. Soon television became interested in the breed, and this coverage led to more and more interest. At every opportunity, Mr. Albright touted the breed's high intelligence and wonderful companion qualities. The results of his personal crusade are evident for there are now approximately 10,000 Shar-Pei in this country and the breed is certainly not the rare oddity it once was.

For those who enjoy owning the unusual, the Shar-Pei is cer- tainly the ideal breed. It is his totally unique appearance that has attracted such widespread interest in the breed. A medium size dog, the Shar-pei usually tips the scales at 35-60 pounds. The tremendously wrinkled puppies seemingly have enough skin for any three pups. The wrinkles diminish somewhat as the dog matures. The Shar-Pei has a very distinctive head, which is reminiscent of a hippopotamus. The muzzle is very blunt and broad, and there is little stop. Extremely blocky and full muzzles are commonly referred to, by breeders, as "meatmouths." The Shar-Pei's body is compact, balanced and very muscular. Two coat types are prevalent in the breed. The somewhat longer length is referred to as a "brush coat." The shorter bristly hair, referred to as a "horse coat," is preferred. The Chinese Shar-Pei comes in a wide and pleasing range of colors. These include a pale cream, various shades of

The impressive Champion Gold's Red Baron, owned by Jim Hodges, of Chester Springs, Pennsylvania.
(Ashbey photo)

fawn, red, chocolate (quite rare), sable and black. Spotted dogs do exist, but these are to be heavily penalized in the show ring and excluded from breeding programs. Like the Chow Chow, one of the breed's distinguishing features is his blue-black tongue and mouth. "Flowered" (blue-black markings splotched or spotted with pink) tongue and mouth markings occur, but these are not desirable. Conscientious breeders strive to retain this distinctive feature. Concerned breeders place great emphasis on the "total" dog, and those interested in the Shar-Pei should not allow themselves to be carried away with the concern for only super-wrinkled dogs. The Shar-Pei matures quickly, with most dogs achieving adult height by six to eight months. Some lines will take one year to reach their full height. Like all other breeds the dogs will continue to mature thereafter.

It may be the breed's unusual physical qualities that first attracted many present breeders, but it is the dog's wonderful mental characteristics and personality that created so many enthusiastic Shar-Pei devotees. "My Shar-Pei have the most beautiful temperament of any breed I have ever owned," says Tommie Sue Mason of Pensacola, Florida. "The Shar-Pei are extremely intelligent, most loyal and devoted to their owners, and very protective of their home and family. They understand everything you say and, like an elephant, they never forget." Indeed, one of the qualities most praised by all Shar-Pei breeders is intelligence, and they are determined to retain this quality. "We don't consider temperament a big problem," says Betsy Davison whose Loong Ch'ai

The superb Champion Gold's Black Magic, exemplifies proper Shar-Pei type. Owned by Gayle Gold, House of Gold, Charlotte, North Carolina.

Kennel is located in Sarasota, Florida. "Most Shar-Pei, if handled sensibly, are bowls of mush with their own families. They are not 'one man' dogs. They make excellent house dogs. They are natural clowns and very intelligent. Many of them are the kissee-type, whose goal in life is to slurp faces." Shar-Pei thrive on their owners love and attention. "This is not a breed that you can place in a kennel and forget about," is a comment heard, universally, from all Shar-Pei owners. The dogs are happiest when they are part of the family. Those breeders who are forced to house their Shar-Pei in kennels, find that it is necessary to establish a rotation system, so that all dogs have as much human contact as possible.

The Shar-Pei tends to be aloof with strangers. They have been described as inscrutable and they seem to stand back and size up newcomers. Puppies are, almost always, friendly and outgoing. Most responsible breeders advise careful socialization of puppies. "This is a breed that definitely needs to be socialized at an early age," says Gayle Gold, one of this country's top breeders. Gayle's House of Gold Shar-Pei have accounted for over twenty-five champions and she, like most concerned breeders, places strong emphasis on temperament. "Every dog must first be a pet and companion, then a show dog," she says. Potential owners should ask breeders about their dogs' temperaments. An occasional dog will be overly aggressive or hyperactive, but most concerned breeders cull these animals from their breeding programs.

Some Shar-Pei are aggressive toward other dogs. They will usually accept other breeds if they are introduced at an early age. "Several Shar-Pei can live quite comfortably together," says Gayle Gold. "Occasionally, you will have spats, as with children, until a pecking order is established. I do know of some studs that live and play together without problems, but, as a whole, I don't find that this happens too often. It's asking a lot to introduce a new male into the household where a full grown stud dog already lives. Some Shar-Pei lines have temperament problems with extremely agressive behavior, but, on the whole, temperaments are great."

The Shar-Pei has been successful in obedience work, and it is certain that more owners will be participating in this sport, as the breed grows. "The Chinese Shar-Pei is highly trainable," says Tommie Sue Mason, of GilSu Kennels. "They are occasionally stubborn, but I believe that it's because they hate to repeat things. They are always eager to move on to something new and they never forget what they've learned. This breed will do anything for praise and love. They crave affection."

Potential Shar-Pei owners must be alert to the breed's medical problems. Perhaps because of the breed's distinctive physical traits or the extremely limited gene pool, the Shar-Pei suffers from several conditions. Those interested in purchasing this breed are advised to quiz breeders about the prevalence of these conditions within their bloodlines. It is advisable to seek references from owners of their puppies. Any breeder who denies having any medical problems should be viewed with extreme skepticism.

Many Shar-Pei have problems with entropion. This inrolling of the eyelids causes the dog's eyelashes to scratch the cornea. The eye will frequently ulcerate and, if left untreated, the condition may lead to blindness. Entropion is correctable with surgery and, if caught at a young age, tacking of the eyelids may prevent the development of the condition.

Some Shar-Pei also are afflicted with a condition termed "tight lip." This is most likely to occur in the large muzzled (often called "meatmouth") specimens. The dog's lower lip tends to roll over the teeth and eating becomes very painful and difficult. In severe cases, surgery is recommended.

Many Shar-Pei are also prone to skin disorders. Most will blow their coats as puberty approaches. Breeders describe the coats as having a "moth eaten" appearance. Generally Shar-Peis can be expected to blow their coats twice annually. Pregnant and nursing mothers almost always suffer from ratty looking coats and this should not cause alarm. Buyers are counseled to ask breeders about other skin conditions they may have encountered.

It is advisable to ask your breeder about diet recommendations and follow his advice closely. Many Shar-Pei have great difficulty tolerating soybean based foods. "I warn people to feed them a dog chow that has a base of meatmeal, cornmeal, and a vegetable such as beet pulp-definitely no soybean," says Betsy Davison. "Many cases of skin problems have been cleared up simply by changing to a chow that has the meat/corn/vegetable base."

Those interested in breeding the Shar-Pei should be advised that the breed experiences problems with hip dysplasia. Betsy Davision, the Chinese Shar-Pei Club of America's representative to the Orthopedic Foundation for Animals, found this out the hard way. When one of her first litters contained several dysplastic individuals, this dedicated woman undertook a strenuous x-ray program. It would be wise to ask breeders if they x-ray their breeding stock. In an effort to eliminate the problem, many reputable breeders are now offering written guarantees.

Gayle Gold sums up the attitude of most responsible breeders, "I am totally in love with this breed...problems and all. It is not the perfect breed for everyone because of the health problems, but it sure is a great breed for me." With such dedication, the future of the Shar-Pei in this country seems assured.

Any breed which is suddenly thrust into the limelight will, inevitably, face problems, and the Shar-Pei has his share. But for those who want the thrill of owning the unusual, this breed more than fills the bill. The Chinese Shar-Pei is an ideal companion for the home. He is not prone to wandering, is an excellent watchdog, a delightful and loving companion, and an entertaining and devoted friend. For those wishing to share their home with these wonderful animals, it is best not to rush out and buy the first adorable puppy you see. The time spent in researching bloodlines, corresponding with different breeders and talking with many Shar-Pei owners will be time well spent. All those who truly love and care for the Shar-pei are devoted to seeing that this dog is not a fad, to be discarded when his "rareness" wears off. The Chinese Shar-Pei will, the author believes, take his rightful place among the world's most loved dog breeds.

This is the super wrinkled appearance of the Shar-Pei puppy. This distinctive and unique appearance has attracted much attention to the breed.

Yokayo Bear, a big, impressive Chinook. This beautiful male is owned by Neil Wollpert, of Kettering, Ohio.

Chapter 18

The Chinook

Of all the breeds of dogs around the world, the Chinook qualifies as the rarest of the rare. Listed in the 1966 Guinness Book of World Records as the world's rarest breed, the Chinook has again captured that dubious honor for 1987. The fate of this uniquely American breed is in great peril. Unless dedicated and conscientious dog lovers step in, before it is too late, we may well lose the Chinook. As of February, 1986, there were only 82 living Chinooks worldwide. Of the 37 females only 17 are considered breedable, and of the 45 males only 28 can be used for breeding. This is a frightening figure. To exacerbate the problem, the Chinook is so rare that few people are familiar with the breed, and it is extremely difficult to find homes for available puppies. This makes it very expensive and frustrating for those trying to maintain the breed. I can think of no other breed whose fate, throughout the years, has remained in the hands of so few people. Dog breeders have often achieved the near impossible, and now is the time to take action. The Chinook needs the support of those who love animals, and it needs it now. It would be a shame if this breed, with its colorful past, was allowed to lapse into oblivion, when we had the opportunity to save it.

The Chinook's story begins earlier in this century, in one of the most exciting periods of American history. Gold had been discovered in Alaska, and many men set off to seek their fortunes. Arthur Treadwell Walden was one such man. In 1869, he left his native New Hampshire for Alaska. He became much more fascinated, however, with the noble working dogs that aided men in the north. He was particularly interested in the larger freighting dogs, and he quickly gained an enviable reputation as one of the most experienced and knowledgeable drivers. He was considered by many as the best "dog puncher" of his day.

Adventurers in Walden's day gave little thought to the purebred status of their dogs. They only wanted a hardy dog with endurance and intelligence, and any dog capable of doing the task, regardless of his breeding, became an invaluable asset. A man's dogs might be the difference between his survival and a lonely, freezing death. It is sometimes difficult for us to accurately trace the ancestry of some of the most famous sled dogs. Furthermore, there were no registries for these sled dogs, and a one word name was most efficient when issuing orders. Walden talks about his first dog named Chinook (meaning warm winds) in his book, *A Dog Puncher on the Yukon.* "One of the best dogs I ever owned was Chinook, a large half-breed MacKenzie River Husky. I got him in Dawson in 1898. The man who owned him used him as a one-man dog. He wouldn't sell him for money, but I traded him for three sacks of flour, worth sixty dollars a sack, and two sacks of rolled oats, making two hundred dollars in all. He claimed that Chinook could start a heavier load than any other dog in the Yukon. He cried when he left, carrying his food." A later dog, also named Chinook, was to gain worldwide fame as Arthur Walden's famous lead dog. Eva B. Seeley and Martha Lane tell us in their book, *Chinook and His Family--True Dog Stories,* that this later Chinook, upon whom the present breed is based, was born in a litter of three at Walden's Kennels, in New Hampshire. In Walden's book, *Harness and Pack,* he describes his lead dog and friend. "Chinook was a large tawny yellow dog, a half-bred Eskimo, with dark ears and muzzle. His mother traced her lineage back to Peary's lead dog when he made his famous trip to the North Pole. His father was a mongrel with perhaps a trace of Saint Bernard." Were these two dogs named Chinook related? We will probably never know.

Chinook gained fame in the First International Sled Dog Race between Canada and the United States, in 1922. The race was a total of 120 miles long. The course was split into 40 mile segments, run on three consecutive days, from Berlin, New Hampshire to Colebrook and then to Lancaster, New Hampshire. On the final day the racers returned to Berlin. Camera crews and the press were there to cover this record setting event, and the Walden team, lead by Chinook, triumphed. It was this event that was to capture public attention and fuel interest in sled dogs. In 1925, Walden again entered a team in the event, but he placed second. A new trend had come to the racing world, and the lighter boned and faster little dogs were now the rage.

Eva B. Seeley heard of the racing event and decided that a race would be the perfect attraction for the winter carnival she was organizing. "Short," as she was called, visited Arthur Walden and his wife Kate, at Wonalancet, New Hampshire, to discuss the possibilities. It was here that the physical education instructor was taken for her first sled dog ride. She was particularly impressed with Walden's lead dog, Chinook, whom she described as "an exceptionally strong dog, massive in body for his 90 pounds of weight, and with drop ears." In 1924, Short married Milton Seeley and they spent their honeymoon at Wonalancet. The Waldens and the Seeleys became fast friends, and the couple left New Hampshire with a son of Chinook. "He was a tawny gentle puppy and he was very friendly," Short later said. They named him "Nook." The couples stayed in touch and when, in 1927, Chinook and Arthur Walden traveled to New York, to attend a charity function at the Waldorf Astoria, they stayed with the Seeleys. Milton was suffering from health problems, and doctors had suggested that a change of scenery might be helpful. Walden suggested that the Seeleys move to Wonalancet. They took him up on his offer and moved, in 1928.

Walden's Chinook Kennels, in Wonalancet, was abuzz with activity. Commander Richard Evelyn Byrd had been chosen to lead an expedition to explore the continent of Antarctica. It was a monumental task, for not only did dogs have to be procured, but drivers had to be located and trained. In addition, it was necessary to make arrangements for sleds, harnesses, kennels and food for the dogs. It was decided that Arthur Walden was the one man who was up to the task. The Seeleys became very involved in the preparations, and before Walden left with Byrd and his

men for the Antarctic, Milton and Eva Seeley purchased a half-interest in his Chinook Kennels.

Eva B. Seeley is the acknowledged matriarch of the Alaskan Malamute breed. She was actively involved with both Siberian Huskies and Malamutes, and an examination of the records reveals that she was the owner of both the first Alaskan Malamute registered with the AKC, and the first champion of record. She was also both the breeder and owner of the first Siberian Husky champion bitch. She was instrumental in gaining American Kennel Club recognition for both breeds, and reorganized the Siberian Husky Club of America. She became a dominant force in racing circles and helped to formulate the standards for both breeds.

At his Chinook kennels, Arthur Walden had been working to develop a superior freighting breed. He had discovered that his lead dog was a prepotent sire, and all the puppies he produced resembled this special dog in both temperament and conformation. These dogs were wonderfully intelligent and tended to be more friendly than other sled dog breeds. He called his newly emerging breed Chinooks, in tribute to his most loved dog. We can only imagine that the future of the Chinook breed might have been very different had Short Seeley taken up their cause. Instead, Scotty Allen, another famous driver, had stirred her passion for the Alaskan Malamute.

Walden left with the first Byrd Expedition for Antarctica. Although Chinook was aging, he accompanied Walden on the adventure, and this great old dog and his descendants (early Chinooks) were of extraordinary help to the men in setting up Little America. Chinook was never to return. Short Seeley has said that he was jumped by a number of other dogs and very seriously wounded. He then escaped and was never again seen. Commander Byrd details the significance of the loss in his book, *Little America*.

"The second incident, perhaps the saddest during our whole stay in the Antarctic, was the loss of Walden's famous lead dog, Chinook. Chinook was Walden's pride, and there was no doubting the fact that he was a great dog. He was old when brought to the Antarctic, too old for hard, continuous labor, and Walden used him as a kind of 'shock troop,' throwing him into the team when the going turned very hard. Then the gallant heart of the old dog would rise above the years and pull with the glorious strength of a three-year-old. The affection between him and Walden was a beautiful thing to see: one sensed that each knew and understood the other perfectly, and it was Walden's rare boast that he never needed to give Chinook an order: the dog knew exactly what had to be done. A few days after his twelfth birthday, Chinook disappeared. We searched the camp for him without success; in the trampled snow about the ship, it was impossible to find his tracks. No doubt he made his way alone. Whether he walked out alone to die, because his days of service were done, is something I cannot vouch for: this was the romantic theory advanced by several of the men. At any rate, his body was never found....All this was a deep disappointment to Walden, who wanted to bury Chinook in his harness."

Whether the loss of Chinook was too much to bear, or he simply wanted to retire, Arthur Walden did not participate in freighting activities when he returned to the U.S. He sold the remaining share of his Chinook Kennels to the Seeleys, and they trained the dogs for the next expeditions. Because of Short Seeley's involvement with the Malamute and the Siberian, all Walden's remaining Chinooks were turned over to Mrs. Julia Lombard. She had worked at Chinook Kennels and assisted Walden in working to form the breed. In 1931, Mrs. Lombard became the sole owner of the world's entire population of Chinooks. She continued to breed the dogs until her retirement in 1940.

Then Perry Greene entered the picture. He was one of those eccentric American characters who are so often found in novels from the early part of this century. A true outdoorsman, tall and lanky, Perry claimed that he had been, at one time or another, a trapper, a gold prospector, a lumberjack, a shipyard worker, and an outdoors guide. He won awards for his prowess with an ax and a crosscut saw. He claimed Mohawk ancestry, and was said to be very able with his fists. In 1940, Perry took a team of seven Chinooks on a 502 mile sled trip. Beginning at Fort Kent, on the Canadian border, and ending at Kittery, on the New Hampshire line, Perry and his dogs ran what was, at the time, the longest sled dog trip in U.S. history. It took 90 hours.

From all accounts, Perry was also a spinner of tall tales, and some of the claims he made for his newly acquired Chinooks were mighty tall, indeed. It was he who kept the breed alive for the next twenty-five, or so, years. He concocted a mystery that surrounded the breed, often declaring that he was the only person alive who knew the true ancestry of the Chinook, and he would never divulge the secret. The colorful Greene drew writers to his Maine home, and articles on the Chinook and Perry appeared in several publications. Perhaps the Chinook would never have survived without Perry's inventive approach, but the sad fact was that he never allowed the breed to grow, even in the face of growing interest. He enjoyed being known as the world's sole breeder of the rare Chinook, and so he refused to allow any unspayed bitch to leave his kennel. He always bragged that he could have had the breed registered with the American Kennel Club, but he declared loudly, "Never, never,

A charming Chinook puppy owned by Neil and Marra Wollpert, of Kettering, Ohio.

never...I don't want the breed ruined. If I didn't have control it wouldn't be long before they would be breeding for narrow heads and no brains." Perry had a somewhat unusual policy relating to the sale of dogs. First, he named all dogs and the owner's last name was added when they went to their new homes. Any necessary correspondence was addressed to the dog. Perry personally selected the pup he thought you should have. The prices were based on his evaluation of intelligence and conformation. He guaranteed that pups would be housebroken within three days and declared, "If it takes longer there is something wrong with you." Furthermore, if you wanted to buy a Chinook you had to go to Maine and submit to Perry's scrutiny. "They're not just pets," he told one reporter. "...They're proud individuals and should be treated with respect. So we never ship them or sell them to strangers." Those who wanted to buy a Chinook had to stay in a guest cottage at Perry and Honey Greene's for at least 24 hours. If the dogs didn't like you, you went home empty handed. Many people came to visit the Greenes and their rare dogs. In one year alone, there were 11,000 visitors.

At the death of Perry Greene, followed shortly by the death of Honey, the Chinooks fell on hard times. Perry had kept no records, and all the extraordinary

77

knowledge that he had garnered, from working with the breed, was lost forever. Neither Perry or Honey had left wills. To complicate matters further, Honey had remarried, and the ownership of the Chinooks and the Greene's entire estate had to be settled by the courts. For several years, litigation prevented anything from being done with the breed. Finally, the court chosen heir was ready to put all the remaining dogs to sleep. Luckily, three Chinook owners stepped in. They took the available dogs and split them up, determined to save the breed. Two of these original three remain active to this day. Neil and Marra Wollpert, registrars for the breed, were one of the three couples. Neil had seen a photo of the Chinook in *National Geographic Magazine* in the 1940s, and, in 1969, he bought his first Chinook. "We love the dogs and do not want to see them become extinct," Marra says. "We want others to share in our love."

In the days when Perry Greene was breeding the Chinook, individuals were large, ranging from 85 to 115 pounds. Old photos show them to be large and substantial, with good bone. Today, the Chinook is smaller, although breeders are working to increase size and bone. Nowadays, Chinook bitches weigh in at 50-65 pounds, while males are generally 70-95 pounds. Dark almond shaped eyes are preferred, although amber eyes are permitted. As befits a sled dog, they have a thick double coat. Chinooks come in various shades of tawny, from a deep reddish gold to a light palomino. They may have black face markings and white or buff on specified areas. Although in Walden and Perry Greene's day, most Chinooks had drop ears, today most Chinooks carry their ears erect.

"The Chinook is very easy going and laid back," says Marra Wollpert, of Kettering, Ohio. "They are gentle with children, yet protective when strangers arrive. As soon as the stranger is accepted, the Chinook relaxes and is very eager to please. They make very good companion dogs. They are not aggressive, although they will stand their ground with a stranger. They do not bite and are excellent with people."

Barbara Martin, of Suisun City, California, is an avid Chinook supporter. "Chinooks are a VERY people oriented breed. They will often attach themselves to one person primarily, even though they will love and be protective of the whole family unit. As pups and young adults, their enthusiastic and boisterous personalities make them very bouncy and active. They will mow you down in their delight to show how much they like you.

"They are not aggressive by nature and are normally very patient with children. My youngest child learned to pull herself to a stand by grasping the hair on Kima's chest and dragging herself up. She was always rewarded by a sloppy kiss--never a growl. We had had Kima only two months when this occurred and Kima had never been reared with children of any age! To this day, Kima has never snapped at any child, and I watch six in addition to my own three.

"Like many breeds with a 'pack' type background, the Chinook will need to be taught from day one that his master is the 'leader'. Chinooks need firm, consistent discipline to keep them obedient. By three, if properly trained and loved, all that is necessary is to express disapproval with the misdeed. Chinooks live to please their human partners."

With his colorful past and delightful personality, it would be our great loss if the Chinook became extinct. It could very well happen within our lifetimes. With total breed population below 100, a serious epidemic could virtually wipe out the breed. Furthermore, the fate of the Chinook, at this time, still lies in the hands of too few dog lovers. Dog breeders around the world have accomplished some great feats, and now is the time for them to turn their attention to the Chinook. Pictures of Perry Greene's old dogs show many of them to be truly magnificent. Surely, we can make a committment and return the Chinook to his former glory.

Chapter 19

The Czech Terrier

The Czech, or Cesky Terrier, as it is known in some European countries, is unique in the dog world. Only recently developed, this stunningly beautiful dog's ancestry can be fully authenticated. With his distinctive appearance and wonderful disposition, the Czech Terrier is making a name for himself in European dog circles, where he has garnered some notable wins.

The Czech Terrier was "invented" by Dr. Frantisek Horak of Czechoslovakia. Dr. Horak, a noted geneticist, worked with the Academy of Sciences in Prague. Articles by Dr. Horak appeared in many publications. He wrote on genetics, dog care, and proper management of horses and ponies. However, his first love remained terriers.

The Scottish Terrier is very popular in Czechoslovakia, and Dr. Horak was one of the country's premier breeders. From 1932 until 1963, his Scotties dominated Czech show rings. But, the Scottie is more than a show dog in Czechoslovakia. While he is primarily a household companion in most countries of the world, the Czechs still use the breed for hunting fox, rats and other small varmints. Dr. Horak, an avid hunter, who also raised Sealyhams, was a member of the Hunting Association of Prague. While he loved the Scottie, he did not find them to be the ideal go-to-ground dog. The breed's large head and broad chest made it difficult for them to corner a fox or rat once it it had been trapped in the hole. Dr. Horak's Scotties, game though they were, would often wedge themselves underground. Also, the breed's hard coat, so important in the show ring, did not allow them to slither easily into the holes.

Dr. Horak finally decided to try his hand at breeding a superior working terrier. He wanted a dog with a narrower, more practical front and longer legs. A hanging ear would help to provide protection from the dirt encountered while digging. This ideal dog would also need a tail long enough to permit the hunter to pull him from the hole. The coat color should be a practical one, with little white. In addition, the dog must be active, have good hunting instincts and be easy to train.

In 1949, Dr. Horak bred a Scottie bitch to a Sealyham male. He carefully charted all breedings and kept meticulous notes. After a total of only four crossbreedings, Dr. Horak had achieved his goal. A silver-blue pup, with silver fox highlights, was born. This fellow, Javor Lovu Zdar, was the dog that Dr. Horak had dreamed about. He christened the breed the Czech Terrier, in honor of his homeland. There were sufficient progeny from these four crossbreedings to enable Dr. Horak to continue his breeding program. To the doctor's delight the little dogs bred true. No further crossbreedings have been necessary. It is a testament to Dr. Horak's knowledge of genetics that the end result was achieved so rapidly.

Javor Lovu Zdar was first exhibited in Leipzig, East Germany, in 1959, as a "point of interest." His appearance caused a sensation, and many dog people stopped to speak with Dr. Horak about his new creation. The breed was officially recognized by the Federacion Cynologique Internationale in 1963, and Javor became the first champion. In only fourteen years, Dr. Frantisek Horak had succeeded in creating a new breed of dog and piloting it to official recognition.

The Czech Terrier is a low slung dog, standing from 10 1/2 to 14 inches tall and weighing

13-20 pounds. The standard says, "Thanks to its size, the Czech Terrier has fine natural qualities as a going-to-ground and open-field terrier. Although his legs are short, he is an agile, rugged dog, tenacious in his battles against game and rodents, but not unduly aggressive." The Czech has a moderate length body. The standard specifies that the "ideal circumference of the body immediately behind the elbows is 15 1/2 - 18 inches." The breed's 7-8 inch long tail is generally carried down although it may be raised somewhat when the dog is excited. The standard calls for two distinct colors. By far the most popular are the blue shades. Puppies destined to be this color, are black at birth. Also permissable is a brown described as "light coffee". Brown puppies are chocolate at birth. The distinctive coat is dense and glossy. The Czech's deepset eyes peer from beneath his overhanging brow. Blue/gray dogs have black eyes, while brown dogs may have light to dark brown eye color. Nose color also coordinates with the coat, with blue/gray dogs having black noses, while dogs in brown tones generally have liver noses. The prescribed method of grooming allows the dog to hunt and still compete successfully in the show ring. Clipping can be done several days before a show. The standard describes the proper method of grooming. The coat "should be clipped, depending on the season and the working requirements. On the forepart of the head the hair should not be clipped, thus forming a thick beard and prominent eyebrows. On the legs, chest and belly also the hair should not be clipped. The dividing line between clipped and unclipped areas should be skillfully tapered, not abrupt. In a dog prepared for showing, the hair on the neck and back should not be longer than 2/3 inch. When it is cut the coat is lighter, finer and moderately wavy; As it grows out it becomes darker, wavier and almost curly. Over the entire body the hair should be dense and with a silky gloss."

Those familiar with the Cesky say that they are magnificent pets. They are clever and have delightful personalities. In addition they tend to be less quarrelsome than most other terrier breeds, and, generally, get along easily with other dogs. The Czech Terrier is quite alert and makes a very good watchdog. Those who own the breed say that the little Czechs are quite loyal and very fond of children.

With his stunning beauty, the Czech Terrier would certainly perform well in American show rings. This great little terrier is versatile and can provide owners with hours of enjoyment. An ideal household companion, an avid hunter, a stunning show dog, the Czech Terrier would make a welcome addition to the breeds that have made their homes in the United States.

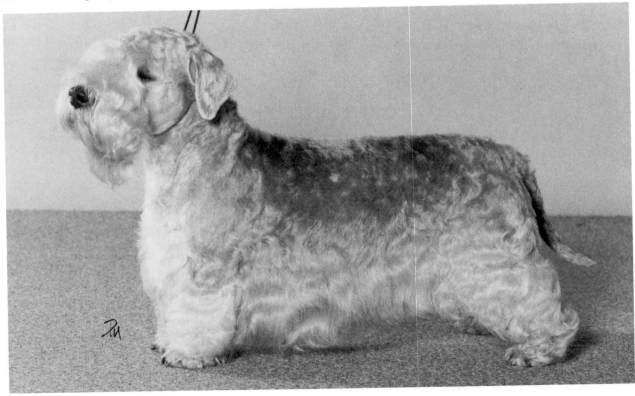

International, Scandinavian and Swedish Champion Neodomansky, owned by Christina Ekh, is a superb Czech Terrier. (Per Undén photo)

Chapter 20

The Dogue de Bordeaux

Meet the powerful and impressive French version of the Mastiff...the Dogue de Bordeaux. The breed was first brought to the United States in the late 1960's. Progress in this country was slow, but with the growing interest in rare dogs, this worthy French breed is attracting much attention. There are currently about twenty Dogues in this country, but the number is sure to grow. Recently three fanciers joined forces to form the Dogue de Bordeaux Club of America, and this organization promises to aid in spreading the word about this wonderful breed.

There are many theories on the origin of this French native. The English have speculated that the breed first came about from a cross of the Mastiff and the Bulldog. Other authorities contend that the breed's predecessor accompanied the Oriental tribe of Alains, when they migrated to France in the Middle Ages. Still others believe that the breed is descended from the Roman war dogs of old. Whatever his precise origin, the breed has long been known in France. The barbaric practice of pitting dogs against bulls, bears and other dogs was just as popular in France as in medieval England. The Dogue de Bordeaux was a worthy competitor. However, even in those early days, the Dogue de Bordeaux was regarded as a multi-purpose animal. "In the Pyrenees and in South France," one authority tells us, "it was kept to protect herds of cattle against the depredations of wolves and bears, and accompanied sportsmen on boar and bear hunting expeditions. Spanish mercenaries took many of these dogs with them in the war against Mexico." If this information is correct, it would certainly appear that the Dogue de Bordeaux actually arrived on the North American continent much earlier than is generally conceded.

"The Dogue de Bordeaux was used in Aquitane, and elsewhere, as a fighting dog against the bull, the bear and other dogs," says the renowned French breed authority Raymond Triquet. "It became its glory and its misfortune, because he acquired a detestable reputation. We say of an irritable man that he has a dogue's temper, but there is not a dog more equable, more balanced and quieter than the dogue." Like the Bulldog, when the days of baiting were past, French breeders concentrated on ameliorating the breed's aggressiveness and selectively bred for his outstanding characteristics. They have succeeded admirably.

The Dogue de Bordeaux is a massive, powerful dog that is somewhat low in stature. Do not be misled by his heavy body, though, for the Dogue is quick, agile and very athletic. He is a well balanced dog of impressive size. While the standard calls for a 23-26 inch height, many large males exceed this size. Males must be at least 100 pounds, and females can be no smaller than 88 pounds. Again, they are, frequently, substantially larger. The Dogue de Bordeaux should have ample muscle, particularly in his shoulders and forequarters. The Dogue's head is a distinctive breed characteristic and is described thusly: "Tremendous, with a characteristic expression and appearance. The skull is broad and short, and its circumference is approximately the same as the height at the withers in males." As befits a former fighting dog, he has very strong jaws. Also contributing to the breed's unique head, is the undershot jaw. Dogues should be undershot by well over 1/4 inch. His body is

A superb male Dogue de Bordeaux owned by Jacque Dive, of France.

massive, and his chest deep and broad. "The circumference of the body, behind the elbows, should be some 10-12 inches more than the height at the withers," says the standard. The Dogue de Bordeaux comes in several colors, although the warm tones are preferred. Most common colors are fawn, golden and mahogany. A distinct black or red mask is a must. Nose and pigmentation, in black masked dogs, ill be black, but is generally lighter in red masked animals.

Although some old books proclaim that the Dogue de Bordeaux has a sharp temperament, those familiar with the breed are anxious to dispel this notion. "I think that it is this gentleness, and that hidden loyalty under his terrible mask, that attracts the actual amateurs," Raymond Triquet says. Steve and Wendy Norris, together with Dr. Phillip Todd, have formed the Dogue de Bordeaux Club of America. Seven grown Dogues and a recent litter of eight puppies share the Norris' Kansas City home. "We have spent nearly five years researching and working daily with our Dogues," Wendy Norris says. Mrs. Norris is effusive in her respect for Raymond Triquet, an economist from Paris. "If

there is one person responsible for the breed not slipping into extinction, it would definitely be Prof. Triquet. He was the founder and President of the Club from the mid-1960's up until 1984, when he chose to retire. He has also owned some of the finest Dogues shown in France in the last 20 years. "One must keep the dogue equable, stable, loving and vigilant," Professor Triquet writes. "A long time ago they made a gladiator of him. One can also make of him a living room dog. The Dogue de Bordeaux has talent for both functions. But he must not be either of these functions, but stay the superb athlete, built like a wrestler, close to the ground, muscle bound, prompt and eager to defend his master and his home."

Those who have had the opportunity to live with the Dogue de Bordeaux know him as an affectionate and loving animal. Although he is large and powerful, he is calm by nature and not prone to hyperactivity. Despite his large size, he is well suited to even small homes, where he will lie unobtrusively until his master beckons him for fun outside. In Europe, he is often kept as a pet in apartments. The Bordeaux is also known for his superior intelligence. This breed seems to have a particular fondness for small children and has gained a reputation for being unfailingly trustworthy.

As a watchdog, the Dogue de Bordeaux is without equal. One breeder calls him the "ultimate guard dog." He is completely fearless and will not tolerate uninvited intruders. However, once strangers are admitted by his owner, he is most accepting. It would take a very foolish individual to challenge a Douge on his home ground. "The Bordeaux Dogue is a companionable and loving dog to the immediate family," says Dr. Phillip Todd. "He enjoys the company of children, but is suspicious of strangers. He will readily accept other dogs and animals, but males tend to be more protective and aggressive toward strange male dogs near their master's property." Dr. Todd has had many years of experience with the breed. A former Bullmastiff owner, this Army doctor acquired his first Dogue de Bordeaux in the late 1960's. "Dr. Phillip Todd should be credited with establishing the breed in the U.S.," Wendy Norris says. "Without his assistance, there would probably be no Dogues in the U.S. today. He started working with Prof. Triquet and the French Club in 1969."

"The Dogue de Bordeaux, under his forbidding look, has a great need for affection," says Professor Triquet. "At the price of a few caresses, you will have a most affectionate companion, the most attentive and best bodyguard that anyone could hope to have." Indeed, Americans are discovering the truth of Raymond Triquet's wise words. The number of Dogues in this country seems sure to rise in the coming years. Fortunately, Steve and Wendy Norris, who have traveled extensively in France and delved into the history of the breed, have been fortunate in obtaining the support of French breeders. They have imported excellent foundation stock and are truly dedicated to establishing the breed in this country. But, the Norrises caution, you must be patient if you wish to purchase a Dogue. The breed is also attracting great attention in other European countries and the Dogue de Bordeaux is not a common breed in France. Wendy tells us that only 250 puppies were born in all of France last year. "**Good** Bordeauxs only come to those who wait," she says. Americans are discovering that, with their many wonderful qualities, these impressive French dogs are well worth the wait.

A trio of excellent Dogues de Bordeaux owned by the esteemed breeder Professor Raymond Triquet, of France.

The lovely Elnora Kazan v. Breezand's Bravoure, dam of four Dutch champions, owned by R. John Farley, Starlyte Dutch Shepherds, Gig Harbor, Washington.

Chapter 21

The Dutch Shepherd

It seems as though most every country has its sheepherding breed. Many people do not understand the derivation of the inherent desire that these dogs so ably display. And yet, dogs have been used for sheepherding for centuries. Man's use of these dogs, for his own purposes, is a testament to selective breeding. Many people have the misguided belief that the herding breeds attend to their duties because of some benevolent characteristic that makes them peculiarly fond of livestock. Nothing could be further from the truth.

Early dogs were hunters, just as man, himself, was. The dog's instinct was to run down prey and kill it. In the days when all dogs were members of packs (and, indeed, feral dog packs operate in the same way today), the swifter dogs in the pack would race ahead of a herd of animals. They would attempt to cut out and turn one member of the herd, so that it could fall into the clutches of the other pack members. It is clear that early man observed the hunting style of the animals and attempted to emulate it himself.

In later times, man began to maintain his own herds of livestock. With the closer association with man, the dog became more responsive to his owners desires and needs. He was now well fed, and his instinct to hunt for preservation and survival could be curbed. Instead of running down and cutting out an individual for his packmates, the dog could cut out a single sheep and bring it to his master. What the livestock owner most needed for this task was a dog that would respond quickly to his commands, and yet have the common sense to think for himself when the situation dictated. This faculty for instant obedience to commands, an innate intelligence and common sense are the hallmarks of the herding breeds. The

Dutch Shepherd, though little known, is a distinguished member of this group.

The Dutch Shepherd, or *Hollandse Herdershond*, as he is commonly called in the Netherlands, is a striking dog. Undoubtedly, he is related to the four varieties of Belgian Sheepdogs and the German Shepherd. This breed is one of the only two surviving sheep herding breeds from Holland. The other, the *Schapendoes,* is somewhat reminiscent of the Bearded Collie.

The skyrocketing popularity of the German Shepherd has had an adverse impact on the herding breeds of Europe. Probably the world's best known breed of dog, the German Shepherd became so popular and sought after that he supplanted many lesser known breeds. As the German Shepherd's star rose, the fate of many other breeds diminished. The Dutch Shepherd was certainly no exception.

The Dutch Shepherd is believed to have evolved in the North Brabant region. There, they gained a reputation as superb herders It was said that this breed had an intense aptitude for herding. This native of Holland was renowned for his stamina, his amazing speed and his efficient ground covering ability as he worked. Early examples of the breed were of extremely diverse type, since the Dutch farmer cared little for looks. His only need was for a strong, rugged and able working dog.

The breed was first recognized about 1870, but it was some time before they were seen in the show ring. The formation of a breed club did much to aid in breed improvement. These native dogs came to the attention of residents of the Netherlands and, in the 1890's, there was a swell of interest in the Dutch Shepherd. As we have seen so often in the history of purebred dogs, sudden success is often harmful. In an effort to fullfil the public's demand, poor quality dogs were bred and touted as excellent examples of the breed. Overall quality declined rapidly and the breed club stepped in to counter the situation. Unfortunately, although motivated by their great love for and devotion to the breed, they overreacted. It was decreed that no dog showing any white marking, no matter how small, could be bred. This caused some truly outstanding individuals to be withheld from breeding. "The very thought of white in a litter, created nightmares for breeders," one Dutch writer said. Some time later, this unfortunate section of the standard would be revised, allowing for a small amount of white on the chest and the toes. Unfortunately, the stringent requirement had taken its toll, and many breeders turned away from the Dutch Shepherd.

Monique Consolazio is a Keeshond breeder in Putnam Valley, New York. As a native of Holland, she is much concerned about the status of the breeds from her homeland. "Regrettably, almost all the native Dutch breeds have been neglected, and only through the efforts of small, interested groups have these breeds managed to survive. Always a highly affluent people, the Dutch found more excitement in expensive foreign breeds." Monique is a member of Keeshond Rescue in the state of New York. "We often hear the Keeshond referred to as a great favorite of the Dutch people, and categorized as their national dog. The truth is that one must travel far and wide throughout Holland to find a Kees, and then it is likely to be an English import!"

We know that over the years, some Dutch Shepherds have been imported to this country. The most recent importations were made by Keith Ranney, of Gig Harbor, Washington. Mr. Ranney and his partner own an importing service, and they have helped other dog lovers bring rare breeds to this country. Keith began in dogs several years ago with German Shepherds, but he was dissatisfied with a decline in quality in the breed. "My personal interest is with the working breeds," Keith says. "When my associate and I began our importing endeavors in January, 1984, we consciously decided that we would keep our eyes open for a rare, all-around working breed to introduce to the United States. The Hollandse Herdershonden, or Dutch Shepherd Dog, fit that bill perfectly. The choice was both business and personal."

Keith Ranney has several of the breed at his Starlyte Kennels, in Washington. "Thus far, I have discovered many similiarities between the Dutch Shepherd and the Belgian Malinois. The Malinois breeders who have come to see my dogs have pointed out many similiarities, and they say that the Tervurens, the Groenendaels (known in this country as the Belgian Sheepdog), the Malinois, and the Dutch Shepherds are much the same dog with very strong instincts toward herding." We should not be surprised by this, as Belgium and the Netherlands are neighbors. There seems to be fairly conclusive proof that this Dutch breed is descended from the Belgian Laekenois (one of the four varieties of Belgian Sheepdogs).

The Dutch Shepherd has a lovely personality, and is extremely intelligent and quick to learn. Not only is he a proficient herder, but the breed has also been used successfully in police work. It has been reported that this native breed is a particular favorite of Dutch gamekeepers, who keep them as guard dogs. Owners report that the Dutch Shepherd is very docile and undemanding in the home, although he benefits from a close family relationship. "All breeds now used for 'man work' appear to suffer from shy-sharpness," says a Dutch publication, "but luckily the Dutch Shepherd Dog has remained in sensible hands, and the dog which will defend its family bravely, will, at the same time, be completely trustworthy concerning people who do not pose a threat, such as delivery boys, mailmen, etc." Indeed, it would be uncharacteristic for these dogs to display unwarranted aggression toward humans. The Dutch Shepherd has a lively and outgoing personality, and is extremely faithful to his owner.

The breed comes in three varieties, distinguished by varying coats. All are a most attractive brindle. The Shorthaired variety is far and away the most popular. The Coarsehaired, Wirehaired, or Rough Coated variety comes next in popularity, but this coat type has not found favor in recent years. Regrettably, the very beautiful Longhaired variety has been steadily losing ground and, many believe, is on its way to extinction. A Dutch publication, written several years ago, stated that only about 200 longhairs remained in the country. That number may have declined further. It is believed that the roughcoat is the oldest of the three varieties and, one Dutch writer warns, "he must not be made into a show dog, with a terrier coat clip, as the latter has resulted in less of an undercoat, making the animal useless for work in the elements. One must also guard against the 'wolf-trot' of the German Shepherd Dog, which is not a functioning working gait."

The *Korthaar,* or shorthaired variety, has a short, dense, flat coat. Even shorthaired dogs possess an undercoat which protects them from the elements. The coat comes in chestnut, yellow or brown, and is brindled, or streaked, with silver or gold. The dog should have a black mask. The wirehaired variety, called the *Ruwhaar* in Holland, is outfitted with a straight hard coat that is quite attractive. They present a distinctive appearance with their moustaches, beards, and the tufts of hair over their eyes. Wirehairs have a somewhat squarer muzzle than the other varieties. The standard calls for their color to be "yellow, red-brown, ash blue, streaked, gray-blue, salt and pepper." Longhaired Dutch Shepherds (or *Langhaars)* have flat, harsh coats with a prominent mane and trousers. Their undercoat is pronounced and wooly. The standard tells us that the ears should never be fringed. They come in chestnut, with gold or silver brindling.

The Dutch Shepherd exhibits great balance and symmetry. Males measure 23-25 inches and females stand 21 1/2-24 1/2 inches tall. The standard allows for a reduced size for the longhaired variety, but they must be at least 21 1/2 inches for males and 21 inches for females. The breed is slightly longer than tall. The body gives the impression of leaness and these dogs have a decidedly elegant quality. Pigmentation is always black, regardless of coat color, and the almond-shaped eyes are dark. They are stong muscular dogs with moderate angulation. All in all, it is a very natural breed, without exaggeration.

It's too soon to tell what kind of future the Dutch Shepherd has in this country. With his striking brindle coloration, he would undoubtedly make a beautiful member of the Herding Group. One hopes that he will find a place here and will be appreciated for both his working qualities and his great beauty. Those attracted to the photos of the Dutch Shepherd, might consider trying to locate one of the longhaired specimens. Old photos show these dogs to be remarkably attractive, and, unless dog fanciers step in soon, this variety may be lost to us forever. Regardless of coat length, the Dutch Shepherd seems sure to make a devoted addition to American homes.

An impressive ten week old Dutch Shepherd puppy from Starlyte Dutch Shepherds, in Gig Harbor, Washington.

A beautiful head study of Bend's Pat. This lovely photo is used to illustrate the English Shepherd Club of America's breed brochure.

Chapter 22

The English Shepherd

"You won't find a better all-around dog than an English Shepherd," says Frank Russell. At his sides sits Max. Although the Alabama resident has never been involved in breeding and, indeed, has owned only one dog at a time, he is an enthusiastic promoter of the breed. "An English Shepherd can do anything," he says. "He will work whatever kind of stock you raise, he will protect your henhouse from varmints, he will be a companion to your children, he will chase away stray dogs and he will protect you with his life. Besides, he's a great friend when you are lonely."

While the English Shepherd is well known in stockdog circles, most dog lovers have never heard of the breed. When I asked several otherwise knowledgeable dog people, what they knew about the English Shepherd, the most consistent comment was, "They aren't really purebred are they?" Yes, indeed, they are. In fact, English Shepherds have been in this country since before the Declaration of Independence was signed. The breed has gained more public attention since its recognition by the United Kennel Club. Still, breeders who do not live in rural areas face problems, due to scant public knowledge, as one breeder, in the Baltimore- Washington, D.C. area discovered. When she had her first litter, she placed an advertisement in the paper. She found that she couldn't even persuade people to come see puppies from a breed about which they knew nothing. This industrious woman did not allow herself to be deterred. She donated two puppies to a local program that trained dogs for the hearing impaired. The service was so pleased with their new English Shepherds, that their representative returned to purchase two more puppies! This would come as no surprise to English Shepherd owners. When you speak with owners of

these dogs, you'll hear some amazing stories. You'll be tempted to take their claims with a grain of salt. Spend some time with one of these dogs, though, and you'll have some stories of your own to tell. Some breeders call the English Shepherd, "the world's best all-purpose dog." They just may be right!

"I got my first English Shepherd in the late 1940's," Frank Russell says. "I was at this feller's farm and he had this dog helping him. He had some pretty wild ton bulls, but he had this dog that could handle them with ease. I was amazed. I'd had dogs all my life, but I'd never seen one that could handle stubborn bulls like this guy. He was fully in control, and whenever this man gave the dog a command, be it by voice or hand signal, the dog reacted with almost lightning speed. I just couldn't take my eyes off that English Shepherd. I spent half the day trying to talk that man into selling me the dog. He must have thought I was just some darn fool and he kept telling me, 'Son, you won't ever have enough money to buy that dog.' I kept pestering him, and I think he was sort of proud that I was so impressed with his dog. Finally, he told me about a woman in the next town that had a litter sired by his dog. The next day, I bought my first English Shepherd, and I've had one ever since. Max, here, is the fifth English Shepherd that I've owned."

Max and Mr. Russell sat on the porch. Frank stroked the dog's head as he spoke of the English Shepherds that had shared his life. Sometimes he would laugh and a few times I thought he was close to tears. "I don't know what I would have done without Max," he says quietly. "When my wife died, I was pretty lonely, and sometimes I just didn't feel like going on. But Max had to be fed, and if I sat around for too long, he would come nudge me. I tried to just let him out of the house, but he'd stand by the front door and whine. He wanted me to go with him. So we started taking long walks. I don't farm anymore. I'm retired and I'd probably just sit around, like so many other old people, if it weren't for Max. He keeps me young. He has a few gray hairs now, but then so do I," he laughs.

Mr. Russell began farming when he got out of the service, following World War II. "I was in the dairy business when I got Chuck, my first English Shepherd. He was one heck of a worker, and I wish I had a nickle for every minute he saved me. That dog would herd anything. I once saw him try to round up and herd some deer that wandered on the property. That was some sight! He worked every day of his life on the farm, and he loved farming as much as I did. Since we had so many people coming and going around here, he was a little friendlier than most English Shepherds. They're usually a little standoffish with strangers, but Chuck was a darned friendly dog. The only time he'd carry on was when someone arrived while my wife or I were in the house. Every day he'd usher those cows in and out of their stanchions so they could be milked. He'd move them from pasture to pasture, and he was great at loading them in trucks when we sold them or took them to auction.

"He was a good stockdog. English Shepherds are what you call 'low heelers.' Do you know what that means?" he asks. "These dogs will circle around and get behind the cattle, and they'll bite the backs of their hocks to get them to move where they want them. They can give them quite a bite, and they have to be very alert and have good reflexes so they won't get kicked. They can be pretty rough when they're working tough stock. My dogs have all had what they call 'grit.' I've seen them be pretty fierce and determined with the big stock, and then turn right around and be amazingly gentle when they were working with calves. When we had our Old George, I was raising hogs. You could make money on them in those days. They used to call them mortgage lifters. Anyway, hogs can be mighty difficult to handle. Some people think that they're stupid, but they couldn't be more wrong. They're stubborn animals, and I think they present more problems to dogs than any other stock. But Old George worked them with no trouble at all and, I believe, almost any good English Shepherd could do the same.

"We were raising our family when we got our first English Shepherd. Those were tough times, and sometimes I had to work at outside jobs. There were many nights when I got home pretty late, and I felt real good that we had Chuck to look after the family. He never really calmed down until I got home. He

Halsell's Roger and Halsell's Chloe at a County Fair. These two lovely dogs are owned by Mrs. F. H. Halsell, who now lives in White Plains, New York.

was a good sized dog and must've weighed about 60 pounds. He had a big bark and wouldn't let anyone in the house at night, unless I was there. These dogs are great with your kids. My wife found that they made great babysitters. She used to carry the youngsters to the garden with her or to the barn when she was doing her chores, and it took her twice as long to get things done because she was always stopping to check on the young'uns. She discovered that our dog was always with the kids. He was a best friend to our little girl. You could trust him to watch over her and play with her in the front yard. We never needed to worry, even though we lived just off a well traveled main road. My wife would be working in the house and she'd hear our little girl crying and yelling. She'd go outside and there would be Chuck holding my daughter's skirt in his mouth. Whenever she tried to go toward the road he'd grab her and stop her. He ripped a couple of her dresses, but he never even nipped her, even when she pulled his ears and tried to ride him. Chuck felt the same way about our sons too.

"There was only one problem. He wouldn't let us spank the kids. I remember the first time I was going to teach one a lesson. Chuck became very upset when I started to spank my daughter. It was the first time he ever growled at me. When I didn't stop, he grabbed my shirt sleeve and just stood there with it in his mouth, his eyes pleading with me not to do it anymore. I never had to spank my kids much, but when it was necessary, we had to tie Chuck up."

The breed shares a common heritage with the other British herding breeds. English Shepherds bear some resemblance to the Border Collie, although there are differences. Some claim that they are related to the Rough Collie. They came to this country with some of the earliest English settlers. These early American immigrants brought livestock with them when they came to settle in the New World. Because they hailed from England, their working dogs were called, simply, English Shepherds or English Collies. Raised on American farms, they were valued for their ability to perform a number of tasks and for their qualities as a fine family dog. They were not taken to shows, and no one included them in fancy breeding programs. The only consideration at breeding time, was the desire to retain fine working qualities and stable, loving personalities. If anyone asked, he was likely to be told that this was a "farm collie."

The English Shepherd is a medium size breed, standing about 20 inches tall and weighing about 50 pounds. He carries a heavy coat that comes in a variety of colors. The standard allows for black and white, black and tan, and tri-color (black, white and tan). These are the most preferred colors, although the standard also lists as permissable, "white ring around the neck, white tip on the tail, white chest, lower legs and face blaze; tan dots over the eyes, on feet, sable color." The English Shepherd's ears are usually half pricked and he should always have round, dark eyes. He is a muscular dog with moderate angulation.

The breed is known for its loyalty and intelligence. These are bright that dogs that learn very quickly. They have a calm steady nature that wins the admiration of their owners. Strong protective instincts make them ideal watchdogs. They are known for their gentleness and patience with children, and many a child has grown up with an English Shepherd as his best friend. English Shepherds are active, energetic dogs who love to learn and can be taught a wide repertoire of tricks.

If you like a versatile dog, you need look no further than the English Shepherd. One hopes that this breed will come to the attention of more and more dog lovers. His greatest fame is likely to come, as it always has, from his excellent working skills. "You just can't beat this breed," Frank Russell says. "I've thanked my lucky stars, many times, that I happened to see that first English Shepherd. I've never regretted choosing the breed. Over the years, I've met many people who've owned them. They talk about their dogs with great fondness. It's hard to forget an English Shepherd."

The English Shepherd is an extraordinary children's companion as this dog, bred by Elizabeth Halsell, of White Plains, New York, illustrates.

Sachem Farms Buster, owned by Vincent Tucci, if Medford, New York, is a superb example of a Fila Brasileiro.

Chapter 23

The Fila Brasileiro

The Fila Brasileiro is one of the newest breeds to be introduced to this country. Although there are examples of this breed in Germany, until recent times it has remained virtually unknown outside Brazil. Now, dog lovers are discovering this, and other, South American breeds. The Fila, the Argentine Dogo and the Peruvian Inca Orchid have attracted much attention and seem destined for greater popularity.

The breed takes it's name from the Portuguese word *filar,* which means "to hold or secure." It is difficult to accurately pinpoint the Fila Brasileiro's precise origins. We do know that Portuguese and Spanish Conquistadors arrived on Brazil's shores accompanied by their dogs. In all likelihood, these were large, powerful dogs that aided their masters in subduing the native population. It is known that the forerunners of our modern Bulldog and the English Mastiff were great contributors to his heritage. Bloodhounds were also used to provide greater scenting ability. Undoubtedly, these dogs were bred with local, indigenous breeds. What early breeders succeeded in producing was a dog specifically suited to the conditions of his Brazilian homeland. Those that still remember Filas of the early 1900's say that the breed has changed little in the intervening years.

The Fila is a multi-purpose breed that has seen many uses in Brazil. In colonial times, the Fila was used to track down Indians who were then doomed to slavery. One can only imagine that the natives must have been terrified by the huge, ferocious dogs. Sugar cane plantations often employed Filas to trail and apprehend runaway African slaves. It is said that the breed accompanied explorers on their forays into the jungle wilderness. They found the Fila to be a dog of great stamina, able to withstand the rigors of the humid, steamy climates, and virtually impervious to the stinging insects. The Fila was a strong swimmer and had no difficulty fording streams. Sometimes, these dogs were used for hunting the wily jaguar or the fearsome wild boar. In some parts of Brazil, he earned the nickname *Onceiro* (or jaguar hunter) for his prowess in the hunt.

While the Fila certainly doesn't fit our concept of a stockdog for working cattle, the Brazilians have, indeed, used him for this purpose. In Minas Gervais, which some believe to be the original home of the breed, he gained a reputation as a valued cattle dog. At times he protected domestic herds from predators and rustlers, but he was also used to round up largely wild cattle that had been turned out to graze. When dealing with recalcitrant bulls, the Fila usually grabbed the large beast by the ears, the nose, or the cheeks and held him until he could be lassoed by the cowboys. Ranches sometimes employed a brace of Filas. While one grabbed the bull's head, another would nip at the hocks to subdue the animal. The Fila was a frequent companion on long cattle drives and served as protection for both men and cattle.

The Fila is a large dog, with males measuring twenty-seven inches at the shoulder and bitches standing twenty-four inches in height. Males should weigh a minimum of 110 pounds, while females should be at least 90 pounds. The Fila is a strong dog with large bone, and he gives an impression of power. He has a massive head with rather houndy ears, which are a remnant of his Bloodhound ancestry. This background is further evidenced by his dewlap and thick, loose skin. He comes in all solid colors except mouse gray and white, and brindles are quite

The impressive International Champion Camburi Do Embirema, at home in South America. Owned by Clelia Kruel, Camping Kennels, Brazil.

common. The Fila has some distinct characteristics that are rarely seen in other breeds. He is one of the few dogs that stand higher at the croup than at the withers. Although it would be considered a fault in other breeds, the natural Fila gait is a pace (called the "camel pace"), which causes the dog's body to rock back and forth with a peculiar rolling motion.

The Fila has gained a reputation for attacking first and asking questions later. Actually, this does not adequately describe the breed's temperament, for the Fila is uncommonly devoted to his owner and his home. Filas bond very quickly and very closely with their families, and they thrive on love and attention. Owners report that the breed seems to have a special gentleness and patience with children. Dr. Paulo Santos Cruz describes the breed's extraordinary devotion to his owner. "You captivate him. He thinks you are fantastic. You are his, and so, no one is allowed to disturb you. His adoration will grow for you as this friendship deepens. He will only be happy when he is near you, and he will only ask to be able to lie by your feet."

The Fila Brasileiro Club of America touts this breed as "the world's best natural guard dog." At the same time, a very old proverb in Brazil, "faithful as a Fila dog," demonstrates the breed's legendary capacity

for devotion to family. The Fila is not a breed for everyone. He is very wary and distrustful of strangers, and vistors to a Fila's home must be formally introduced to the dog. There is great responsibility in owning this breed, for they have a natural aversion to strangers and, when they perceive a threat, they will attack. With proper socialization, they will become valued family members who can discriminate between a real threat and an unintentional occurance. Vincent Tucci, a Medford, New York, breeder of Filas, says, "Much has been written of late of the aggressive nature of this breed. This is not to be interpreted as condoning irrational savagery. or as being a danger to his own family. An agitated or restless disposition is highly undesirable. Good specimens, although they are ready to attack on provocation, will demonstrate the firmness of nerves in the calm way of walking, serene and self-assured, and they pay no attention to commotion or strange noises." Indeed, many owners have found that the Fila is calm and quiet when he is away from his home. They say that he will react aggressively only when he is confronted by a direct threat.

Clelia Kruel, a noted Brazilian judge, has raised many different breeds in her thirty years in dogs. This energetic and dedicated woman has done much to popularize the Fila Brasileiro in this country. "We have had Filas for ten years," she says, "after making a careful selection for a reliable guard dog. We wanted a strong, faithful, courageous and fearless dog to guard our two children when we were traveling. After screening the most probable breeds, we selected the Fila Brasileiro, and we've never been disappointed. The Fila is the only dog that has a natural attack against strangers, and that is humble, obedient and very sweet to his owner and his family, especially to children.

Connie Himes poses with a group of Fila puppies from Sho-Win Kennels, Chester Springs, Penn.

Buddy Boy, an outstanding Fila-puppy owned by Margaret E. Jackson, of Collegeville, Pennsylvania.

"The main difference between the Fila and other guard dog breeds is that he attacks and defends his territory without going through any training. Quite the contrary. Obedience training is a must and can be done in six months time to have the dog absolutely under control. In the ring, the judge is able to put his hands on the Fila as long as he has been trained to accept such a situation."

Those who regularly temperament test both puppies and adults have been able to observe, first hand, the Filas natural aggressiveness toward strangers. As puppies, they routinely test in the most aggressive category. In temperament testing adults, the Fila is awesome. While other breeds' reaction to stimulus is mainly attributable to their training, the Fila reacts instinctively in a very aggressive manner. They will not tolerate a threat, and the tester is immediately confronted with a bold and angry dog that leaps, in a suprisingly agile manner, for his throat. He should not be faulted for such reaction as it is an inherent breed characteristic. Because of this propensity, it is essential that owners follow Mrs. Kruel's advice and make sure that they have a properly trained dog that can be controlled by his master. The Fila is forceful and strong, but he will provide you with great security and devotion if you take the time to work with him.

The Fila Brasileiro is the most popular breed in Brazil today where more than 8,000 are registered annually. He has become an esteemed protection dog for city dwellers, and is often used to guard factories, warehouses and other places of business. Brazilians have discovered, in Clelia Kruel's words, that "his greatest value is not in beauty or in his admirable and impressive structure, but in the unique character of the dog." Many Americans have been attracted to the breed for just this reason, and are finding that Clelia Kruel is correct.

"The Fila is what you want him to be," Clelia says. "He may be a killer or sweet as a lamb, it all depends on his owner. It is the entire responsibility of the breeders to preserve the temperament of this unique breed, and to keep the image of the faithful, obedient, loyal companion that he is, besides being a terrific guard dog."

The lovely Finnish Spitz, Champion Jayenn's Auburn Anow, poses with his Pomeranian friend, Jayenn's Windfire. Both are owned by Joan Grant, Jayenn Kennels, Golden, British Columbia, Canada.

Canadian and FSCA (American) Champion Jayenn's Firebrand Finn, C.D., an outstanding example of the breed, owned by Joan Grant, Jayenn Kennels, Canada.

Chapter 24

The Finnish Spitz

"Finnish Spitz resist contact, but only to get your attention. They resist training, but only to convince you they already know it all. They will do everything possible to assume the top dog position, yet are very satisfied to have you there," says Joan Grant, of Golden, British Columbia, Canada. "This breed is independent, loving and intelligent."

Above all, Finnish Spitz are lively dogs. Many owners describe them as having the character of a big dog in a small dog's body. They are very alert and curious and their mobile ears are often a barometer of their feelings. While they are independent by nature, they do love attention and are excellent and trustworthy with children. They are small enough to fit comfortably in a city home, but these sturdy and active dogs derive immense enjoyment from country life, as well. "I've lived and worked with many breeds," Joan Grant says, "but, I've never found a better house pet than the Finnish Spitz. They house train very easily and can be taught to respect property within a few lessons. They are great with children and with other animals. Here they live with a variety of animals, ranging from chickens and geese, to pigs and horses."

In Finland, the breed is known as the *Suomenpystykorva,* which translates as the Finnish Prick-eared or Cock-eared dog. Undoubtedly this is a very old breed, originally descended from the Spitz-type dogs of Central Europe. His first masters were nomadic hunters who gradually traveled northward. One can only imagine that the breed's cheery personality added joy and warmth to the long, cold days. Indeed, the breed's history is inextricably intertwined with the history of the Finnish people. He is even mentioned in the *Kalevala,* the national epic of Finland. Eventually, the early Finnish tribes split. Some stayed in southern Finland, where the dogs would be interbred with other breeds. Other tribes, however, settled in the northern backwoods regions where game and fish were abundant. It was in the north country that the true Finnish Spitz was maintained through the centuries.

The world would probably have never known of this unique breed were it not for the work of two Finnish foresters. Hugo Sandburg and Hugo Roos were avid hunters and they were impressed with the abilities of this native breed. They had become alarmed, however, at the ever decreasing number of true specimens. In 1890, an article by Mr. Sandburg appeared in *Sporten* magazine. He related his experiences with the Finnish Spitz and extolled the breed's ability as a hunting dog. The article included a description of the authentic Finnish Spitz, and urged readers and the Finnish Kennel Club to save the breed before it was too late. The appeal was successful and, in 1892, the Finnish Kennel Club recognized the breed. The first standard was based on Mr. Sandburg's description. Although never a breeder himself, Mr. Sandburg was accorded the privilege of judging the first appearance of this Finnish native in a show ring.

Hugo Roos, however, did breed Finnish Spitz. His committment to the breed led him into remote areas of the country in quest of truly typical breeding stock. He gathered beautiful specimens from backwoods areas and, for more than thirty years, was an active breeder. Most of the world's Finnish Spitz today can trace their ancestry to dogs selected by Mr. Roos. When he retired from breeding, he became a very prominent judge.

The first Finnish Spitz were imported to England

in 1927. While on a shooting and hunting expedition in Scandanavia, Commander Sir Edward Chichester had an opportunity to shoot over the Finnish Spitz. He imported a brace of dogs and, later, an unrelated stud joined him in England. Fortunately, the breed attracted the attention of Lady Kitty Ritson and several other fanciers. Lady Ritson became so fascinated with the breed that, in 1933, she traveled to Finland to see the dogs in their native environment. Other imports arrived in England, and enthusiasts formed the first club.

As in so many countries, World War II was a trying time for dog fanciers in England. It was difficult to obtain food, and many breeding programs were disbanded. As a result, the quality of the breed dropped dramatically. After the war, strengthened by the addition of several imports, English breeders made a concerted effort to improve their breeding programs, and the results have been amazing. Many of the world's top-winning Finnish Spitz have come from British kennels.

In the 1950's, the first Finnish Spitz were imported into the United States. It was not until 1966, however, that a concerted effort was made to acquire breeding stock. Mr. Henry Davidson, of Annandale, Minnesota, and Mrs. Aino Hassell both succeeded in importing specimens of the breed. While Mrs. Hassell's pair produced several litters, the results of her breeding program have lapsed into obscurity. Mr. Davidson, however, continues as a breeder to this day. The Finnish Spitz Club of America was formed in 1975, and imports from Finland, England, and Canada have bolstered the breed in the United States.

It was a native Finn, Ray Rinta, who was responsible for obtaining recognition of the Finnish Spitz in Canada. In his homeland, the Rinta family had always owned the breed. In 1968, Mr. Rinta visited his brother in Finland. He was so captivated by his brother's dog that he decided he had to have a Finnish Spitz of his own. When he returned to Canada, he discussed the situation with his wife and dashed off a letter to a prominent Finnish kennel. Six months later, two puppies, a male and a female, arrived on Canadian soil. It was to be a tragic start. Mr. Rinta had mistakenly understood that the puppies had been given distemper innoculations before leaving Finland. Sadly, they had not. Two months later, the puppies were ill, and the Rintas lost their male. While the female survived, she never reached her full potential.

Once again, Mr. Rinta wrote to Finland. This time he obtained nine month old male and female pups, as well as a two- year old bitch. The adult bitch had already produced one litter in Finland and she was bred again before being sent to Canada. On New Year's Day in 1969, Mr. Rinta's first litter arrived.

"We enjoyed our Finnish Spitz," Mr. Rinta said. "I do a lot of hiking in the mountains in the summertime, and my male dog accompanied me on most of my trips." Mr. Rinta enjoys talking about his treks with his dogs. "On June 21, 1972, a neighbor, who had an Irish Setter, and I, with my Finnish Spitz, decided to go on a week long hiking trip about 200 miles east of Vancouver. It is beautiful alpine country. We slept in the camper at night and rose at six in the morning to hike into the mountains. At two in the afternoon, my Finnish Spitz smelled something in the bush. It was a bobcat." The Irish Setter showed little interest, but the Finnish Spitz, ignoring Mr. Rinta's cries, took off after the cat. Mr. Rinta and his neighbor had equipped their dogs with packs to carry all the food on their trek into the high mountains. The Finnish Spitz sported a four layer thick denim backpack. The little dog battled the cat in the bush for almost fifteen minutes. Mr. Rinta feared that his beloved companion would be killed. When the dog emerged from the bush, he was very much alive, but the pack on his back was in shreds. "That pack probably saved his life," Mr. Rinta said.

Ray Rinta worked energetically to obtain Canadian Kennel Club registration for the breed. He devoted more than three years, and countless hours of work, toward this objective. He submitted a great amount of material, much of it procured from Finland, to the Canadian registry. There was much disagreement as to how the breed should be classified within the existing groups. The Canadian Kennel Club originally proposed listing the breed in the non-sporting group. The Finnish Kennel Club, however, strongly objected. Since the sporting dogs listed in Canada's Group One are all silent hunters, the Finnish Spitz was admitted, in 1974, to the Hound Group.

Although he has seen little use as a hunter outside Finland, in his native country the Finnish Spitz is considered an excellent bird dog. They are extremely proficient in use on the *capercaillie*, a large game bird similiar to our wild turkey. In the field, the dog ranges ahead of the hunter, constantly scouting the area for birds. When he finds one, he will trail it until it settles in a tree. The dog then runs back and forth, and begins to bark. Hunters say that the birds are mesmerized by the movements of the dog's tail. The Finnish Spitz's bark begins softly, then increases in volume until it carries over a vast area. The hunter can, thus, accurately pinpoint the game's location. The dog's barks obscure the sound of the approaching hunter. It is said that the most adept and experienced dogs will purposely lure the bird into shifting position so that the bird turns his back to the gun, thus giving the hunter a decided advantage.

Considering their purpose in Finland, it is no wonder that this breed is an accomplished barker. "Anyone thinking of acquiring a Finkie," (as the breed is sometimes nicknamed), says Joan Grant, "should be told about their history of bark-pointing. In order to be successful hunters, they must have this instinct. A good hunter feels it should point out every robin or sparrow in sight. They might also point or retrieve your domestic fowl. Training can effectively curb these tendencies, but, if not controlled, they can become neighborhood problems."

"They are very beautiful dogs," Ray Rinta says. "Some people say that they bark too much, but I believe that if you teach them correctly, this is not a problem. We have had neighbor's dogs that bark much more than ours do. Of course, if I let them bark as much as they wanted, they would be excessive barkers." While this may be an undesirable trait to some, most Finnish Spitz owners are successful in curbing this tendency through proper and consistent training.

This lively, alert nature and inclination to bark does, however, make the breed an ideal watchdog. "They alert you rather than guard you," says Mrs. Grant. "I prefer them to other breeds which might attack unnecessarily. I have had one attack a man who seemed to be threatening me. If they feel it necessary, they can protect the ones they love with their lives."

All breeders agree that the Finnish Spitz makes an ideal companion. This hardy breed requires minimal care. "I would hate to see this dog living in confined quarters," Joan Grant says. "They will keep themselves in tip-top condition if they have access to an outside run. If this type of run is not available, then every effort should be made to get the dog out regularly for exercise. They become fat and lazy otherwise. If the dogs get plenty of exercise, grooming can be minimal. Even the twice yearly shed-out of their coat presents few problems, as the hair does not mat. I do like to see them receive a monthly brush out, though. I very rarely find it necessary to bathe this breed. Their coat sheds dirt easily and they groom themselves like cats."

Due to their independent nature, Finnish Spitz present challenges to obedience trainers. While Mrs. Grant characterizes the breed as "eager to please," she admits that standard obedience training instruction should be varied for best results. "They seem to wonder why repeating what they already know is so important." With a training routine that keeps the dog interested and enthused, good results are certainly possible. "There are a few dogs here in Canada who have earned their C.D.'s, but only one dog in the world, as far as I know, has a C.D.X.

"I tell all prospective owners to be sure to be firm when the question of who is boss comes up, or

Ten week old Varpo already demonstrates the Finnish Spitz's curious nature. She is owned by Joan Grant of Jayenn's Kennels, Golden, B.C., Canada.

the dog will certainly take over." Most owners fully agree, for as one Finnish Spitz breeder summed it up, "They must be gently, but very firmly, handled during puppyhood, as their ability to take over the household is unsurpassed!"

A very natural dog, the Finnish Spitz constantly attracts attention for his great beauty. His proportions are square and balanced. Most people comment on his fox-like appearance. The breed's luxuriant coat contributes to his distinctive look. He has a short, dense undercoat, and a lush standoff outercoat. Males generally have a pronounced ruff. His beautiful coat may vary from a light honey gold to a deep chestnut red. His 23-30 pound weight, sparkling brown eyes and jet-black nose make the Finnish Spitz a very handsome companion. With his striking looks and lively personality, the breed is certain to catch the eye of judges once he is admitted to American show rings.

Indeed, the breed has enjoyed considerable success in Canadian show rings, and there are now more than fifty champions in that country. Joan Grant has enjoyed great show ring success with her Finnish Spitz. Her first import arrived in 1975, only the seventh of the breed to be registered in Canada. Cullabine Isadora, imported from England, was bred prior to shipping. Out of a litter of four, three remained in Canada and completed their championships. Joan retained the only male,

The world renowned English and Canadian Champion Cullabine Tarik, owned by Joan Grant, Jayenn Kennels, Golden, British Columbia, Canada. The outstanding Tarik is a famous Best in Show winner.

the hands of show breeders who are non-hunters."

The Finnish Spitz has recently been granted Miscellaneous Class status by the American Kennel Club. Like Joan Grant, those dedicated to the breed hope that the fine qualities instilled over the centuries will be preserved. The national dog of Finland is finding a loyal and enthusiastic group of fanciers in this country. Supporters hope that very soon he will take his rightful place in American show rings.

Champion Jayenn's Cullabine Kotka, who became the first group placing Finnish Spitz in the country. In 1976, Mrs. Grant imported another male. Her Champion Cullabine Tarik scored a number of group placings enroute to his championship, and earned a Best in Show. Fortunately, he has passed on his outstanding qualities and sired a number of champions.

Mrs. Grant has raised Pomeranians for many years at her Jayenn Kennels in Canada. In 1973, she acquired her first Norwegian Elkhound. "I found the Elkhound too strong for me at times," she says. "I knew I got along well with spitz personalities, and I researched a number of breeds. I was fascinated by the Finnish Spitz, then newly recognized in Canada. At first, I confused them with the American Eskimo Spitz because of the name similiarity. Many people still do. The Finkie turned out to be the answer for me."

"I haven't done any true hunting with my dogs," Mrs. Grant says, "although my partner, Til Labovich, has been out a few times with one of our co-owned females. This bitch, Champion Jayenn's Happy Harakka, has a yen to hunt. She also went Best in Show at the National Specialty in Minneapolis. I do get requests for hunters, usually from Finlanders. I like to take every pup out into my bush to see what natural instinct it has. I do go bird watching with my dogs, and they are very adept at pointing out birds for me. I want dogs who have hunting instinct, yet are tops in conformation. I would hate to think that this historical trait could be lost because the breed is in

Chapter 25

The German Pinscher

No, your eyes aren't deceiving you. This small dog does strongly resemble the Doberman Pinscher. In fact, a successful Doberman breeder, examining a photo of one of these dogs, remarked at the exceptional quality of this nice "puppy". However, she was viewing a full-grown adult German Pinscher. Sometimes called the Medium Pinscher, the Standard Pinscher, or simply, the Pinscher, this breed is attracting great attention in this country. And rightly so, for the Miniature Pinscher and the Doberman Pinscher are exceedingly popular around the world. The German Pinscher predates the Doberman and is at least as old as the Min Pin. It seems only right that he should take his place among these related breeds.

The German Pinscher has always been a multi-purpose breed. Originally, his primary function was that of ratter, guard dog, and possibly, herder. Though many have referred to all the Pinscher and Schnauzer breeds as stemming from old terrier-type dogs, none of them was ever used for go-to-ground hunting. While the breed is believed to be centuries old, it was not until the 1800's that any serious breeding took place. A moment must be taken to explain the use of the term pinscher. It may have been derived from the English word "pinch" (to seize, nip or squeeze) or from the French term of the same meaning, *pincer*. Reichenbach, writing in 1836, speculated that these dogs were formulated by crossing either the Pug and the Dachshund, or the Greyhound and the Dachshund. While this seems unlikely, it does show that the breed was well known even at that early date. The breed was first officially recognized in 1879.

A breed referred to, in old texts, as the *Bibarhunt* bears a striking similiarity to the German Pinscher of today. The acknowledged expert on Schnauzers and

Pinschers, Berta, discussed the state of these breeds in 1890. He found that Pinschers came in a very confusing array of sizes, colors, types, and hair textures. Indeed, in the early days, with the exception of coat, there was little difference between the Schnauzers and the Pinschers. The Pinscher Club was formed in 1895, and the Friends of the Schnauzer was established in 1907, in Munich. In 1921, the two clubs merged to form the Pinscher-Schnauzer Club. This organization issued the first joint stud book in 1924, and continued to publish a yearly volume until the advent of World War II. Prior to that time, each club maintained separate registries. Recorded in the first edition of the *Pinscher Zuchtbuch*, published in the 1880's, are a number of *Glatthaariges*, as the smooth coated German Pinschers were then known. Records from the 1890's indicate that it was quite common to crossbreed coat and size types. A total of eight *Glatthaariges* are included in the studbook, and five of these have wire-haired parents. One Miniature Schnauzer recorded in the volume had a Min Pin as his sire, and a Min Pin bitch was reported as being out of a Standard Schnauzer mother.

The 1902 book on German breeds, *Gebrauchs- und Luxushunde*, by Emil Ilgner, offers an illustration which is remarkably similiar to the German Pinscher of today. Also included are drawings of the *Reuhhaariger Deutscher Pinscher* (or Wire-haired German Pinscher) that we know today as the Standard Schnauzer. It was not until about 1920 that moves were made to standardize type and separate this confusing mix into distinct breeds. The Pinscher-Schnauzer Club adopted a policy whereby no dog could be registered which did not breed true to type for a minimum of three generations. For example, all smooth coated German Pinschers were required to have three generations of smooth coated forbears in order to qualify for registration. These early discrepancies in type were even seen in this country. A long time authority on Miniature Schnauzers stated that she had seen smooth coated puppies whelped from Mini Schnauzer parents. Interestingly, she found that bitches of this coat type, when bred to properly coated males, produced high-quality, exceptionally hard coats.

The stringent registration policies instituted by the Pinscher-Schnauzer Club have done much to achieve proper type. The German Pinscher now breeds true, and it would be extraordinarily unusual to have an off-type coat in a purebred litter. Further, size has been firmly entrenched, and the German Pinscher is seen only in one size. The Pinscher-Schnauzer Club still registers the breed in Germany today.

There is one other type of Pinscher currently registered in Germany. This unique dog is the Harlequin Pinscher. The small dogs share the looks of the other Pinschers, but are midway in size between the German Pinscher and the Miniature Pinscher. They stand 12 to 14 inches in height and are characterized by their unusual harlequin markings. Their color, according to the German standard, is "white or light coat with markings; grey with black or dark markings; streaked, with or without tan markings."

The German Pinscher is a very attractive breed and, for those who appreciate the sleek looks of the Doberman and the Min Pin, the German Pinscher should be very appealing. The breed typically weighs between 25 and 35 pounds, and stands 16 to 19 inches tall. He exudes elegance, yet is strong and muscular. In motion, he is agile, quick and remarkably graceful. His square body is free of exaggeration. A Pinscher should never be allowed to become so fat that his musculature is not visible. His eyes are oval and of medium size, and the standard says that the Pinscher's expression is one of "intelligence, keenness and alertness." The ears are usually set high on the head and cropped. The breed's long, arched neck contributes to his elegance. The German Pinscher's tail is docked

The impressive Wolfgang von Munchhof, owned by Kevin Fitt and Rodger Brasier, Von Alsdorf German Pinschers, Moreno Valley, California. Wolfie is a group winner. (Poole photo)

in the manner of the Doberman and the Min Pin. His feet are always catlike. His short coat is smooth, sleek and glossy. The German standard for the breed allows for a wide array of colors. German Pinschers may come in black and tan ("with the more tan markings the better"), stag red or roebuck brown, brown, chocolate, solid black, salt and pepper, and blue-gray trimmed with yellow or red markings.

Rodger Brasier, publicity director for the newly formed German Pinscher Club of America, is enthusiastic about the breed. While Rodger had always liked Dobermans, large dogs were prohibited in his condominium home. "We saw an ad for German Pinschers in a local paper and, although we knew nothing about them, we wanted to see this 'little Dobie' in person. Luckily, we were able to get one." Rodger found that, while the breed's size made them suitable for condo living, his new dog tended to be very alert and territorial, and barked when anyone walked by. He has since moved to a home where the dogs have adapted beautifully. Rodger Brasier and Kevin Fitt raise their Von Alsdorf German Pinschers in Moreno Valley, California. Their lovely bitch, Baroness von Hexenhausen, "Nadia to her friends", was purchased from Mike Mueller, president of the German Pinscher Club of America, in Huntington Beach, California. Mr. Mueller imported a pair of these rare dogs from Germany several years ago.

"These are very sharp and alert dogs," Rodger Brasier and Kevin Fitt explain. "They are very intelligent, yet wonderfully loving toward their masters. They are easy to train, but take a firm hand. You want to handle them firmly, but with patience. A German Pinscher will surely remember if he is mistreated. These dogs want very much to please you."

Rodger and Kevin have discovered that the German Pinscher is an excellent watchdog. "They always know what is happening. These dogs do have a natural tendency to be aggressive. We know of dogs that are very tough, but that's what their owners wanted. They encouraged them to be that way. Our dogs have been socialized since puppyhood and they enjoy people. If anyone tried to enter our home without permission, though, they would be quite surprised at the reception these little guys would give them."

The German Pinscher is a hardy dog, and breeders in this country have yet to encounter any health problems. These dogs are extremely active and alert. As Rodger Brasier and Kevin Fitt discovered, the breed has long been recognized for its excellent guard dog capabilities. Indeed, most German Pinschers are quite suspicious of strangers, and care should be taken to properly socialize them, so that they will feel at ease and confident in the presence of strangers. At home, these little dogs have a docile and delightful personality, and a reputation for becoming uncommonly attached to their owners.

This short coated, small dog requires minimal care. He does not shed excessively and an occasional brushing or rub down, to remove dead hair, will keep him in tip-top condition. Cropped ears allow for good air circulation and prevent ear infections. His convenient size makes him suitable to a wide variety of households. He might be successfully kept in apartments, but owners must be aware of his alert nature and curb any tendency toward excessive barking. They should also keep in mind that this is an active breed that will need adequate exercise.

With his many attributes, it is expected that the German Pinscher will have a great future in this country. There is absolutely no reason that this little dog cannot enjoy the same popularity that the Doberman and the Min Pin share. The breed is quite rare today, even in his homeland. Introduced only in the past few years, there are now 29 known German Pinschers in this country. Owners have chosen to register their dogs with the Universal Kennel Club. With the enthusiasm being generated in this country, the German Pinscher is a breed that seems destined for much greater success and more widespread ownership. A dog of elegant bearing, sleek good looks, and devoted temperament the German Pinscher will make a marvelous addition to the breeds currently recognized in this country.

Glen of Imaal Terrier (Artist Pat Elkins, Chicago, Illinois)

Chapter 26

The Glen of Imaal Terrier

One of the newest terrier breeds to be introduced into the United States is the Glen of Imaal Terrier. Like many of the other terriers, he has abundant spirit and a desire to hunt. In Ireland today, however, the breed is generally maintained as a pet and show dog. The Glen has a very unusual appearance that will not suit everyone's taste. One official of the Irish Kennel Club described the breed as resembling a small Soft-Coated Wheaten Terrier, with a head reminiscent of a Dandie Dinmont. Still, those who have had a chance to become acquainted with the sturdy Glen of Imaal, are impressed with the breed's delightful temperament and personality.

"There is a glen, Imaal, in the Wicklow Mountains, that has always been, and still is, celebrated for its terriers," wrote Rawdon Lee in the early 1900's. Located on the eastern coast of Ireland, County Wicklow is south of Dublin. In this rocky, mountainous region, the "Glen," as he is commonly called, was popularly used as a hunting dog. It may be that the breed was first developed in the Wicklow Mountains, near Tinahely and Mullacer. The British brought Hessian and Lowland troops to colonize the area, and they found great enjoyment in hunting the rugged hills, which abounded with game.

The little Glen excelled in use on badger. In sporting competitions, in Ireland, he often competed successfully with the longer legged Irish breeds, such as the Soft-Coated Wheaten, the Kerry Blue and the Irish Terrier. In the early days, Glens were extremely diverse in type, but this was to be expected as they were, traditionally, maintained on small farms strictly for working purposes. Since homesteads, in those days in Ireland, were unfenced, it can be assumed that there were many misalliances. Some have suggested

that Bulldog blood was introduced by English garrisons, and others have speculated that the Scottish Terrier contributed to the heritage of the Wicklow County native. None of this can be proven.

Unlike other terrier breeds, the Glen is generally conceded to be a silent hunter. He is a very strong and tenacious digger, and has great agility and substance to help him in his work. He draws his quarry from the hole instead of barking and worrying the game to dislodge it. The Glen's power and spirit was also tested in another way. He became a valuable contender in Irish dog fights. The farmers who kept the Glen often enjoyed gathering at mills on a Saturday evening. Amidst plentiful drinking and gambling, the Glen was pitted against other dogs. He proved a tough competitor. Enthusiasts found that the Glen's harsh coat provided him with extra protection in the weekly bouts. This is probably unique, as all the other breeds used for fighting have short, sleek coats.

The Irish Kennel Club granted the breed recognition in 1933, but the Glen was seldom seen at shows. The breed was in danger of extinction when, in the 1950's, Willie Kane of Rathfurnham and Paddy Brennan of Tinahely dedicated themselves to saving the Glen. They did much to revive interest in the breed and stabilize conformation type. Until 1966, all Irish Glen of Imaal Terriers were required to demonstrate their hunting skill before being awarded conformation championships. The English Kennel Club recently recognized the breed, but he is still rare in Britain. Only a few specimens have been imported to the United States and Canada.

The Glen of Imaal has a rough and ready appearance. Upon first seeing the breed, terrier lovers may note his resemblance to the Soft-Coated

Wheaten, the Dandie Dinmont and the Sealyham. He weighs about 35 pounds and stands no more than 14" at the shoulder, making him a convenient size for city or country living. This breed is strong and agile, despite his low to the ground appearance. The Glen has a deep body that is longer than tall. His ears are either half-pricked or rose. The Glen should always have a wide chest and great bone. Quite distinctively, his front legs should be bowed. He carries his tail gaily. The Glen comes in either blue or wheaten (ranging from a light wheaten to a golden reddish) colors and his coat is harsh in texture. Usually shown naturally, stray hairs may be trimmed to neaten his appearance for the show ring.

"We are happy to promote any interest in these remarkable terriers," says George and Pat Grunnill of Chester, Ireland. "Although to some the look of this terrier is not really attractive, they soon endear themselves to their owners. In our experience, they are quite intelligent, quick to learn and respond, quite playful at times, but will easily settle down for quiet periods." The Grunnills enjoy their Glens and have recently had much success in the show ring with their "Pentreva Beanie." "Puppies we have sold to families, have settled in happily, proving adaptable, easy to train and handle, and they enjoy playing with small children. We have been in the company of families with children, exhibiting these terriers, and we have not seen any signs of difficult temperament.

"The Glen of Imaal is a true terrier bred to hunt and, if history is to be believed, to fight. These days are long gone," George and Pat say. "But, the terrier spirit remains, and rightly so. However, a terrier, correctly bred, will retain a terrier spirit, without undue aggression. These terriers, in the home, are amenable and pleasant, but alert housedogs. Our own live with Scottish Terriers and Yorkshire Terriers, and are good friends. In the show ring, there is no fighting, even though the dogs show an awareness of strange dogs. They are controlled without difficulty."

The Grunnills maintain their dogs as housepets, but they have often heard the adage that terriers are only suitable for country homes. They strongly disagree. "Many people, dog owners and non- dog owners alike, seem to think that dogs need acres of ground to be happy and fit. In our opinion, this is not so. Dogs require human companionship and, ideally, also a doggy friend. They need warm, comfortable quarters, good feeding and exercise. These requirements can be fulfilled in town or country. Only size and family accomodations should dictate the choice of breed," the couple says. Most knowledgeable dog owners would agree. "The Glen of Imaal is a powerful dog with a medium sized, compact body. He does not need masses of room, but he is energetic and, therefore, needs exercise. In the puppy stage, he is happy to play in the yard or garden, with a ball or other playthings. Ours love to carry sticks around in their mouths, or romp with each other. When they are older, good steady walks are necessary for daily exercise, but free play in a spacious area should also be included, as this is appreciated."

The dedicated and conscientious Grunnills suggest that those interested in the Glen deal with responsible breeders. "We stress temperament in our breeding program. Experienced breeders will give detailed instructions to new puppy owners. They are always available for advice, and they keep in contact, in the event any difficulties develop. A responsible breeder is only too happy to help if any difficulty arises."

For those who enjoy terriers and their dynamic personalities, and want to share their homes with a rare breed, the Glen of Imaal should definitely be considered. These terrific little dogs are endearing and loyal companions that can fill your days with much joy. One hopes that the delightful Glen of Imaal will be seen more frequently in this country.

Chapter 27

The Greater Swiss Mountain Dog

Switzerland is a country of majestic snowcapped mountains and lush emerald green valleys. It is home to a number of breeds, but the oldest are the heavy bodied dogs of the mountains. These large and powerful dogs are firmly rooted in the history of this alpine country. The *Sennenhund* (literally translated as "dog of the Alpine pastures") breeds are the most strikingly beautiful of the native Swiss dogs. All are characterized by their brilliant tricolor markings. The Bernese Mountain Dog, with his long coat, has been known for years in this country. Now his cousin, the Greater Swiss Mountain Dog, is capturing the attention of dog fanciers. While the Greater Swiss' physical conformation is impressive, breeders contend that his real beauty lies in a noble and endearing character.

The history of these mountain dogs traces back to the earliest settlement of Switzerland, which was then known as Helvetia. In approximately 50 B.C., the Germanic tribes from the north began a determined push into Helvetia. In desperation, the native peoples packed their belongings and fled westward, to territory controlled by the mighty Roman Empire. Julius Caesar, however, had no intention of welcoming these newcomers. He sent armed troops into the mountains to block the German advance and the resulting Helvetian migration. For hundreds of years, thereafter, Helvetia would be part of the Roman Empire.

Armies traveled with huge entourages in those days of old. Complete families accompanied the soldiers, and it was necessary to sustain this large number of people. Herds of cattle were brought along to provide food for the occupiers. With them, the Romans brought dogs to serve a variety of purposes.

On their treks, these canines drove cattle to the newly established garrisons. They protected their masters and their property, and, undoubtedly, fought beside them in battle. It was said that they were formidable guard dogs that struck terror in the hearts of captured peoples, who were then, sometimes, enslaved. The most authoritative experts contend that these large and substantial dogs were direct descendants of the ancient Tibetan Mastiffs.

In the following centuries, these dogs would be adopted by the residents of the mountains and valleys. On isolated farms, a number of related, but distinct breeds, would develop. While these dogs varied in size and length of coat, all shared distinctive tricolor markings. Perhaps it is a testament to the dominance and beauty of these markings that they were retained despite the differences of location. They became versatile helpmates to the local residents and were sometimes called "Swiss Cottage Dogs." At Vindonissa, a pottery lamp from Roman times was discovered. It shows a dog that is clearly identifiable as the breed we now know as the Bernese Mountain Dog.

While the Swiss mountain breeds served their owners as cattle drovers and watchdogs, they were, perhaps, most outstanding as draft dogs. Many turn of the century drawings and photographs clearly show the Greater Swiss Mountain Dog engaged in this activity. It is difficult for us, in this day and age, to appreciate how useful draft dogs were to the Swiss, the Belgians, and the Dutch, all of whom extensively used dogs for this purpose. Dogs pulled the wares of small business people to the markets and on their rounds. Gardeners, butchers, bakers, milkmen and coalmen all made use of draft dogs. It was said that these dogs were capable of hauling the same weight as a donkey and, yet, were much more economical to feed and care for. Undoubtedly, they made better pets, too.

Professor Dr. Albert Heim, one of the saviors of all the Swiss Mountain Dog breeds, was an enthusiastic promotor of the draft dog. He firmly believed that the Greater Swiss Mountain Dog was the world's best draft dog. It was said that the Greater Swiss' inherent instinct to pull was so strong, that it took only a few minutes of training in harness for him to be ready to work. At one time the breed was known as the *Metzgerhunde* or Butcher's dogs...a tribute to their usefulness. "The work enobles one," Professor Heim said, for he believed that "the workless dog constitutes a misfortune, just as a workless man."

Dogs in these European countries were generally worked singly or in pairs, although we know that, in a few cases, as many as five dogs were harnessed to a cart. Some countries formed societies for the improvement of the draft dog, and they often enacted regulations for the protection and welfare of these workers. The famed Belgian authority, Dr. Reul, helps us to appreciate the importance of the draft dog in daily life. "The dog in harness renders such precious services to the people, to the small trader and to the small industrials (agriculturists included)...that never will any public authority dare to suppress its current use. A disastrous economic revolution would be the consequence. Penury and poverty would enter thousands of homes where a relative affluence is apparent now."

Advocates of draft dogs took great pride in their animals' working ability. Competitions, called "coursings," were held to determine the strongest and fastest haulers. Societies were formed to ensure the welfare of these valuable companions. It was in Belgium that the most progressive regulations were instituted. There were detailed specifications for the construction of carts, and exact requirements for all harnesses and traces to be used. These stringent laws dictated the proper treatment of draft dogs, and violators could be fined and their dogs impounded. Some of these regulations may be of interest to fanciers of the draft breeds.

1. It was forbidden to harness dogs who measured less than 24 inches at the shoulder.

2. Dogs which were in poor health, or those that were too old, could not be used.

3. Dogs which were too young were prohibited from use.

4. Bitches that were pregnant, or nursing young, could not be used.

5. No dog could be harnessed with another species of animal.

6. The care of a cart and its dogs could not be entrusted to anyone under fourteen years of age.

7. People were not allowed to ride in any dog drawn vehicle.

8. Dogs could not be left harnessed in the hot sun.

9. Any part of the harness that came in contact with the dog's body had to be padded.

10. All carts must have springs and brakes, and be well greased.

11. No dog was permitted to pull more than 300 pounds, and the load for two dogs could not exceed 400 pounds.

12. No cart could ever be left unattended.

13. During stops in inclement weather, the owner was required to provide shelter for their dogs and to have a blanket to cover them.

14. In snowy weather, the dogs had to be provided with a waterproof tarpaulin.

It can be clearly seen, from these regulations, just how important the draft dog was to the local economy. Unfortunately, with the advent of the railroads, the use of the local draft dogs declined dramatically, and these breeds suffered. Other breeds came to the fore, and the Saint Bernard, the Leonberger and the German Shepherd became popular choices. By the turn of the century, the Greater Swiss and others of the mountain dogs were considered almost extinct. Fortunately, a few examples of these breeds remained on isolated farms.

We are indebted to Dr. Albert Heim for saving the four breeds of *Sennenhund*. Dr. Heim was a renowned geologist and professor, but his great love was dogs. Along with Richard Strebel, an artist from Munich, and Max Siber, the head forester from Winterthur, Dr. Heim conducted research on the native Swiss breeds. He became an acknowledged expert, a sought after judge and an esteemed dog writer. It was the research work of these gentlemen that led to the classification of the four distinct *Sennenhund* breeds. Dr. Heim, who hailed from Zurich, encouraged breeders to help rescue these native dogs. It was as a result of his urging that breed clubs were formed and the breeds survive to this day.

The long-coated Bernese Mountain Dog is the only one of the *Sennenhund* breeds to gain official recognition, thus far, by the American Kennel Club. The remaining Bernese were discovered in Dürrbächler (a district of the canton of Berne) by Franz Schertenleib, in 1892. They were first exhibited, under Professor Heim, at a Berne show, in 1904. The *Entlebucher Sennenhund* was first shown at

Langenthal, in 1913, once again by Mr. Schertenleib. In 1925, he presented several of these rare specimens to Dr. Kobler, a veterinarian from St. Gall. The following year, Dr. Kobler established a club which worked to rescue the breed. The *Appenzeller Sennenhund,* or Appenzell Mountain Dog, is the smallest of the *Sennenhund* breeds. In 1909, a club was formed under the direction of J. Gründer. Today, the Appenzell is seen on farms and in city homes.

The Greater Swiss Mountain Dog, or *Grosser Schweizer Sennenhund,* is the largest of the four breeds. In 1908, Franz Schertenleib, of Rothîhe, Burgdorf, exhibited the first Greater Swiss Mountain Dog at the Langenthal show. While the dog was entered as a short-coated Bernese, the judge, Dr. Heim, quickly realized that it was one of the few remaining Greater Swiss Mountain Dogs. He strongly urged breeders to save these wonderful dogs,

and, in 1910, the breed was recognized by the Swiss Kennel Club. A butcher from Olten, Mr. J. Jaussi, formed a club for the breed in 1911. The organization was very successful, and breed popularity has increased in the intervening years.

The Greater Swiss Mountain Dog, fondly called the "Swissy" by his fans, is a large breed, standing 25 1/2 to 28 1/2 inches at the withers. He generally weighs 120-140 pounds. Heavily boned and muscular, he has a sturdy and rugged appearance. His short coat comes in a brilliant tricolor. The background color is black, although one will sometimes see a bronze tinted hue. He has crisp white markings on his feet, chest and tail tip. All Swissys are required to have a white blaze on their faces. Rich red is found above the eyes and on the cheeks, and the red forms a separation between the black and white markings. With a broad head and dark brown expressive eyes, the Swissy

The Greater Swiss Mountain Dog (artist: Pat Elkins, Chicago, Illinois)

always appears intelligent. The Greater Swiss is slightly longer than tall. As befitting a draft dog, he has a very strong back, powerful thighs and moderate angulation.

Several American dog lovers saw articles on the Swissy and were interested. In 1967, Mr. and Mrs. J. Frederick Hoffman and Mrs. R. Klem saw the breed at the German Bundessieger Show, in Frankfurt. They were impressed. In 1968, the Hoffmans, Mrs. Klem and Mr. Perrin Rademacher imported the first Swissys to this country. Mrs. Klem and Mr. Rademacher were well known for their top winning and producing Rottweilers. Indeed, their outstanding imports and homebreds did much to improve the quality of Rottweilers in this country. The first four puppies to arrive (two females and two males) were selected with the assistance of the Austrian and Swiss clubs for the breed. These new imports attracted much attention, and, in 1970, the first litter was born in the United States. A breed club was formed, and many other imports have followed. In 1985, the breed was admitted to the American Kennel Club's Miscellaneous list. Recently, an American Swissy was exported for breeding purposes to Switzerland. This is a tribute to the progress the breed has made in this country.

Breeders of the Swissy say that this breed is the "ideal family dog." The Swissy is easily trained and naturally quite obedient. This breed seems particularly fond of children, and they has occasionally been used as a rescue dog. A remarkably docile dog, the Swissy has a very sound and stable temperament. He is bold and quietly confident with people, and should never be nervous or hyperactive. Owners are quickly won over by his charming personality, for the Swissy is patient, faithful and, despite his great size, amazingly gentle. Owners say that these dogs are always eager to please and enjoy attention. Indeed, they reach their full character potential when they are allowed to become a part of the family. They adapt easily to a variety of climates and require very little grooming. They are not given to roaming and will appreciate being included in family activities. Just hitch your Swissy to a cart, or strap on a backpack for a day of hiking, and the dog will enjoy the activity every bit as much as you will.

Mrs. Liselotte Lenhart, of Gunnison, Colorado, is originally from Austria. She has owned Swissys for many years and is an enthusiastic supporter of the breed. Her sister, Mrs. Christiane Adrian is a Swissy breeder in Vienna, is an esteemed judge. These two women were responsible for first bringing Swissys from Switzerland to Austria many years ago. "This breed has a great rapport with women," Mrs. Lenhart says. "In the past, they often guarded the women and children, while the men were away at work. Swissys

get along well with other dogs. They are not fighters. They also are very trustworthy with livestock. I raise angora rabbits and can fully trust my dogs. When I place a rabbit on the ground, the dogs will lick it. They seem to adopt the rabbits. I consider this natural, as in the past they helped with livestock duties in the summer and stayed on the homestead where the animals were confined in winter." Mrs. Lenhart believes that the Swissy makes an ideal watchdog. "While they are not excessive barkers, they will let you know when a stranger arrives. When I admit a stranger, they will accept them. They will even be friendly. However, if I leave the room, they will place themselves by the door and not allow the person to leave." She tells the story of a couple who went away, but asked friends to check the house to ensure that their pipes wouldn't freeze. Their Swissys cheerfully greeted the visitors and allowed them into the house. Then they refused to allow them to leave. The police were finally summoned and they arranged for someone who knew the dogs to come and assure them that all was well. With the Swissy's size and deep bark, though, it is not likely that a burglar would want to enter a home where one of these vigilant dogs resided.

The Swissys' recent move to the Miscellaneous Class is sure to bring more attention to the breed. He would make an impressive addition to the Working Group in this country. Perhaps, one day, the other *Sennenhund* breeds will gain a following here. It just may be that Greater Swiss Mountain Dog fanciers are correct when they say that this is an "ideal family dog". For those who want a large companion that is not aggressive, and can be fully trusted with children, it would be hard to find a breed better than the Swissy. With his striking looks and wonderful temperament, he seems destined for greater popularity.

Chapter 28

The Havanese

"I have a whole file of letters from Havanese owners. Every one of these people are absolutely convinced that they have the smartest and the best dog in the whole wide world," says Dorothy L. Goodale, of Montrose, Colorado. "These letters really make you feel good. This type of response makes dog breeding rewarding." It's no wonder that the Havanese is winning friends and admirers throughout this country. This delightful little dog must surely be one of the most exciting toy breeds to make an appearance here.

The Havanese is a member of the Bichon group of dogs, which include the Bichon Frise, the Bolognese, the Coton de Tulear and, possibly, the Maltese. We know that this group of small, longhaired dogs is very old, extending back to 230 A.D. One dog historian, in the 1930's, mentions the Havanese and says that Maltese, in France, were mistakenly called *Havanais*. Indeed, the description he gives seems to more closely resemble the Maltese than the Havanese of today. This text also mentions a breed known as the *Manilla* which weighed as much as 15 pounds. While the Maltese is thought to have originated in Melita, the Manilla came from Malta.

It is difficult to accurately pinpoint the origin of the Havanese. One writer theorizes that Italians, from Emelia, moved to Argentina with their Bichon-type dogs. In this South American country their little dogs were bred with the Poodle to create a new breed. Later, the dogs made their way to Cuba, where they became known as the Havanese. The esteemed writer Dechambre clearly believed that the Havanese was a direct descendant of the Maltese. He believed that the breed accompanied Spaniards to the West Indies, where they were known as the Havana Silk Dog. Still others theorize that the breed arrived in Cuba during the days of the expanding Spanish Empire.

We do know that the breed was popular among the wealthy residents of the island of Cuba. He was most popular in the capital city of Havana. Sea merchants, engaged in trade, arrived on this Caribbean island. Their financial success depended on the support and business of wealthy Cubans. They discovered that, by presenting wealthy wives with a small rare dog, they could win entrance to homes that might not otherwise welcome them.

The Havanese became the pampered pet of wealthy Cubans. Owners jealously maintained the exclusivity of Havanese ownership, and these dogs were never allowed in the hands of the peasants. It was said that on Sunday afternoons following mass, wealthy women, decked out in their finest clothes, would ride through the streets of the capital in their carriages. Beside them would be their precious Havanese. The little dogs were bred, but they were never sold. If you were fortunate enough to become a favored friend, you would be presented with a little Havanese puppy as a gift. One of the most noted Cuban breeders was Catalina Laza. The wife of a wealthy sugar baron, Señora Laza was said to have presented many Havanese to her friends.

The Cuban Revolution nearly destroyed the breed. Many wealthy residents fled their island homeland, and we do not know if any Havanese remain in Cuba. Since they were associated with the ruling class, those that remained may not have fared well. Thousands of people fled the island. Among them were the Fantasio and Perez families. They succeeded in bringing their dogs with them during the early Cuban airlifts. Their pride in their dogs and their

Havana's Show Girl and Havana's Topsy, two charming Havanese owned by Dorothy Goodale, of Montrose, Colorado.

are 8-10 1/2 inches at the shoulder, and weigh between 7 and 13 1/2 pounds. They are not, however, fragile. Sturdy little dogs, Havanese have great energy and stamina. They have a rectangular body shape, being longer than tall. They're dark eyes are round, but should never bulge. Their beautiful profuse coats come in an array of lovely colors. Most common and popular are the champagne, white and golden shades, although black and white and parti-colors are born occasionally. The Havanese coat, which may be wavy or curly, is non-shedding and has no doggy odor. The coat does require grooming, but a twice a week brushing should be sufficient, although show dogs may be groomed more often.

"The Havanese has a mellow, happy-go-lucky

breeding efforts saved the breed from extinction.

Other Havanese did escape Cuba with their owners, however, as Dorothy Goodale, of Montrose, Colorado, discovered. The President and registrar for the Havanese Club of America, Mrs. Goodale has long searched for any information on the breed. Several years ago she took a bold and innovative step. She placed advertisements in Latin papers in Miami, offering to buy Havanese. She received only one response. A Florida man wrote to say that a friend of his had five Havanese that he wished to sell. The elderly man had fled Cuba, but instead of coming to the United States, he had settled in Costa Rica. He had decided to move to Texas, to live with his daughter, but could bring only two dogs with him. Fortunately, his friend had seen Mrs. Goodale's ad. A check was sent to the gentleman, but Dorothy heard no more. "I began to think that we had been taken," the Colorado resident said. "Six weeks later, I received a phone call from the airport in Grand Junction, saying that they had some dogs for me. It was a pleasant surprise. It seems that the man brought the dogs to Texas with him and shipped them from there. We were delighted to have these new dogs. They gave us two new bloodlines to work with. One of the difficulties rare breed fanciers face is a limited gene pool. Knock on wood, we have been very fortunate with the Havanese. We have had no health problems with these dogs."

The Havanese is certainly a beautiful dog. They

attitude," says Dorothy Goodale. She and her husband have been raising Havanese for 11 years. Several of these delightful dogs make their home at the Goodale's Havana Doll House. The temperaments in this breed are excellent. Dorothy has been involved with purebred dogs for more than 30 years, but nothing has given her more delight than her work with the Havanese. "I used to raise terriers. While I loved their temperaments and they were great with people, terriers are aggressive with other dogs. The

The beautiful Havana's Ladybug owned by Monika Moser.

Havanese is not at all aggressive. I have five males who spend the day together in a fenced playyard. They all live peacefully. My girls share an adjoining playyard and there's never any trouble, even when several of the females are in season. Oh, there's bound to be whining and begging," Dorothy laughs, "and they'll run up and down the fence, but not once has there been any fighting. I find this quite remarkable and very refreshing. It's one of the qualities that I love about the breed.

"They are very intelligent dogs and very eager to learn. In this regard they are quite similiar to the Poodle. They are very easy to train and love the attention that it brings. It is said that after the Havanese became established in Cuba, owners took them back to Europe, and they were used in traveling circuses. That's very easy for me to believe. Mrs. Gaglione, our Club's secretary, has trained her dogs to perform a variety of tricks. They walk on a two-by-four set on edge, climb a ladder, jump through hoops, and stand up and push a doll carriage. They love tricks and appreciate the chance to show off. They're such wonderful little clowns. They just love the attention and acclaim. If you clap and laugh, it makes them so happy. They're so pleased with themselves and they're so cute."

While the Havanese is lovable and friendly with his family, he is also very alert and this makes him an ideal watchdog. These bright dogs always seem keenly aware of everything around them. "As puppies they are very friendly," Dorothy Goodale says. "However, when they're grown they become a little wary of strangers. They will not allow strangers to touch them. They won't bite or act aggressive, but they will be standoffish. When we allow a stranger into the house, they will sit back and make up their minds about them. Once they see that I have accepted them, they will come over and introduce themselves. I like this. I don't have to worry that my Havanese will be easily stolen. By the same token, they are marvelous with the family. You couldn't ask for a better disposition in a small dog."

An added bonus is the breed's unusually robust health. They are hardy and long lived. You won't be visiting your veterinarian often, except for routine matters, if you choose the Havanese. "My Havanese are in outside kennels," says Sadie Stomberg of Lockhart, Texas. "They withstand temperatures from 10 to 100 degrees with no ill effects. They are adaptable to any situation."

The Havanese has attracted a great deal of attention and, undoubtedly, will continue to do so. 487 Havanese are currently registered with the Havanese Club of America, and the breed has recently been exported to Europe. The Europeans have been very interested in the breed and are anxious to start their own breeding programs. America, however, remains the bastion of the breed. If you are interested in obtaining one of these little charmers, you may have to wait a bit, as there is usually a waiting list. Still, the opportunity to own one of these rare little dogs, is certainly worth the wait.

The impressive Havana's Sno Sprite, owned by Dorothy Goodale, Havana Doll House, Colorado.

A basketful of Havanese puppies owned by Cathy Cashen.

Ayan von der Nussbaumschule, owned by Mrs. Ebba Grumieaux, with his dumbbell.

A head study of Bonso, a Hovawart, owned by Mrs. Ebba Grumieaux, of Greenwich, Connecticut.

Ayan von der Alten Nussbaumschule poses on the deck of the Grumieaux home in Greenwich, Connecticut.

Chapter 29

The Hovawart

"My life has been irreversibly changed, since I have my lovable and huggable companion, Bonso, a Hovawart," says Ebba Grumieaux, of Greenwich, Connecticut. Such enthusiasm and devotion comes as no surprise to those familiar with this German breed. Probably the rarest breed in the United States today, the Hovawart is attracting much attention. The first litter in this country was recently born in California.

The Hovawart is both a new and an old breed. His story begins far back in the Middle Ages. The name Hovawart has been variously translated as guardian of the farm, the estate or the court. He is first mentioned in the *Sachsenspiegel,* a medieval law book that was so popular it was commonly used in Germany, Poland, and parts of Hungary and Russia. Published in 1220, the book gives us our first mention of the Hovawart. In fact, the writer, Eike von Repkow, tells us that, when he was a baby, the castle where he lived was assaulted by an unfriendly tribe. He was saved by a wounded Hovawart, who carried him to a neighboring castle. A Germanic people called the *Hundinge,* literally "those with the dogs", owned Hovawarts. The *Schwabenspiegel,* written in 1275-1280 and based on the earlier *Sachsenspiegel,* describes the Hovawart as a watchdog, and there were penalties for anyone who stole such a dog. If someone stole a Hovawart during the night, he had to replace it with another dog of equal value and pay a penalty of three schillings. If a Hovawart was stolen during the daytime, the thief must replace the dog and pay a fine of one schilling. This has led historians to conclude that dog breeding may have been widespread in these early times or it would have been difficult to obtain a substitute dog.

While some writings lead us to believe that the Hovawart was a dog of the court, he is also sometimes described as a peasant dog. An early legend, with social overtones, tells us of a peasant's Hovawart who creeps into a nearby castle and steals food from the table of the owner. He grows very strong and powerful on this rich fare and waits until the master's hunting dogs come back, exhausted, from a day in the fields. He then drives these dogs away and becomes the only dog at the castle. Early writings indicate that the Greyhounds and other hunters were more in vogue among the nobility at that time. Hovawart owners believe that the breed was pictured in Albrecht Durer's 1513 woodcut of the "Devil, Death and the Knight."

Over the years, the Hovawart became virtually extinct. Karl König, however, began to reconstruct this ancient breed in the 1920's. He had read about them in old writings and scoured the remote countryside for dogs which resembled the Hovawart. He secured specimens in the Black Forest, the Hartz Mountains and other isolated villages. König crossed German Shepherds, Kuvasz, Newfoundlands, and Leonbergers with the dogs he had collected in the Germany countryside. Also introduced was the blood of a breed called the African Wild Dog. A prepotent dog, Castor Meyer-Busch, born in 1932, helped in establishing breed type. The gene pool was officially closed in 1944 and no other crossbreedings were done. The Hovawart's good qualities were much admired, and a Rumanian king was reported to have offered 3,000 gold marks for one Hovawart.

World War II brought Hovawart breeding to an abrupt halt, and it is a wonder that the breed did not become extinct once more. Many Hovawarts starved and others were killed with their owners, in bombing raids. Furthermore, many Hovawarts had been pressed into war service and none returned. Some Hovawarts did remain in East Germany, but the political complications, after the war, prevented them from being used. However, there were a few breeders who banded together to save the breed. The Hovawart is now found in Switzerland, Austria, Denmark, the Netherlands, Finland, Sweden and a few other countries. He has recently been introduced to the United States.

The standard describes the Hovawart thusly: "A robust working dog of medium weight, the Hovawart is strong and highly weather resistant, a good runner and jumper, brave, attentive and quick to react. It is a splendid guard dog...His voice is deep, full and powerful." Males measure 23 1/2 to 27 1/2 inches and weigh 66 to 88 pounds. Females should be 21 1/2 to 25 1/2 inches and weigh 55 to 77 pounds. The Hovawart is a strong, rugged dog that is well muscled. The breed is slightly longer than tall. His hair is long and dense, and some have slightly wavy coats. In color he may be either black, black and tan, or an attractive flaxen (yellowish gold).

In recreating the Hovawart, great emphasis was placed on temperament and abilities. This has resulted in a very stable and useful animal. Hovawarts easily accept other dogs, as the recreators wanted a dog that could live peacefully with other animals Indeed, he enjoys other dogs and will engage in rough play. This breed has never been used for hunting, and so is not tempted to leave his home and chase wild animals. Great emphasis was placed on ensuring that the Hovawart would stay close by his home, even if not fenced, and guard the property. The early breeders also insisted on an easily trained dog, and the Hovawart seems to take a special delight in learning. Training affords him an opportunity to exercise his many skills, channel his energies and develop a rapport with his owner.

The Hovawart makes an excellent guard dog. He is affectionate and loving with his family, but somewhat wary and distrustful of strangers. However, when visitors are accepted by the owner, the Hovawart will readily make friends. Only when he perceives a real threat, will the Hovawart attack. As with all breeds, it is important to adequately socialize the Hovawart puppy. The protective instincts do not fully manifest themselves until the dog begins to mature, and as puppies the Hovawart greets both humans and dogs with joy. Hovawarts quickly learn the perimeters of their property, and will protect and defend their domain if necessary. Very sensible dogs, they are not prone to nuisance barking. This breed loves children and will play with them for hours on end. While they enjoy the outdoors they also love creature comforts. In fact, the author of one German book on the breed laughingly calls one of her dogs a "sofawart"...guardian of the sofa!

Ebba Grumieaux was first introduced to the Hovawart many years ago, when she was a teenager in Africa. Friends gave her parents their first Hovawart. The dog had been living with his owners near a mine, but the constant exposure to limedust produced problems with eczema. "The change in environment cleared the skin problems and the dog lived to the ripe old age of 16," Ebba says. "I got my present dog while living in West Germany, just prior to moving here. He is our first dog and has proved to be a never- ending source of pleasure, fun and enjoyment.

"Since he reached the age of six months, we have been active in a local dog obedience club, and Bonso has proven an eager and fast learner, although his temperament does get the better of him (and me) at times! All obstacles notwithstanding, we have managed to get an 'All American' Companion Dog title and are aiming for a Companion Dog Excellent and Tracking Dog title this year.

"Caring for Bonso has proved a delight. His coat is waterproof and requires minimal grooming. A good brushing once or twice a week is all that's necessary," Emma says. "Since this breed is not prone to wandering, he remains on our unfenced property, even when left alone outside. This is a great asset in our part of the country, where few yards are enclosed. A disadvantage for some may be the fact that the Hovawart needs a lot of exercise. We are very active and walk several miles daily, and Bonso has become a great companion on these excursions.

"Bonso is a regular snow-buff and thrives in our winters. In fact, every time we have had a fresh snowfall, he does what we call his 'snow dance' outside, racing around, jumping up and down, and chasing imaginary animals, as well as rolling over and over with his legs in the air, quite beside himself! He has joined us on ski vacations in Colorado, and has proven very adaptable to flying, car trips, staying in strange hotels and being left alone in those rooms or in the car. We do a lot of traveling and more often than not, he comes along.

"We have two grown children and, although Bonso is basically my dog, he is very loving to and protective of the other members of the family. Our children no longer live with us, but he is overjoyed when they return for a visit, and he accepts their pets without a complaint."

With so many wonderful qualities, the Hovawart is sure to attract a loyal following in this country. He is a medium size dog of rugged beauty, with a unique and winning personality. His great asset of staying close to home, combined with his trainability and watchdog capabilities, should make him a popular choice for rural homes. While currently the rarest of the rare in this country, I believe that we will soon see many more Hovawarts in the United States.

Chapter 30

The Iceland Dog

"I find them to be quite the best house dogs," wrote Mrs. Wingfield-Digby, in 1923, of the Iceland Dog. "They are good watchdogs. It would be a great shame if this ancient breed became extinct, particularly when some other breeds which have neither the length of pedigree or the attraction of the Icelandic Sheepdog are being actively promoted." The Iceland Dog, or the Icelandic Sheepdog, as the breed is known in Great Britain, is still in need of promotion. While the dogs have some following in the Scandinavian countries, they are scarcely seen in the rest of the world. This is, indeed, a great shame, as everything written about the breed refers to their wonderful and loving personalities.

A very ancient breed, the Iceland Dog is somewhat of a rarity, in that we can find early, documented proof of the breed's existence. Indeed, his history extends back over a thousand years. This may have been the same breed whose bones were discovered by archaeologists in Denmark and Norway. The Finnish Spitz and the Norwegian Buhund are probably descended from old specimens of this breed. The breed first arrived with the Vikings when they emigrated from Norway to settle Iceland in approximately 880 AD. The Icelandic Sagas tell us that the Vikings brought sheep to the country, and small sheepdogs accompanied them. Other references to the breed and its prevalence in Iceland are noted in 1492 and again in 1555. "The farm dog follows man wherever he goes," says the *Sturlunga Saga,* written in 1492, "and a dog always accompanies man between farms and on long journeys." Indeed, the breed's primary function appears to have been sheepherding, rounding up ponies and serving as a watchdog for the *Tun* (home or meadow).

The breed was first introduced into England in the Middle Ages. There was a good deal of trading between Great Britain and Iceland, and this small spitz breed made its way to British soil. The English were said to have become quite taken with the breed in the 1500's, and on their visits to Iceland they sought out good puppies. In 1650, Sir Thomas Brown wrote, "To England there are sometimes exported from Iceland...a type of dog resembling a fox and these are said to be bastards of the dog and fox. Shepherds in England are eager to acquire them! I sometimes wonder whether there is a little Icelandic Sheepdog in our own Border and Rough Collies." Well, we know that the breed certainly wasn't half fox, and it is doubtful that either the Border or the Rough Collie owes any heritage to the little dog from Iceland, but it is testament to the breed's herding ability that Sir Thomas pondered the association.

No less a figure than Shakespeare referred to the breed. Shakespeare is not known for his flattering quotes on dogs and the Iceland Dog is no exception. "Pish for the Iceland dog! Thou prick-ear'd cur of Iceland," he wrote in Henry V. As a British observer of the spitz breeds commented, this quote is quite notable in that most of the breeds known in England during the Bard's day had floppy or drooping ears. He concludes that Shakespeare must have had some acquaintance with the breed.

The Iceland Dog is depicted and mentioned in Count de Buffon's 1755 work, *Natural History.* "Of the Iceland Dog which belongs to the Spitz group, embracing roughly fifty distinct varieties of dogs, the Huskies of the Western World account for about one-third of these, whilst the Laika of the Western Hemisphere represents the majority of the remaining two-thirds including the Spitz-which had wandered from their original home- Pomeranians, Wolfespitz, Keeshonden, Iceland Dog, and others." The Count also included a Genealogical Table of the Different Races of Dogs, although it showed very few breeds. Still, the Iceland Dog was widely enough known to be included.

While the breed may have been gaining in popularity and reputation in the Elizabethan age and for some time thereafter, they did not fare so well in recent history. In the late 1800's, there was a terrible distemper epidemic in Iceland, and it was said that more than three-quarters of all the dogs in the country died. It was a near devastating blow for the little sheepdog.

The first known importation to England, in modern times, came in the late 1800's. The breed's first show ring appearance came in 1880, in London. Britain's Kennel Club first recognized the breed in 1905. It was not until 1921, however, that a second member of the breed was registered. The breed did make appearances in Danish show rings, though, until the advent of World War I.

In the 1920's, Mrs. Wingfield-Digby, the world renowned Keeshond breeder (although she had yet to make this name for herself), became extraordinarily interested in the breed. It was on a fishing vacation to Iceland that she first saw this small dog. A male accompanied her when she returned to Britain, and she arranged for the purchase of a female. Sadly, her plans for breeding the Iceland Dogs met with disappointment from the very start. Her male died only a couple of months after the bitch cleared quarantine, and they were never bred.

It was an American Keeshond breeder that became interested in the Iceland Dog in the 1950's. Mark Watson, owner of the Wensum Kennels, in California, was fascinated with the breed and alarmed at the disappearance of true breed type. He traveled to Iceland to search for outstanding specimens, and a number of them joined him in California. He started a serious breeding program and even exported a few dogs to England. Unfortunately, there was not sufficient interest in the breed. We do not know what has happened to the dogs resulting from Mr. Watson's breedings.

The breed does not seem to have been highly valued in his native homeland, until recently. Iceland Dogs continued to be crossbred, and it seemed certain that the breed would eventually become extinct. A

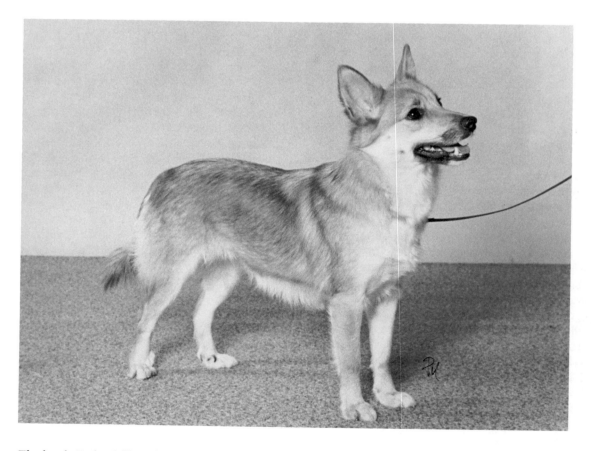

The lovely Iceland Sheepdog bitch, Swedish Champion Loa av Björnli, owned by Repeta's Kennel, Inga-Britt and Bengt Johansson, of Sweden. (Per Unden photo)

confirmed dog fancier, Mrs. Sigridur Petursdottir, of Olafsvellir (located in southern Iceland), became very alarmed. In 1967, she rounded up many specimens and began an intensive breeding program. It is said that she has had considerable success, and that her dogs are of high quality. Dogs of Mrs. Petursdottir's breeding have been exported to various European countries. We are also told that she sent Iceland Dogs to both the United States and Canada, but there appears to have been no serious attempt to promote the breed in either country.

From all accounts, the Iceland Sheepdog makes an ideal home companion. They are attractive, small dogs that lend themselves well to city or country living. They are said to be quite adaptable and very alert. While they are friendly, the breed's alert nature makes them ideal as a watchdog. The Iceland Dog is very loyal and attaches himself readily to his human family. They are not known to be aggressive with other dogs. Additionally, they are very clean dogs who housebreak easily. They tend to clean themselves in the manner of cats. They are a low maintainance breed whose coat requires only occasional grooming. Iceland Dogs are active and lively. Those who have owned the breed say that they are exceptionally bright, learn quickly and are remarkably affectionate.

The Iceland Dog stands 14-18 inches tall and tips the scales at approximately 30 pounds. He shares the spitz characteristics of a wedge-shaped head, prick ears, and a tail which, generally, curls over his back. The breed comes in an array of colors, including white with fawn markings, and various shades from a light golden to red with black tips. It is said that black specimens appear occasionally. His nose is black and his eyes are dark brown.

For those interested in a rare breed that is noted for its intelligence and affectionate nature, it is worth considering the Iceland Dog. While so many of the spitz breeds are said to have an inherent hunting instinct, this is not the case with the Iceland Dog. He is not particularly interested in pursuing game, but prefers to stay around the home. It is reported that he is, still an excellent herder, and he might well be used for that purpose in this country. Perhaps soon, Americans will discover what Mrs. Wingfield-Digby did so many years ago when she said, "The Icelandic Sheepdog is a delightful breed in every way."

Nestor Acorn, a frequent winner at working terrier trials, owned by Catherine Doran, of Geneseo, New York. (Peter Hiaber III photo)

Blencathra Badger, owned by Paul Ross, of Conway, New Hampshire, was conformation champion at the J.R.T.C.A. National Trials in 1985.

Chapter 31

The Jack Russell Terrier

"Jack Russell Terriers are people trapped in dog bodies," laughs Catherine Doran, of Geneseo, New York. "I have never known a more intelligent breed. They are incredibly sensitive to human contact and can sense your mood. I believe that they view us as their pets. They are faithful, cheerful, intelligent, willing, willfull, determined and steadfast. In short, they are like no other canine on earth! They have ruined me for any other breed. Jack Russell Terriers have totally captured my heart." Owners of these small terriers would certainly agree with Ms. Doran. They know that owning a Jack Russell is a wonderful delight, and are firmly committed to protecting these hardy terriers.

The breed is named after Parson John Russell, better known as Jack, who was born in 1795, in Dartmouth, England. Like his father, Jack Russell was an avid and devoted hunter. While a student at Plympton, he spent all his spare time riding to the hounds and, it is said, that his studies took second place to his passion for hunting. It is rumored that he was almost expelled. Later, he attended Exeter College, at Oxford and, in 1820, he was ordained. For most of his professional life, he lived in Swimbridge.

He was fortunate in selecting a wife that shared his enthusiasm for hunting and dogs, and they often rode together, covering many miles. Parson Russell was one of the original founders of England's Kennel Club, in 1873. In 1874, he judged Fox Terriers in the first Kennel Club sanctioned show in London. While he remained a Kennel Club member for the rest of his life, he did not exhibit his own dogs.

In his later years, Jack Russell gained reknown as something of a local character. He was highly opinionated, had a strong and forceful personality, and came to be regarded as somewhat of an eccentric. Although he was an able minister, he still had plenty of time to pursue his favorite pastime...hunting. He became a legendary figure, and many stories were recounted in the local pubs of his exploits in the field. We are told that he rather enjoyed his reputation. One poem about him indicates the good natured ribbing bestowed on the Parson.

> But who's that, may I ask, who in grey hue is
> clad,
> Riding wide of the pack, and tight hold of his
> prad?
> 'Tis a rare sort of parson, and if there's a run
> The Rector of Swymbridge will see all the fun,
> His phiz I can't see--by his figure I twigs
> It can be no other than Russell on Figs.
> If hunting's salvation, he's nothing to fear;
> His soul has been hunting for many a year.

Jack Russell died in 1883, at the age of 88. Until the end, he had remained active and vital. He continued to enjoy riding to the hounds, and his terriers were his great love. So beloved was he that more than 1,000 mourners attended his funeral service in Swimbridge.

It was in 1819 that Parson Jack Russell acquired his legendary Trump, who was to be the foundation for his strain of working terriers. While he was studying at Oxford, he decided one bright May afternoon to walk to nearby Marston. On the way, he met a milkman who was accompanied by a terrier bitch. So impressed was Jack Russell with the little dog, that he purchased her right then and there. He considered Trump the "perfect terrier" and her likeness

Blencathra Nettle and Blencathra Badger are ready for action. These two lovely Jack Russell Terriers are owned by Paul Ross, of Conway, New Hampshire.

can, today, be seen on the painted sign for the Jack Russell Inn at Swimbridge.

Many people do not realize that Jack Russell bred a working strain of Fox Terriers. Indeed, early drawings and depictions of old Fox Terriers bear a striking resemblance to many JRTs, as the breed's name is often abbreviated. The Fox Terriers in Parson Russell's day were smaller than the representatives seen in modern show rings. The wirehaired dogs were also much less heavily coated than their modern counterparts. Mr. Russell considered the ideal terrier to be about the size of a European vixen fox. This is generally conceded to mean about 14 inches at the withers. He preferred his terriers to be primarily white, as he felt that this made them easy to differentiate from the fox.

It is fortunate that the Parson placed great emphasis on temperament. No terrier should ever be timid, but Jack Russell was just as appalled by overly aggressive dogs. While he maintained a kennel, several favorites were always kept as house dogs. He often spoke out against "hard" dogs. "A real terrier is not meant to murder," he once stated, "and his intelligence should always keep him from such a crime." The Parson's terriers were used exclusively on fox and they would go to ground to bolt the fox, so that it could be pursued by waiting hounds and men on horseback. A "hard" terrier that wanted only to fight and kill the fox, could not be heard baying underground. There was also the real possibility that he might be very seriously injured in the encounter. You can well imagine how frustrating this attitude

would have been. There were dozens of men waiting on horseback for the little dog to bolt the fox. If the quarry were killed underground, it would have deprived them of their sport.

While Parson Russell did not show his dogs, it would be wrong to conclude that he placed no emphasis on conformation and type. Indeed, it was not show dogs *per se* that he despised, but rather the attitudes of their owners. He firmly believed that terriers were sporting dogs, and the true measure of any good terrier was his degree of gameness. He thought the show ring was a poor arbiter of a terrier's essential spirit, courage and eagerness to work. It annoyed him that, with the advent of dog shows, many owners considered their dogs too precious and too valuable to engage in the task for which they were originally bred.

The Jack Russell Terrier is a compact, small dog with a totally balanced appearance. He should always appear active and alert. The standard describes the breed as being, "a sturdy tough terrier, very much on its toes all the time." Like all other terriers, he should have a very powerful jaw. His intelligent eyes are dark and almond shaped. A Jack Russell's tail should be about four inches long, and is set rather high and carried gaily. The breed comes in either smooth, rough or broken coats. Following Parson Jack Russell's preference, the coat is primarily white with black, tan or brown markings. In the show ring, JRT's are divided into two classes according to their height. They may be shown in the 10 inch to 12 1/2 inch class or the 12 1/2 to 15 inch class. Currently, the leggier dogs are more in vogue. Regardless of size, there are a couple of characteristics which any good Jack Russell must have. Above all, he must retain those qualities that enable him to successfully go to ground. Most important is a small chest. "The chest should be small enough to be easily spanned behind the shoulders, by average size hands," the standard says. The Jack Russell must also be totally flexible, to allow him to maneuver underground.

The Jack Russell is a happy, bold and energetic dog. "Jack Russell Terriers are action dogs," says Catherine Doran. "They seem to need to be out of doors. I think this is why they fit in so well with equine lifestyles. They require lots of activity both mentally and physically. They like human contact and keep well in a pack, playing endlessly. Then they'll sleep soundly, but they are ready for more action at the move of a muscle. They run like lightning, and need room to spread their wings without potential disaster. The working qualities have been preserved so far because they have remained in the country. I don't think they are any more suitable to city or suburban homes than a horse is!"

Many JRT breeders agree with Catherine Doran.

They refuse to sell their puppies to city homes. Some Jack Russells have successfully made the transition to urban living, but those interested in the breed must understand that these dogs have a need for activity. It takes a very special owner to cater to the JRTs abundant energy. If they are left alone during the day, they may well turn that boundless energy to destructive activity.

The Jack Russell requires firm and consistent handling. "If you are weak then they will seize the upper hand and the control," Catherine Doran says. "They are little clowns and very determined. They will, however, do just about anything you ask if it has purpose and meaning. I find them obedient without submissiveness. They are bold to the point of abandon, which may be their undoing. They want to be important to people and won't allow themselves to be ignored. These little folks are center stagers every minute."

Jack Russells are terriers and some may be aggressive toward other dogs, however, many JRTs live peacefully with other canines. "The courage of the Jack Russell is never in doubt," says the Jack Russell Terrier Club of America, "but this does not mean he is vicious or could become a nuisance by attempting to fight with other dogs. It is rather he knows he could better them if he wanted to, so he is, therefore, quite content to remain either aloof or friendly, as the situation demands."

The Jack Russell gets along well with well behaved children. Many a child and one of these small terriers have become inseparable friends. "One of the Jack Russell's most surprising qualities is a gentle and kindly nature," says the JRT Club of America. "He has a very soft mouth, in spite of having been bred, for countless generations, to overcome his enemy. He usually is particularly friendly towards young children. The few instances of bad temper can nearly always be traced to the fault of the owner, who provided no early corrective training, or actually encouraged a display of aggressiveness."

Bred for years as a hunter, the Jack Russell still excels at the task. They will go to ground at any given opportunity. They are excellent on rats, rabbits, woodchucks and fox. "I personally work my terriers to groundhog, raccoon, and when possible fox," says Paul Ross, of Blencathra Kennels, in Conway, New Hampshire. Catherine Doran finds her terriers very useful on her New York farm. "Foxes have killed many of my ducklings, peafowl and full grown hens," Ms. Doran says. "Our terriers know not to disturb fowl, but well known when to work fox, chuck or rat. They can break the neck of a rat faster than the snap of one's fingers." Like many terrier owners, Ms. Doran cautions people not to leave their dogs unattended. "A Jack Russell will go hunting if you don't watch them and they are not afraid of anything on the planet. They have been known to stay in an active den for two weeks, without food or water, because there was something at home in the hole. It's maddening to be sent to the woods after errant dogs. You are so frightened that your anger is dulled by the panic in your heart. I make certain that my dogs respond to the recall. I have trained mine so that they will come to the sound of my voice, a whistle or, if they are out of range, the blasting of the truck horn. I make a big deal out of their return with much praise. If I have to go get them, like children gone wrong, they get grounded!"

The JRT, although willful, is surprisingly obedient. "You must obedience train a working hunting terrier," Catherine Doran says. "I go to obedience classes. I am not interested in competing, but I find that it helps to better develop my dogs' minds and improve my communication with them. Obedience training could well save the live of any dog. JRTs can be very good at obedience if you make it both fun and rewarding."

This small terrier from the British Isles is attracting a host of loyal and devoted followers. He is a favorite with fox hunters and country dwellers. He is esteemed not only for his working attributes, but also for his superb qualities as a companion. Indeed, the Jack Russell is equally at home sleeping on your bed or bolting a fox. Like Catherine Doran, many owners are discovering that Jack Russell Terriers have captured their hearts.

Blencathra Badger, a broken-coated dog owned by Paul Ross, has the narrow front so essential to a good J.R.T.

123

Two Jagd Terriers treeing a racoon.

A Jagd Terrier prepares to enter the water.

A Jagd Terrier retrieving a duck.

A Jagd Terrier proudly looks over the results of the season's first duck hunt.

Chapter 32

The Jagd Terrier

The Jagd Terrier is little known in this country, although the breed enjoys widespread popularity in Germany and throughout Europe. It seems a shame, as this is a very distinctive and unusual little terrier with multi-purpose hunting skills. *Jagd* means "to hunt" in German and it is certainly an appropriate name for this sturdy little dog.

The Jagd (pronounced Yakt) Terrier came to the attention of Americans in the early 1950's, and, within the next twenty years, the breed made slow, but steady, progress. Interest seems, however, to have diminished in the intervening years. Considering the tremendous interest in the Jack Russell Terrier, one would think that the Jagd Terrier, or German Hunting Terrier, as he is sometimes called, would find a receptive audience here.

"We introduce to German shooting men, the German Jagdterrier, the little, unassuming working dog, the keep of which suits the lightest pockets and any domicile," wrote Count von Schwerin in *Der Hund*. The Jagd Terrier is one of only three terrier breeds created outside the British Isles. He is, however, descended from British breeds and may be very reminiscent of some of the early terrier types. In the early 1900's, the industrialist C.E. Gruenwald, the renowned hunting writer Walter Zangenbert, Chief Forester R. Fiess and Dr. Herbert Lackner began to develop a new hunting breed. They used the old Black and Tan rough coated terriers and crossed them with the Fox Terriers of the time. Some have said that the Jagd Terrier contains Welsh Terrier blood, but this claim is usually disputed. If you examine the history of the German developed sporting breeds, you will see that sportsmen of this country prefer non-specialized hunting dogs. The Weimaraner and the German

Shorthaired Pointer are considered utility hunting breeds that are able to point birds, hunt large game and retrieve. The Jagd Terrier follows in this tradition, and these German gentlemen succeeded in producing a tough little working terrier that combined the sporting nature of the hunting strains of Fox Terriers with the physical strength of the old British terrier. As one breeder said, "They wanted the best qualities of the old working terriers, along with the style and flash of recent terriers. We believe they succeeded." They developed both short and rough coated varieties, although the smooth coat is no longer considered acceptable. These four men worked arduously to create just the breed they wanted. It is said that they maintained a large kennel, containing some 700 of these new terriers, before they were convinced that they had, indeed, created an ideal breed that reproduced totally true to type. In 1926, they formed a Club and introduced the breed to German hunting advocates.

Max Thiel, Sr. and his family relocated to Bavaria after World War II. They had lost everything in the war, and that included their beloved hunting companions, Jagd Terriers. Max had been associated with the breed since 1938 and, once settled, he promptly purchased two females. Asta vom Mairhof and Naja von der Kammlach joined the Thiel family. The Thiels emigrated to the United States in 1951 and brought Naja with them. Asta was left behind to be bred, and she arrived, in whelp, in August of the same year. From Asta's litter came Freia von der Walkmuhle, who was to be of major importance to the breed in the United States. Although breed progress was slow, many people were impressed with Mr. Thiel's little hunters. One of the new enthusiasts was Armin Schwartz, Sr. and, in 1954, he imported

Axel vom Elsterbusch, who had sired champions in Germany. In his homeland, the Jagd Terrier was required to compete successfully in both hunting and conformation events in order to be bred and obtain titles. These dogs formed the basis for the breed in America, and subsequent judicious imports enriched the gene pool. The Jagdterrier Club of America was formed in Saint Louis, Missouri, in March 1956.

Word of this new breed spread, primarily among hunters. The Jagdterrier Club of America continued to thrive, and about 500 Jagds were registered in the American studbooks. The Club was strongly affiliated with its German counterpart and established breeding rules based on the German guidelines. All Jagd Terriers were dual registered in the United States and Germany, and the Club maintained meticulous records. At the time, the Club stated, "The ultimate goal of the J.C. of America is to gain recognition by the A.K.C., with intent not to over popularize the Jagd, but to place him more readily in homes with hunters. Likewise, American breeders appreciate that a stimulus to maintaining good type would be provided by participation in conformation classes in approved A.K.C. shows." Sadly, this did not come about. The Club lapsed, and we no longer know how many Jagd Terriers are still in the United States, although it seems logical that some remain. Adele Abe, the former Club registrar and publicity chairman, says, "To the best of my knowledge, there isn't a Club in the U.S.A. At present, the people who worked so hard in the late '50's and early '60's have lost interest and, if they still have Jagds for family and hunting, don't care if the A.K.C. registers them."

The Jagd Terrier is a sturdy, compact little dog. He stands 16 inches or less in height, which makes him ideal for working purposes. At 19 1/2 to 22 pounds for dogs, and 16-18 pounds for bitches, the Jagd is a convenient house size companion. He is strongly built and well muscled. The Jagd's dark eyes have a very determined expression. His ears are set on high and V-shaped. His tail is always carried at the level of the back and never gaily. The standard describes his gait as "rigid, rather like that of a wader." While most of the Jagds brought to this country were black and tan, the German standard allows for a range of colors, including "black, black mixed with gray, or dark brown with lighter markings, brown-red-yellow on the brows, muzzle, chest, legs and vent. The mask may be either dark or light. A little white on the chest and toes is allowed." Those who have an opportunity to see a group of Jagd Terriers are often surprised at the amazing uniformity. These are inherently sound dogs, and overall breed quality is extremely high. It is said that there are often only very minor differences between placings at dog shows. Indeed, many breeders comment that totally unrelated dogs from different countries resemble littermates.

As a working dog, the Jagd is hard to beat. He is often used as an all-round hunter and, if you could keep only one dog, the Jagd would be an excellent choice. He has plenty of gameness, and is tough as nails when going to ground. In addition, he has proved adept on birds. When working fowl, the Jagd flushes birds in the style of spaniels. The little Jagd has won much praise for his retrieving ability. It is said that he will retrieve to hand anything that he can carry. He is very accomplished at water work and is an able and enthusiastic swimmer. The Jagd has been used on squirrel and raccoon, and it is said that he is quite fearless. In Germany, the breed was used successfully for tracking work. There are several accounts of him finding wounded game on a 36 hour old track. Strange as it may seem, the game little Jagd has even been used on wild boar. When tackling this large animal, the Jagd makes use of his amazing agility and, generally, approaches the large animal from the side. Leaping, he grabs the boar's ear and hangs on for dear life. By his actions, he is able to slow the boar down until the hunter can arrive.

"Our family found the Jagdterrier easy to keep," Adele Abe says. "They do not have the profuse furnishings of many of today's terriers. They have a fun loving attitude that makes the Jagd easier to keep in the house and with children, and they love to roam over field and stream. For us, as nonhunters, he represents all we deem desirable in a terrier breed. Hardy, sturdy, tough-as-nails constitution, a hint of the terrier independence, but coupled with a sensible attitude and a willingness to work with his people at any task they desire." Mrs. Abe first became interested in the breed when a close family friend acquired a Jagd Terrier. She fell in love with the breed. She advises that training is mandatory, and that the Jagd can sometimes be stubborn. The Jagd Terrier is quarrelsome with other dogs. "They are very much terriers," Mrs. Abe says. "Perhaps, the most outstanding thing to us is his sensible level headedness. He is not silly or foolish, except perhaps in play. Rather he has a very high degree of plain common sense. I believe the Jagd could be an outstanding dog in obedience work. His high level of intelligence, coupled with a very sensible attitude to be a working dog, are prime necessities for top obedience work."

One hopes that the Jagd Terrier will come to be more appreciated in this country. This dynamic little dog is sure to be a hit in hunting circles and working trials. His overall breed quality should enable those importing the breed to obtain good specimens. With his sharp good looks, he could also be quite successful in American show rings. For those who enjoy hunting, and would like a versatile companion, you need look no further than the Jagd Terrier.

Chapter 33

The Karelian Bear Dog

The Karelian Bear Dog, or the Karelian Bearhound, is striking in appearance. With his flashy black and white markings, this breed is one of the most distinctive and attractive members of the spitz family. The breed's original name, in Finnish, is the *Karjalankarhukoira.* In Sweden he is called the *Karelsk Bjornhund.* The Karelian Bear Dog is a very close relative of the Russian Laika breeds, although it is said that he is more domesticated than the other breeds in this class. Like the other Laika breeds, he is an alert, active and very lively dog. Incidentally, the term *Laika* is derived from the Russian word, *layat,* which means "to bark." Those familiar with the Karelian Bear Dog, say that the term is applicable.

The Karelian Bear Dog is an old breed, believed to have existed in the Viking era. He takes his name from what was, at the time, the Finnish province of Karelia. The breed was particularly numerous in the eastern part of Karelia, Finland's easternmost province. Karelia was a remote area of vast forests, abounding with game. There, the Karelian Bear Dog was a family guard and a hunting companion. The farmers liked nothing better than a big game hunt, and their Bear Dog was a hunter *par excellence.* He was used on a variety of game, including elk, lynx, deer, rabbit, wolf and, of course, bear. It was said that the breed was agile and strong enough to battle a full-grown wolf successfully. Unfortunately, as with so many breeds, the Karelian Bear Dog was often cross-bred and, for a time, the breed seemed endangered. However, untainted specimens were discovered in a few of the isolated villages to the east of Salmi. The Finnish Kennel Club recognized the breed in 1935 and established a standard.

The World War II period was a very trying time for the breed. In a peace treaty agreed upon in 1941, Karelia became Russian territory, and the Bear Dog's home is now known as the Karelo-Finnish Soviet Socialist Republic. There were many refugees and some brought their dogs with them to south-central Finland, following this cession of territory. It is also reported that some army officers searched for specimens of the breed before the region left Finnish hands. While this added to the number of Karelian Bear Dogs in the country, it also cut off breeders from the original source of future breeding stock.

The Russians still breed the Karelian Bear Dog, although they have altered it to suit their own purposes. They wanted to breed a "super bear dog" that exhibited greater courage and even greater stamina, and they appear to have succeeded. The original Karelian Bear Dog was crossed with the Utchak Sheepdog, a breed reported to be extraordinarily aggressive when battling other animals. It is said that the Russian version of the Bear Dog is very aggressive, and will readily fight with a bear.

The Karelian Bear Dog was recognized by the Federacion Cynologique International in 1946 and, many will be surprised to learn, the breed was recognized by the Canadian Kennel Club in 1980. They are still extremely rare in Canada and seldom, if ever, seen at shows. The breed is still used in Finland for hunting a variety of animals. They win high praise for their stamina and courage. The breed still excels on bear, and it is said that these dogs have an amazing ability to detect the winter dens where the bears hibernate. The Finnish Bear Dog Breed Council has been particularly devoted to maintaining the breed's ability in the field. While a Karelian Bear Dog

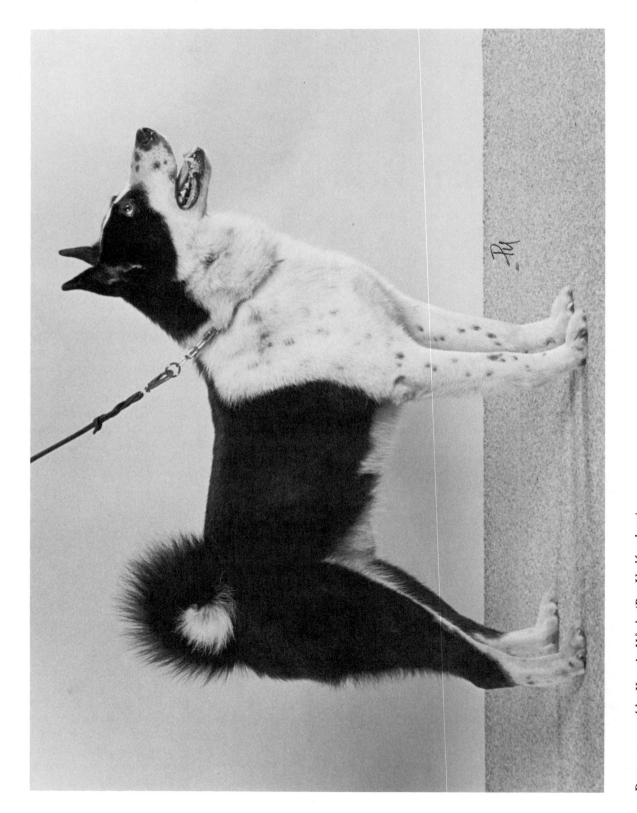

Dragos, owned by Karstin Hård. (Per Undén photo)

may become a show champion in Finland, in order to become a full champion (this would be our equivalent of a dual champion), the dog must demonstrate his ability in a field trial, where he is required to hunt elk.

The breed has improved a great deal since being accorded official recognition. Early on, many Karelian Bear Dogs were bobtailed, and their coats were often brown or grey. One seldom sees these faults today. In the show ring, the athletic and muscular Bear Dog makes a striking sight, and many owners have taken to showing their dogs. However, as one noted international judge says, "There is no evidence they like it. Alas, impressive as this breed is, I doubt if they have a show future. At best, they are a surly bunch, good enough with their owners, but hard-nosed to the rest of mankind. With other dogs they are totally predictable. Drop the lead for one second, and they set straight to work grabbing and hanging on to the nearest available dog."

Indeed, the Karelian Bear Dog does have a reputation for being highly aggressive toward other dogs. This seems to have been true through the ages, and for this reason the breed has always been considered a solitary hunter. Those who have had the opportunity to spend time with Bear Dogs say that they are absolutely fascinating. They are, however, somewhat of a handful, as they can be highly individualistic and quite stubborn. Writings on the breed have characterized the Karelian Bear Dog as sullen and intractable.

The above comments should not be construed as meaning that the Karelian Bearhound is without redeeming temperamental qualities. They are said to be very intelligent, remarkably clever and courageous, and extremely devoted to their owners. They tend to become deeply attached to one master and exhibit incredible loyalty. Karelians make wonderful guard dogs, and will not hesitate to defend their owners with their lives. Those who live with the breed find that they are quite docile in the home.

The Karelian Bear Dog is an extremely attractive, medium- size dog. The FCI standard calls for males to be 21 to 23 1 /2 inches, while bitches should measure 19-21 inches at the withers. The Canadian standard differs somewhat, calling for dogs to be 21 1/4 to 23 1/2 inches, while bitches should be 19 1/4 to 21 1/4 inches. The breed has the traditional spitz characteristics of prick ears and a tail that curls over the back. The head is wedge-shaped and somewhat broad in the backskull. He has a wide chest and is moderately angulated in the rear. The nose is always black. His eyes are brown and said to have an alert and fiery expression. The breed has a double coat that is more profuse on the neck, upper thighs and the back. Karelian Bear Dogs are, generally, black with some white patches. The black should be somewhat dull, and may be brownish in color. White is usually found on the chest, head, belly, legs and neck. While wolf-grey coloring and white with black markings are permitted by the standard, they are not at all desirable, and such a dog would not be likely to win in the show ring. The Canadian standard for the breed includes an additional fault, "savage disposition toward humans".

There are, presently, Karelian Bear Dogs in the United States, although we have no idea of the exact number of dogs. There have, however, been some recent importations to the midwest. At one time, there was a Karelian Bearhound Association of America and they had a promising start, but I have been unable to determine if this organization is still in existence. While it seems likely that some Bear Dogs accompanied Finnish immigrants to this country, the first serious imports for the purpose of establishing the breed in the United States, came in 1972. In that year, a Nebraska resident imported two puppies. Shortly thereafter, two other Nebraska residents imported more puppies. The one photo that I have seen of one of these dogs, showed a superb quality specimen. This should not come as a surprise, as all the original stock was specifically selected for these new owners by the Finnish Karelian Bear Dog Council. One would hope that the descendents of these superior imports have continued to be bred.

The Karelian Bear Dog will make a fascinating addition to the ranks of dog breeds seen in this country. The breed's strength and power is very reminiscent of their relative, the Norwegian Elkhound, and I think you, too, will find them fascinating. Their striking good looks should make them top contenders in the hound group. Owners of this breed should take special care to socialize their dogs so they will be amenable when out in public. With the present growing interest in rare breeds in this country, you may well see a Karelian Bear Dog at a show in the near future.

A trio of Kyi-Leos, Lin-Kai Ko-Me, Lin-Kai Mitzi and Kai-Jo of Lin-Kai, all owned by Harriet Linn, of Concord California.

Chapter 34

The Kyi-Leo

If anyone had told Harriet Linn that she would be the pioneer of a new breed of dog, she would certainly have told them they were crazy. And yet, that's precisely what this industrious woman has done. Little did Harriet dream, one summer day in 1965, when Sandi, her youngest daughter, begged for a puppy, that she would become the "mother" to a brand new breed. In response to Sandi's request, an adorable three-month old puppy joined the Linn family in their Concord, California home. This little charmer was destined to change the course of Harriet's life. "Mitzi," as the black and white shaggy coated baby was named, captivated not only the Linn family, but everyone else who saw her. "She accompanied us everywhere," Harriet says, "always drawing a crowd of admirers." Indeed, most people were so impressed with Mitzi that they wanted to know where they could buy one just like her.

"Mitzi was very intelligent and seemed to understand everything we said to her. She readily learned tricks, and her sitting up and begging was irresistable. She soon learned it could get her anything she desired. Another trait that fascinated us was the dexterity of her front feet. She used them almost as hands in playing with her toys and holding her chew sticks. She also delighted us with sudden exuberant outbursts of energy when she would make wild figure eights around the living room or the back yard."

Although the Linn family had originally planned to have Mitzi spayed, they decided to breed her. "She became more beautiful in looks and personality as she matured, and we decided a litter of her puppies would be very special," Harriet says. But, a very special sire was necessary for little Mitzi. Being an informed consumer, Mrs. Linn began to do research and ask questions. Frequent trips to the library and the purchase of numerous dog books and magazines, helped Harriet gain much information. She inquired into Mitzi's background and finally traced her roots to a breeder in San Jose, California.

In the early 1950's, the San Jose breeder had obtained a pair of dogs from a San Francisco family. These dogs were the result of several generations of Lhasa x Maltese crosses. Her male was a beautiful black and white parti-color and the bitch was a gold and white. This California breeder's soon to develop line was also augmented by a small black and white male Lhasa and a gold and white Lhasa-Maltese male. She carefully line bred on these original four and called their progeny "Lhasa-Maltese Shaggies."

Harriet Linn visited the breeder and was impressed with a small linebred black and white stud. "Impy" became the sire of Mitzi's litter and the first official Kyi-Leo litter was born. In 1967, when Mitzi's puppies, arrived the breed had not yet been named and the Linn's did not yet know that the adorable little tykes who shared their home would form the basis for an exciting new breed. "Kai-Jo," the only male in the litter, joined the Linn household. He was to become the breed's most influential stud dog.

If the Linn's thought Mitzi was special, they quickly learned that "owning a pair of these dogs was double the fun." Kai-Jo inherited Mitzi's loving ways and irrepressible personality "and came up with a few antics of his own. When the two of them walked together on a brace lead," Harriet recalls, "they made a striking pair and always drew a crowd. Once when walking through a local shopping mall, people lined up ten deep just waiting to ask questions about our dogs." The two dogs were inseparable companions and playmates. Rawhide chew sticks remained a great favorite of Mitzi's, but the little imp preferred to have Kai-Jo chew and soften them for her. "She'd sit patiently waiting while he chewed. When it became obvious he wasn't going to give up his prize, she'd run to the front door and bark! Of course, Kai-Jo couldn't resist joining her. The minute Kai-Jo reached the door, Mitzi would quickly run back and claim the chew stick."

When the San Jose breeder decided to retire in 1969, Harriet quickly purchased Impy. Together, Mitzi and Impy would produce four litters, totalling 14 puppies. To the Linn's delight all were a striking black and white. "Ko-Mi," a bitch from Mitzi's final litter, also joined the household.

Kai-Jo became an extremely popular stud. He was bred to many females from the San Jose line. Harriet was impressed with the uniformity of Kai-Jo, Mitzi and Impy's litters. Particularly pleasing was the strong inheritance of temperament. Other owners found the personality as endearing as the Linn family had. Harriet began keeping detailed records of all puppies produced by her dogs and her scrapbook of photos grew. When she phoned or visited owners, she was constantly treated to stories about the dogs' entertaining antics. By 1972, the Linn's "family strain" totalled 60.

It was time for these little dogs to have a name of their own. After a great deal of research, the breed was christened the Kyi-Leo (*Kyi* -Tibetan for dog; *Leo* -Latin for lion). A club was formed and the first of many "reunions" was held. Quite different from formal dog shows or matches, these annual reunions

An adorable twelve week old puppy, Po-Ku of Lin-Kai, owned by Harriet Linn.

afforded owners an opportunity to meet other Kyi-Leos and share stories with their devoted families. "Everyone 'shows off' their Kyi-Leos at our family reunions," Harriet says. "There are no losers! Everyone goes home feeling his dog is a winner, because even though he may look and act like other Kyi-Leos, theirs is surely the best!"

Those unfamiliar with the breed are certain to recognize the resemblance to the Lhasa Apso, the Tibetan Terrier and the Shih Tzu. There are, however, differences. The Kyi-Leo's nose is a little longer than that of the Lhasa and most of them sport a natural scissors bite. Harriet says that the Kyi-Leo's eye is not as prominent as that of the Lhasa and "the iris

The lovely Nan-Di of Lin-Kai makes her home with the Linn family, in Concord, California.

Five month old Tai-Li of Lin-Kai, owned by Al and Harriet Linn, poses for the camera.

Ko-Me, Mitzi and Kai-Jo relax at the Concord, California home of Al and Harriet Linn.

A lovely head study of Lin-Kai Ko-Me.

practically fills the whole eye, with very little white showing." The breed's silky coat is more natural in appearance than these other breeds and rarely reaches the floor-sweeping length of the Lhasa or the Shih-Tzu. Kyi-Leos usually come in a striking black and white parti- color, although gold and white and solid colored dogs do occur. The Kyi-Leo is slightly longer than tall and 8-12 inches in height making them a convenient size for the home. They are extremely bright and alert, and make ideal watchdogs.

There are now about 190 Kyi-Leos registered with the Club and three generations of puppies now carry Harriet's "Lin-Kai" prefix. Others have become interested in seriously breeding Kyi-Leos and Margaret Keim, of Sacramento, California, has been

very successful in exhibiting her "Kei-Mar" dogs in rare breed events. Owners keep in touch through a newsletter, and the number of breeders seems sure to grow. The breed has grown slowly as Kyi-Leo litters are small (3-4 puppies) and there seems to be a preponderance of males. If you are interested in obtaining a Kyi-Leo, be prepared to be patient. A waiting list exists, but as most current owners will agree, it is certainly worth the delay.

"All Kyi-Leo owners agree that they have the most adorable, smartest, most fascinating dogs in the world," Harriet enthuses. "Kyi-Leos don't know they are dogs. I'm sure they think they are people and should be treated as equals, which, of course, most of them are!"

French and Luxembourg Champion Sapho de l'Orchiidee Noire relaxes at her home in Huppaye, Belgium.

Chapter 35

The Laekenois

"The Laekenois is a very attractive breed, that many people feel is endangered and on its way to extinction. I have devoted myself to writing on the breed, which has become my 'passion', in an effort to save these unique dogs," says Mme. Liliane Lambert-Equerme, of Huppaye, Belgium. "The Laekenois is still very rare in Belgium and France. He is more widely known in Holland, and ownership there represents more than ninety-percent of the worldwide Laekenois population. It is very sad that this native breed is completely ignored by most of my fellow citizens. Most of the books devoted to the Belgian Sheepdogs devote only a few lines to this hard-coated variety, and there are numerous books that state that there are only three varieties of Belgian Sheepdogs: the Groenendael, the Tervuren and the Malinois. They completely ignore the existence of the Laekenois. It is impossible to get people interested in the breed when it is rarely written or spoken about. Photos of the breed are extremely rare.

"My country has made huge efforts to promote all kinds of things, but when it comes to dogs, these are often left behind. At one time, we had the famous *Malins Belges,* but this breed has completely disappeared and is now considered extinct. Even the *Petits Griffons Bruxellois* (Brussels Griffon) is not well known in my country. It would be a shame if a breed as wonderful as the Laekenois were to disappear entirely."

The Laekenois (pronounced Lake-n-wa) is the "other" variety of Belgian Sheepdog. Only in the United States are the Belgian Sheepdog (the Groenendael) with its long, solid black coat, the Tervuren with its gorgeous long fawn coat, and the Malinois with its short fawn coat, considered as

separate and distinct breeds. All other countries consider these as varieties under the general category of "Belgian Sheepdogs." The black Groenendael was the first of the Belgian sheepdog varieties to be introduced to the United States, and the American Kennel Club erroneously dubbed the breed the Belgian Sheepdog. When, in later years, the Tervuren and the Malinois made their debuts, the AKC granted them separate breed status. Americans, as yet, have not discovered the Laekenois, although a few of the breed can be found in Canada, where they can be registered and are eligible to compete in show rings.

This seems a profound shame when one considers that the Laeken is the oldest of the four varieties. All Belgian Sheepdogs, Belgian Tervuren, Laekenois, Bouvier des Flandres and Dutch Shepherds trace their ancestry directly to a Laeken, specifically, Voss I de Laeken. All of the world's Malinois descend from Lise de Laeken.

Mme. Lambert-Equerme is one of the world's most enthusiastic supporters of the Laekenois. Her stunning Champion Sapho de l'Orchidee Noire has won many friends for the breed. Liliane has written extensively on this variety and is currently at work on a book devoted to the Laeken. She calls the breed's history, "fabulous, but very sad at the same time." In Flanders, in the latter days of the last century, Belgian industry was in high gear. Particularly prized was Belgian produced linen cloth, which gained a reputation for high quality throughout the world. There were vast fields where flax was grown. The stems of the plants were made into thread, which was then woven into the finest of cloth. The Belgian people would wash the cloth in neighborhood streams and spread it out to dry on the meadows. Similiar

The Laekenois has a rustic, natural beauty.

fields were known, in England, as "bleachcrofts." Thieves often coveted this valuable cloth and, to protect their merchandise, the residents employed coarse-coated dogs to keep watch over them. These dogs, early Laekenois, gained a reputation as being remarkably intelligent, but they were also very distrustful and would not hesitate to bite an intruder. At the same time, they were remarkably devoted to their families and stayed particularly close to the women and children.

Some time later, a shepherd from the Brussels area raised these rough coated dogs. He found that the dogs were hardy, and that the Laeken's rough coat provided him with abundant resistance to all weather extremes. The shepherd and his wife had obtained the dogs from their parents, and they personally knew all the dogs that had contributed to their stock. The couple spoke only Flemish and this prevented them from communicating with many other breeders. In retrospect, this may have been fortunate, as it meant that they bred only Laeken to Laeken. These rough coated dogs were quite adept at herding and protecting the couple's sheep. The man secured permission to allow his sheep to graze on the royal grounds at Laeken Castle. They were seen by many people and attracted much attention. King Leopold and Queen Marie Henriette were very fond of the shepherd and had the opportunity to see his dogs. When it was announced that this was the Queen's favorite breed, the Laekenois became quite famous. More and more breeders appeared in and around Brussels, and the Laeken's future seemed assured.

"But success is not always a good thing!" Liliane Lambert- Equerme reminds us. The demand for the breed skyrocketed, and rough coated dogs of any color were bred. Light or dark fawn, beige, light or dark grey ash, yellow and even black rough coated dogs

were bred in an attempt to satisfy demand. When the standard for all the Belgian Sheepdogs was recognized by the Saint-Hubert (the Belgian Kennel Club) in the 1890's, there was much controversy over the Laekenois. "A decision came out as a knife strike," Mme Lambert-Equerme says. "The hard-haired Belgian Sheepdogs would only have the ash-grey color. Any other color would be rejected for exhibition and for breeding." This move almost sounded the death knell for the Laekenois. "This unfortunate comedy lasted about ten years and, as the Laeken sheepdogs were fawn colored, they were considered inadequate. The ash greys gradually disappeared and the fawn colored hard haired sheepdogs obtained the right of existing once again. They were then called the Laekenois or *Berger de Laeken*." Color continues to be a much debated subject, and one has only to introduce the topic among Belgian Sheepdog fanciers to start a lively and heated discussion.

"During this difficult period, when the true Laeken was denied the right to officially exist, the Dutch people came into the game. They were most happy to welcome dogs which had so many qualities, and they granted them laurel wreaths when they were exhibited, and would have so loved to make them their own. There still remained, however, a few Belgian supporters who struggled along, and they didn't let this happen." The Dutch must have, indeed, been fond of the Laekenois, as they used them as the formation stock for the Dutch Shepherd. Although there is some dispute in the matter, many authorities also believe that the Laeken made a significant contribution to the Bouvier des Flandres. The Laekenois has maintained its great popularity in the Netherlands, although many believe that Bouvier and Dutch Shepherd blood has been introduced into the line, and that the dogs from Holland do not represent the original, and called for, type. "It might sound unfair to talk this way," Liliane says, "because, after all, the Dutch saved our variety of sheepdogs, and the biggest part of the worldwide stock exists there. Unfortunately, the Laekenois which exist in Holland look different from those which one finds in France and Belgium. They look much heavier, and their coats are more profuse and they need frequent grooming."

Over ten years ago, an effort was made in France to restore the Laeken to its original type. L'Orchidee Noire Kennels imported a male from Holland and bred it to a Malinois bitch in an effort to recapture true Belgian type. They had amazing success and their Laekenois are now considered to be of the highest quality. However, Laeken breeders outside of Holland still face problems. These stem mainly from the public's lack of knowledge about this variety. Breeders are never sure if they will be able to place their puppies, and so breedings are few and far between. If there was increased public demand for the

Laekenois, it would enable these dedicated breeders to feel more confident and expand their breeding programs. I normally prefer not to list selling prices for dogs, but it might be helpful to provide you with an approximate price for a Laekenois puppy. These prices are, of course, variable, as they are dependent on the current rate of exhange, and are intended only as a guideline. As of this writing, a Laeken puppy, in France, generally sells for $225-300 and in Belgium the range is from $280-460. I believe that breeders in Holland command higher prices. Mme. Liliane Lambert- Equerme (see the appendix for her address) will be glad to direct you to reputable breeders.

"The Laekenois exhibits all the qualities that one expects in any Belgian Sheepdog," Liliane says, "intelligence, rusticity, elegance, and fidelity." Liliane first became interested in the Laekenois about ten years ago, after she and her husband purchased a male Groenendael. Soon a female joined the couple's home, and Liliane began to research the breed's history. She found frequent references to the Laekenois, but little information on this variety. "The breed was alone and on its way to disappearing, and there was no one to defend this type of dog," she says. "We decided that we had to have a Laeken." It took three years from the time they ordered the puppy until Sapho arrived in Belgium. It was certainly worth the wait, though. Sapho is the only female French champion, and has titles in Belgium and Luxembourg. She has been shown widely, and has captivated audiences with her beauty and character. Sapho is probably the best known Laekenois in the world.

Enthusiasts of the other Belgian Sheepdog varieties are often put off by the Laekenois' appearance. "People are often surprised at first sight. They don't feel attracted by this type of dog, but contact with the breed quickly changes their minds. Caress a Laekenois, live with him and you will understand. Anyone who has had one Laekenois keeps an extraordinary memory of him. In character they are very close to the other varieties, but slightly different. These dogs have a strong personality. Some training is a must, as they have a tendency to dominate their master. This must be straightened out from the very beginning. The dog must know, absolutely, that you are the master. If this is done, you will enjoy living with a fantastic friend," Liliane says.

"The Laeken needs a family life and, just like any other sheepdog, he needs to play, run and relax every day. He is a very affectionate dog that does not bark too much, and he would fit in very well with many families. He is an excellent guard. He doesn't trust people he doesn't know, but he will give all his affection to the people he lives with." Laekenois have been used very successfully as working dogs. Two Laekenois currently guard a royal property in Belgium and they have become quite famous. Several years ago, a televison crew filmed a documentary there, and many Belgians caught their first glimpse of the breed. They were amazed, and breeders received many requests for information. Laekenois have been employed by Belgian police, as well as army brigades, where they have been exceptional workers who were greatly admired. In the army they were used as liaison dogs. However, breed popularity has inhibited their use. Because Laekenois are so rare, most breeders search for serious owners, who are interested in showing and breeding. They feel that it is essential to promote the breed if it is to have any chance to survive.

The Laekenois is a very hardy dog. "While they like the contact of their master's family, they also enjoy being outdoors, no matter what the season. Their coat protects them from all types of weather," Liliane says. "They do go through shedding periods and it is imperative, at that moment, to remove the dead hair. In no case should they be trimmed or

This little known variety of Belgian Sheepdog is the oldest of the four varieties. This lovely bitch is owned by Liliane Lambert-Equerme, Huppaye, Belgium.

The beautiful French and Luxembourg Champion Sapho de l'Orchidee Noire, owned by Liliane Lambert-Equerme, poses for the camera.

I hope that people in other countries will become interested in the Laekenois. Certainly, the pictures of Sapho show just how beautiful this breed can be. Unlike some others, I do not find the breed's rough and natural appearance unpleasant. To the contrary, I find them extremely attractive. I sincerely hope that Americans will open their homes and their hearts to this deserving breed. Then, perhaps, the Laekenois can take his rightful place with his cousins, the Tervuren, the Malinois and the Belgian Sheepdog, in this country.

groomed." In Holland, however, where the Lakenois tends to be larger and coarser, the breed is often trimmed for the show ring. Mme. Lambert-Equerme thinks that when groomed in this fashion, they resemble "teddy bears". She finds the look very unattractive, and strongly prefers the natural type. This manner of presentation often makes it difficult for judges to ascertain quality, as the coat does not have the required natural look, and texture may be altered.

In Europe, the standard for all the varieties of Belgian Sheepdogs is identical except for the references to coat. The Laekenois description reads as follows:

COARSEHAIRED: Characterized by harshness and by the dryness of the coat which, moreover, is tangled. The length of the coat is almost equal on all parts of the body and measures on the average 2 1/4 inches. The hair on the muzzle and around the eye should never be so long as to give the head the appearance of the typical head of Berbets or Briards. However, the presence of feathering on the muzzle is obligatory. The tail should not have a flag. Dogs of this variety are called Laekenois, if they have hard fawn hair, with traces of black, especially in the muzzle and the tail. FAULTS: Hair too long, bristly, curly, wavy or short; tufts of fine hair in the hard hair; excessive length of hair around the eyes or on the lower extremity of the head; tufted tail.

Chapter 36

The Lapphund

Photos of the Lapphund in dog encyclopedias have spurred great interest in the United States. Imports of this Swedish breed, known as the *Lapplandska Spetz* in his homeland, should be arriving shortly. There is good reason for this outpouring of interest, for the Lapphund is a beautiful dog. He hails from the Scandinavian countries, although he is probably descended from the Central European spitz breeds. Indeed, with the exception of his dark coat color, he is very reminiscent of several of our already recognized breeds.

The Lapphund was the companion of reindeer herders in Lapland. Large reindeer herds grazed the vast northland, and the Lapphund was an invaluable herder. His black coat made him easily visible against the white snow. Reindeer were essential to the people of Lapland. The large beasts provided milk and meat, and their hides were made into clothing. Huge herds grazed the countryside, and in winter they would paw away the snow to feed on the lush moss below. Over the centuries, the Lapphund developed into an able herder and he was said to be quite swift and very gentle with his antlered charges.

Many of the spitz breeds have been used with great success in hunting, but the Lapphund seems less inclined in this regard. Perhaps, this is one of the reasons that the breed makes a better guard dog than many others in the spitz group. He prefers, generally, to stay close to his home and master. It is said that the Lapphund is very devoted and affectionate with his family, but makes a vigilant guard dog and can be quite suspicious and courageous when dealing with intruders. He has an excellent reputation as a child's companion, and is particularly gentle and protective of his small charges. The breed is very intelligent and

easy to train. There are reports that the Swedish army recently began raising Lapphunds for use as guard dogs. In Sweden today, the breed is considered a fine home companion and watchdog.

We do not know exactly where the breed originated, although he has been known in the Scandinavian countries for some time. It was in Sweden, however, that the breed gained a following, and dog lovers there have adopted the breed. The standard was first drawn up in that country and, in 1944, the Lapphund was recognized by the Federacion Cynologique Internationale. The Lapphund is often seen at Swedish dog shows, where there are many outstanding champions.

The Lapphund is a beautiful dog that shares many characteristics of the spitz family. He is double-coated, has a tail which curls over his back and, of course, prick ears. The Lapphund is a medium size dog. Males measure 17 1/2 to 19 1/2 inches, while females are 15 1/2 to 17 1/2 inches. The Lapphund's head has a broad and slightly domed backskull, and a rather short and pointed muzzle. His nose should be jet black, and his eyes are dark brown and tend to be somewhat prominent. Ideally, his ears are pointed, although the standard says that some specimens show a slight tip. The breed is longer than tall and has very heavy bone. He is a muscular dog and has only slight rear angulation. Among the most outstanding breed features are the Lapphund's very abundant coat and profuse, bushy tail. Indeed, the luxuriant coat often makes dogs appear larger than they actually are. It should be noted, however, that naturally bobtailed specimens are occasionally born, and the standard permits a docked tail. His heavy, stand-off coat is rather harsh to the touch, waterproof and insulates

seen. The Lapphund may have some white on his chest, feet or neck and the breed is permitted to sport a white collar.

We are sure to hear more about the Lapphund. It seems that he will be making his appearance at rare breed shows in this country in the near future. His medium size, wonderful disposition and natural ability as a watchdog should make him very suitable as a pet. Those looking for a striking and unusual companion should consider the Lapphund. This Swedish breed has much to offer dog lovers in this country.

International Champion Snöstjärnans Kaise-Vaisa, bred and owned by Kennel Snöstjärnan.

him wonderfully in the cold weather of his homeland. The breed does shed seasonally. Lapphunds generally come in black or dark brown. While solid colors are most desirable, brown and white dogs are occasionally

International and Scandinavian Champion Rillo av Torro, bred by Mary Stephens and owned by Kennel Snöstjärnan, in Sweden.

Chapter 37

The Leonberger

This breed takes its name from the city of Leonberg, Germany, near Stuttgart. Heinrich Essig, who lived from 1808 to 1889, was the highly respected mayor of Leonberg. Herr Essig was an avid animal lover. Many varieties of chickens, ducks, geese, turkeys, pigeons, deer and fox lived on the Essig property. Heinrich Essig was also a dog lover, and many breeds could be found in his kennels. He seems to have had a particular fondness for large dogs, for we know that Great Danes, Newfoundlands, Great Pyrenees and Saint Bernards were housed there. Indeed, he ran a commercial kennel and was said to have sold 200-300 dogs annually. Much as modern breeders may condemn such a massive breeding operation, it should not detract from Herr Essig's very worthy accomplishment. Breeders are often creative people, and Heinrich Essig began to dream of creating a breed that would resemble the lion. He was a patriotic man who was extremely proud of the city of Leonberg, and the official city crest featured a lion.

His first experimental breeding began with a Landseer (black and white) Newfoundland bitch that was a great favorite of his. He bred her to one of the large male St. Bernards that he had obtained from the St. Bernard Hospice in Switzerland. Indeed, Herr Essig had become friends with the monks at the Hospice. All of the puppies from this initial breeding were black and white in color, and Herr Essig was most impressed with their temperaments. He continued his breeding experiments for four more generations and then visited the St. Bernard Hospice, to show the monks the results of his new breeding program. They liked what they saw, and he traded two of his puppies for a large adult male. Sometime later, the Abbot told him that these pups had become

favorites, for they were every bit as hardy and strong as the Saints and, in many respects had proven more adept at work. In those early days, Heinrich Essig decided that he wanted more white on his puppies and so he bred some of the progeny from these Newfoundland-St. Bernard crosses to one of his Great Pyrenees.

In 1846, a dog was born that combined all of the qualities that Herr Essig wanted. He felt that he had finally achieved a blending of all the admirable qualities of the Newfoundland, the Saint Bernard and the Great Pyrenees. Type was not yet stabilized, and these new Leonbergers varied somewhat in coat color. Sometime before 1870, Herr Essig's new dogs made their first official appearance in public at Munich's annual Octoberfest. Newspaper accounts of the time describe the dogs as being lion-like, both in size and color. The press reported that the loveliest of the dogs were a yellowish brown with black shadings. These dogs impressed the people who came from all over Germany to attend Octoberfest, for they combined the cleverness and intelligence of the Great Pyrenees with the rugged beauty and usefulness of the Saint Bernard. They had the imposing size of the Newfoundland and shared that breed's enthusiasm for water.

In 1870, the Empress Elizabeth of Austria, known fondly as "Sissy," acquired the first of seven Leonbergers, and the breed's fame spread. This was the first Leonberger brought to Austria and he was described as having a silver-white coat. Indeed, he became Sissy's favorite dog, and she could often be seen walking him in a royal park. She was reputed to have paid 1,400 silver guilders for him.

By 1873, it was reported that 374 Leonbergers were exported at a price of 1,000 guilders each. The

K.K.'s Apollonia de Chiavari, a female Leonberger. Hansi is owned by Vicky and Tim Niver, Saskatoonberry Leonbergers, Howard City, Michigan.

Leonbergers enjoy attention, even in a group setting. Owned by Mary and Reiner Decher of Bellevue, Washington.

breed had become much sought after and the Prince of Wales, Emperor Napoleon III of France, the famed Italian hero Garibaldi and the King of Belgium all owned Leonbergers. Garibaldi's dogs were even said to have fought Sicily's wild bulls. Not that the breed was ignored by Germans, for Leonbergers became the favored companions of Bismarck and the famous composer Richard Wagner. It was the Russians, however, who developed a real passion for the Leonberger. They were so fond of the early imports that, by the end of the 19th century, they were importing approximately 300 dogs each year to the Czar's court.

In 1889, Heinrich Essig died. While he had created the breed and guided it on the road to public acceptance, fame and popularity, few had appreciated just how pivotal his presence was. After his death, vocal critics of the breed emerged. They were scathing in their condemnation of Herr Essig's breed, and one is left to wonder if perhaps they lacked the nerve to speak out while he was alive and could rise to the breed's defense. In Strebel's noted book of 1905, on German breeds, he speaks out against the Leonberger, which he characterizes as unpleasant and describes as merely a crossbred St. Bernard. One translated quote will adequately describe the attitude of this dog historian. "What one cannot define, that one regards as a Leonberger." Luckily, the breed had made a few friends and, in 1895, they formed the first club.

Both World Wars nearly devastated the breed, but the Second World War was a particularly trying time. With food scarce and bombings in many cities, few

Leonbergers survived. While more than 300 dogs had been exported to Russia in 1894, there were fewer than this number of dogs to be found in all of Germany after World War II. Those dedicated to the breed gathered specimens and started to revive their breeding programs, but the going was not easy. In 1945, only five litters were born, containing 43 puppies. Of these, only 22 survived. In 1946, 49 puppies were born, but the times were hard and only 17 lived. In the intervening years, the Leonberger population has since increased, and these dogs can now be found in most European countries and, recently, in the United States. While he is still not a common dog, there are good turnouts at shows on the Continent.

The Leonberger is a large impressive breed. Males measure a minimum of 30 inches, while females are required to be at least 27 1/2 inches. They are strong, broad and powerful dogs. This breed generally has webbed toes and is a strong swimmer. Their beautiful, lion-colored coat varies from a light yellow to a reddish brown and, like the lion, they have a pronounced mane or ruff on the neck. Most desirable is a black face mask, and the coat may have black points. Some Leonbergers have a white star on their chests, and a few white hairs on the toes are permissible. Their brown eyes are very friendly and intelligent.

It may be the impressive appearance of the Leonberger that first attracts the attention of new owners, but it is the breed's extraordinary personality that makes them devoted friends. The Leonberger is an extremely calm and even tempered dog. Indeed, it would be difficult to imagine a breed more tempermentally stable. He is faithful and devoted to his family, and there is a great deal of love in his massive body. Although noted for his calmness, the Leonberger is not a large, lazy dog. Indeed, he has a lively character and seems to greet everything in life with special joy and enthusiasm. Just ask him if he wants to go for a walk and he will jump, run and bark with glee. Owners should be forewarned, though, that, in his great enthusiasm, objects placed on low tables are likely to be swept off by his eagerly wagging tail. Leonbergers are very affectionate, and to develop properly they need a great deal of love. By socializing your new puppy you will be rewarded with a lifetime of devotion.

One of the qualities that owners find most impressive is the Leonberger's fondness for children. This breed must be considered highly trustworthy, and they have extraordinary patience, even with the most rambunctious child. The author of one German book on the breed describes seeing a large 130 pound male with two toddlers. While we will cringe at her observations, it does best demonstrate the breed's tremendous patience. The author watched as the kids inserted pencils into the dog's nostrils and turned them. Then, these little hellions tried to pull the Leonberger's tongue out of his mouth. The dog never showed any aggression, he only whined. When he had had enough, he got up and left. We would hardly approve of these children's behavior, but their canine playmate seemed to take it in stride. The author goes on to tell us that she has five Leonbergers that are great favorites with all the neighborhood children, and never once has any of her dogs growled at any of the small visitors. The Leonberger generally gets along well with other dogs, particularly if he has been raised with them. Occasionally, one will find a very

dominant male who does not tolerate other males.

The Leonberger, with his great size, is an able home protector. His protective instincts do not seem to manifest themselves until he is from one to one-and-a-half years of age. Young Leonbergers greet strangers with joy and want very much to be petted. As he matures, the dog will decide for himself who he likes and who he doesn't. If he doesn't like you, the Leonberger will probably turn his back and walk away. Above all he is calm, and will take confusion, excitement and noise in stride. As a watchdog, his size and strength make him formidable, but he is not a nuisance barker. Those who want a very aggressive and vocal watchdog may find the Leonberger disappointing, but his calm protectiveness is an advantage in city neighborhoods. However, he is an able watchdog, and any uninvited stranger entering a Leonberger's yard, does so at his own risk. He will not tolerate threats to those he loves. As one breeder says, "The Leonberger is always there when you need him." This breed loves to be included in family activities and will gladly accompany you on trips to the beach (he loves to swim)and on backpacking hikes. He can be trained to pull carts and sleds, and will provide you with hours of fun. The breed is even said to have been used for hunting and herding in Germany.

Kerilyn Campbell, of Santa Barbara, California, is the president of the newly formed Leonberger Club of America. She had heard of the breed from an uncle living in Germany, but first saw them at the Saint Bernard Hospice in Switzerland. "I fell in love with the breed and continued on to Germany to see Leonbergers there," says the California resident who has imported several dogs from top German conformation and working lines. "They're a big breed,

Bimbo, the much loved pet of Sylvia Marburger, of Truckee, California.

Anna von Klingelberg and Deuke, owned by Mary and Reiner Decher, of Bellevue, Washington.

The lovely Hansi relaxes at Saskatoonberry Leonberger Kennels, owned by Tim and Vicky Niver, of Howard City, Michigan.

and when people first see them they are put off. A Leonberger is fearless and will approach a stranger. If he is provoked, he will bite, but you don't ever have to worry about these dogs just biting someone. I've never met a Leonberger who has ever forgotten a friend. They have a deep bark and visitors to my house are sometimes frightened, but with a word from me, my dogs will calm down and accept anyone I allow into my home.

"We currently have 86 Leonbergers in this country. It has been difficult to obtain top quality breeding stock from Germany," Kerilyn says. "We have very high standards for the breed in this country. To be bred, all Leonbergers must be x-rayed for hip dysplasia and registered with the Orthopedic Foundation for Animals. We are following German guidelines in setting up our club. This will enable us to have access to top German bloodlines and to join the Leonberger Union. We will then be eligible to receive frozen semen from Germany's top studs." With such a dedicated start, it seems that Leonberger breeding will be wisely guided in this country.

For those seeking a large dog with a gentle personality, the Leonberger can't be beat. They are very capable of protecting you, but remain trustworthy. Beneath that beautiful lion-like body lies a devoted heart of gold. The Leonberger asks only to share your home and love, and he gives unselfishly of

himself in return. This breed is a welcome addition to the fine German breeds that have found homes in this country.

Chapter 38

The Lowchen
(Little Lion Dog)

He was the delightful companion of nobility. His engaging antics brightened the homes of aristocrats. He even figured in legends and, yet, this charming breed was listed, only a few years ago, as the rarest purebred dog in the world. Now, this small dog, groomed to resemble a male lion in miniature, is making a deserved comeback. With his delightful personality and eye-catching appeal, the Lowchen, or Little Lion Dog, is coming to the attention of more and more dog lovers. They have discovered that sharing their homes with a "pride of lions" is great fun.

In those wonderful days of knights and ladies, there was a custom. A knight who was killed in battle would have a lion emblazoned on his tomb. Should he come to his end in a less valiant endeavor, his tomb would be engraved with a depiction of the Little Lion Dog. The companion of Florentine nobility, the Little Lion Dog should never be confused with the so-called Lion Dogs of the East. These eastern dogs came by their names from myths which attributed to them a "lion-like" courage. The Little Lion Dog gained his name solely from his appearance. The breed is, undoubtedly, related to the Bichon family of dogs, which includes the Bichon Frise, the Bolognese, the Havanese, the Tenerife and the Coton de Tulear.

We know that the Lowchen was highly regarded in the 1500's, in both Spain and France. He was a popular subject for Renaissance artists and, on a tour of European museums, you will see many depictions of the breed. The Lowchen is pictured in the "Lady and the Unicorn" tapestries and in the works of Albrecht Durer. Durer was particularly taken with the breed and included these dogs in many wood cuts. He seems to have captured not only their physical likeness, but also their delightful personalities, for they cavort with unabashed joy throughout his works. The Lowchen was also pictured with the Duchess of Alba, in a 1795 painting by Francisco Goya. It is believed that the Duchess owned several Little Lion Dogs. Dr. Walter wrote about the breed in 1817, referring to them as the *Leoninus* meaning lion-like. It seems incredible that a breed so popular and treasured could become endangered, but, for many years, the Lowchen teetered on the very brink of extinction.

In the early days of this century, the future of the Lowchen seemed particularly bleak. There were only one or two breeders in all of Europe. Madame de Connick, of Dieghem, is credited with keeping the breed alive during this trying period. It is said that by the time World War II rolled around the Lowchen was almost lost forever. One breeder was reported to have turned all of his dogs out on the streets to fend for themselves. Madame Bennert, an eccentric elderly woman, scoured the streets of Brussels, Belgium, in search of the Little Lion Dogs. Slowly, she began to rebuild the breed, and she dedicated the next twenty years to their perpetuation and improvement. When she died, Dr. Richert (sometimes spelled Rickard) of Germany, stepped in to carry on her work. Photos of two of Dr. Richert's "living antiques" were carried in an American dog magazine in the 1970's. It was said that, at that time, there were only 40 Lowchen in existence and that Dr. Richert owned 10 of them. It seems amazing that the breed survived when its fate remained, for so many years, in the hands of so few

Sonjay Glemby at Pepperland, a Challenge Certificate and Best of Breed winner, in England. This lovely bitch is owned by Leslie Samuels Healy, of Pepperland Kennels, San Angelo, Texas.

breeders. Dog lovers owe these individuals a debt of gratitude.

The first Lowchen arrived in the United States in 1971. An article in *The New York Times* appeared announcing that a couple had brought back a *Petit Chien Lion* from England. This announcement caught the eye of Robert and Carole Yhlen, of Hopatcong, New Jersey. "We are both Leos and were intrigued with the Little Lion Dogs," the couple says. A short time later, Bob and Carole managed to acquire their first Little Lion. It was to be the first of many, and the Yhlens have acquired other breeding stock, including some from Germany. They began promoting the breed and have worked tirelessly in behalf of the Little Lion Dog Club of America. Bob currently serves as President, while Carole is the breed registrar.

Lowchen were first imported to England in the 1960's, but were not registered until 1971. In just five short years they were granted championship status. Fifty or more Lowchen can often be found at British championship shows, and many English imports have enriched the gene pool here in America. One English book says, "their growth in popularity has been one of the phenomena of the British dog scene." One hopes that the same will hold true here in the United States.

Leslie Samuels Healy moved to the United States in 1981 and brought several Lowchen with her. The San Angelo, Texas, resident has had notable success not only with her Lowchens, but with Border Collies

and Bearded Collies (which she raised in England). "I was on a coach with my Beardie heading north to a Scottish dog show," Leslie says. "Sitting in front of me was a lady with an Old English Sheepdog. This was Susie Dutson. She told me that her mother had just imported three very unusual dogs. They were Lowchen from Germany. I decided to visit these dogs when they got out of quarantine. My best English friend, Justine Warren (owner of Quinbury Bearded and Border Collies), went along with me to Sudbury, Suffolk, to visit Judy Dutson at her Rossglen Kennels. That was it," Leslie says. "We were smitten. And since 1973, I've always had a pride of lions."

Leslie and Matthew Healy have had notable success with the Lowchen at their Pepperland Kennels. Leslie owned America's only English Champion Lowchen, the late Quinbury Gatanya Fondue at Pepperland. Fondue also became an American Champion and a multiple Best in Show winner in this country. Also accompanying Leslie on her move to this country, was the charming particolor, Pepperland Footstep, a grandson of Fondue and a Junior Warrant winner in England. Mrs. Healy believes that the Lowchen is a very intelligent dog, and she has competed with great success in the obedience ring, too. Her American Champion Rossglen Charlie Brown at Pepperland, C.D. is the breed's first and only obedience title holder. Charlie Brown, as this much loved dog is known, has attracted a great deal of attention for the breed. "He is such a clown and loves showing off," Leslie says. "When we take him to shows, he carries a sign saying, 'My name is Charlie Brown. I'm a Lowchen (Little Lion Dog)' and he'll sit on top of a crate

Footprint of Littlecourt in Pepperland, owned by Leslie Healy, of Pepperland Kennels, is England's youngest Junior Warrant Winner and winner of a Best Puppy in Show Award, in England.

146

holding that sign forever. He makes sure that people stop and talk to him. We explain how smart the breed is, and tell them that it only took Charlie two weeks to learn to write," Leslie laughs. "We tell them he wrote the sign himself!"

The Lowchen is a sturdy little dog that is quite strong for his small size. He has a square, well balanced appearance and, although he somewhat resembles a Poodle, has more bone, a broader head and is more substantial in build. The American standard calls for an 8-15 inch height, which allows for a wide size variation. In the United States, the Lowchen competes in the Non- Sporting Group. In England and Europe the breed is classified as a toy, and must not exceed 13 inches.

One of the great delights in breeding Lowchen, is the amazing array of colors that are permissible within the breed. While the golden shades most clearly resemble the lion, Lowchen can come in any solid or particolor, although whites are rare. The first question from those unfamiliar with the breed is likely to concern the Lowchen's coat. "The hair normally grows naturally in a rough lion pattern with a ruff about the head and shoulders," says the Little Lion Dog Club of America. "The coat is usually clipped to emphasize these lines. A rough appearance is preferable. The coat should never be finely chiseled. The tail is carried high over the back and has a plume at the tip. The breed's elegance comes from its well-bred stance and easy, graceful movement rather than from fussy grooming." Your Lowchen will enjoy a daily brushing, and the clipping is not as complicated as grooming a Poodle. Given some time, novices should be able to groom their own dogs with ease. One of the big advantages to owning a Lowchen is that these little dogs do not shed.

With his distinctive looks the Lowchen is an eye-catcher in the show ring. When a good Lowchen makes an appearance at a rare breed show, exhibitors know they will have strong competition. Robert and Carole Yhlen's outstanding male, Champion Low-Ray's Cricket, has exceled in his ring outings. Cricket has garnered several Best in Show wins, as well as many group placements. This showy little dog is the top winner, to date, in the United States. Interest in the Lowchen as a show dog, has increased in the past few years. There are now more than one dozen American champions.

Lowchens make delightful pets. These little charmers are lively, yet not hyperactive. They are, by nature, friendly dogs that are said to alternate "between impishness and innocence." The breed gets along very well with children and quickly becomes a true member of the family. They are quite sturdy and hardy, and rarely suffer from medical problems. Their happy, outgoing nature quickly wins friends for the

American Champion Rossglen Charlie Brown, C.D. This impressive dog has won many friends for the breed. He makes his home with Leslie Healy, at Pepperland Kennels, San Angelo, Texas.

breed. "While small enough to dwell in a city apartment, and travel conveniently in a car, it is very sturdy and enjoys an active rough and tumble life," the Little Lion Dog Club of America says. "The Little Lion has an outgoing, affectionate and inquisitive personality. It loves people and is not particularly aggressive with other dogs."

"Lowchen are super little dogs that think they're big dogs. Mine are brought up with the Border Collies," Leslie Healy says, "and don't realize that they're supposed to be pampered toy dogs." A recent incident at Leslie's Pepperland Farms illustrates this point. "We were bringing on a young Border Collie and working him on some very domesticated goats. Our Charlie Brown was watching with interest from the back porch. When we finished the Collie's lesson, we returned to the porch and Charlie slipped out. It was as though he was saying to us, 'Betcha I can do that, too' and, you know, he did. He penned those goats with hardly any effort at all, and then came back to say, 'See, Mum, I can do that, too.' If only we'd

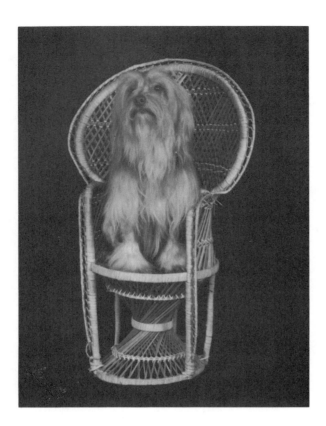

American Champion Rossglen Charlie Brown, C.D., is the only obedience titled Lowchen in the U.S. He earned his obedience degree just before his 12th birthday. Owned by Leslie Healy, Pepperland Kennels. (Olan Mills photo)

had a movie camera that day," Leslie laughs.

It was the breed's personality that first attracted Gini Denninger, of Walworth, New York, to the Lowchen. "I lived with a woman who had one that was given to her," Gini says. Gini's interest in the Lowchen spurred her interest in other rare breeds. This dedicated woman is one of the founders of the Western New York Rare Breeds Association. "The personality of this breed is very lively and friendly," Gini says. "They become very attached to their owners and want to please them. They are also clowns, and it is sometimes tempting to put a tutu on one and ask it to dance. They were circus dogs at one time. I do recommend that new owners make sure to socialize their dogs, as they will, sometimes, withdraw if this is not done."

If you are looking for a small dog that can charm his way into your heart, you need look no further than the Lowchen. With his captivating personality, he is sure to become a treasured friend. However, you may find that only one Little Lion Dog isn't enough. Soon you will be inviting friends over to visit your very own "pride of lions."

Chapter 39

The Maremma-Abruzzese Sheepdog

A great family of white livestock guarding breeds extends throughout Europe. Undoubtedly, these breeds, sharing so many similiar characteristics, sprang from the same source. Over the years, they have acclimated to their respective countries, but they still retain many similarities, most notably imposing size, an independent spirit and a white coat. The noted agricultural writer, Lucian G. M. Columella, spoke of these dogs in the second century when he said, "Shepherds wish to have white dogs in order to avoid confusing them with wild animals, since, when the wolf attacks in the twilight, it is important that there be a color difference between the dog and the wolf; otherwise the sheepherder might strike his dog, thinking he was killing a wolf. The first duty of the sheepherder's dog is to chase off the wolf, to pursue him for a long time and, when he flees with his prey, to force him to release it so that he in turn may regain possession of it and bring it back." We see clearly from this quote that the great white sheep guardian breeds have long been considered an integral part of flock or herd management. Over the years, the breeds have adapted to the needs of local shepherds and the conditions in their homelands. They have done this with great success, and we see these dogs in Hungary (the Kuvasz and Komondor), in Czechoslovakia (the Slovak Tchouvatch), in Spain and France (the Great Pyrenees), and in Poland (the Tatra Sheepdog).

In keeping with this tradition, Italy is home to the Maremma- Abruzzese Sheepdog. In his native country, the breed is known as the *Cana de Pastore Maremmano-Abruzzese*. When the breed was first imported to Great Britain in the 1930's, they were called simply "Maremma Sheepdogs" and that name,

although inaccurate, has since been used throughout much of the world. In years past, the Maremma and the Abruzzese were maintained as separate breeds in Central Italy. Large white dogs had long served the shepherd in the mountainous Abruzzi area, while very similiar dogs were the helpmates of sheep farmers on the Maremma, a plains region. There were only minute differences between the two types of dogs and, in the 1950's, after observing both dogs in their native environments, Professor Solaro determined that they were, in fact, the same breed. He drew up a standard for the breed and both the names of Maremma and Abruzzese were retained.

The Maremma-Abruzzese has protected the livestock and property of the Italian shepherd for thousands of years. The first mention of the breed is included in the writings of Marcos Terentius Varro, penned more than 2,000 years ago. Contrary to some writings on the breed, the Maremma-Abruzzese was never a herder. He was the dog that lived with the flocks of sheep and protected them from predators. In the earliest days, attacks usually came from wolves and bears. While an occasional European brown bear or wolf can still be seen in the Abruzzi, in modern times, the Maremma generally encounters packs of stray dogs or human rustlers. The Maremma-Abruzzese becomes an integral part of the flock. He moves effortlessly, slowly and quietly among the sheep and is accepted as one of them. During the day, he is often left in charge of the flock, although there may be human shepherds to oversee his work. At night, Italian shepherds confine their flocks, and the Maremma protects them from any disturbances. Bitches are bred by the strongest and most fit dogs, and often whelp their litters in a simple hole dug in the ground or a clump of bushes, apart from the other dogs. When the puppies are weaned, the mother will gradually introduce them to the flock. She remains ever ready to step in to prevent them from playing roughly and possibly harming the sheep. The dogs are commonly fed a diet of oatmeal and whey. The Maremma-Abruzzese still performs these functions in his native homeland, where there are about 7,000 of the breed today.

Major Arthur Hammond, of Torup, Sweden, is an avid Maremma-Abruzzese enthusiast and one of the most knowledgeable students of the breed outside of Italy. A former official of the Maremma Sheepdog Club of Great Britain, Major Hammond now maintains a kennel of Maremmas in Sweden. He has visited Italian shows and had the opportunity to view the breed at great length in their native habitat. He provides us with a clear picture of the breed's use.

"Many have supposed that the dog has an inherent independence brought about by it being required to guard the flock, night and day, without the benefit and presence of the shepherd. This is not true," Major Hammond says, "although there may have been isolated occurances of the dog being left alone with the flock." Italian sheep flocks generally spend the winter months on the rich plains pastures and in the summer they are moved to fresh feeding grounds in the mountains. "The winter pasture where the dog spends the greater part of the year," Major Hammond says, "is a permanent farm where the flocks spend the night in permanent buildings or in adjacent pens. Mornings see the flocks milked before being turned out to pasture with a shepherd or shepherds present unless the pasture is immediately adjacent to the farm buildings. The flocks, with both shepherds and dogs

International and Nordic Champion, NV '85 Sonyer Fantasia Of Maremmano. "Gemma" surveys her domain at Kennel Maremmano, in Sweden.

present, graze until mid-afternoon when they return to their folds for the evening milking. The shepherd's dog, and there may be a great number of them, spend the evening and night sleeping, or half-sleeping, in the farm buildings, the adjacent pens and the farmyard. The permanent farm buildings which we see today, would not always have been a feature of the environment but, in earlier days, the winter quarters of the flocks would have been a permanent, or semi-permanent encampment with a number of flocks, their shepherds and the shepherd's families present.

"In summer the entire flocks of the farm, which may amount to several thousand sheep, are moved to the mountain pasture where, if it doesn't already exist, a base-camp is established by the shepherds of whom there will be a considerable number with a large flock. The flocks and shepherds of one farm will therefore consist of a tightly knit community and living accomodations for the shepherds will be permanent or semi-permanent in nature. During the hours of the evening and the night, the flocks will be 'netted' round this encampment and a number of dogs will be 'on duty' throughout this time whilst others will enjoy the companionship of the shepherds in their quarters. After morning milking, each flock (a farm having some 3,000 sheep would have some ten flocks with perhaps as many as fifteen shepherds and thirty or more dogs), will move from the base camp with a shepherd and two or three dogs to graze on the pastures. Here they remain until 4 p.m. or so when they return for evening milking and are 'netted' for the night.

"It should be seen from this short resume, that the free grazing of the flocks is limited to some eight hours a day and that this is always during the hours of daylight. It should also be noted that the dogs have the company of the shepherd, not only during this

The beautiful Swedish and Norwegian Champion Maremmano Eloquent Guard. "Foppa" is owned by Arthur Hammond, of Torup, Sweden.

period, but invariably during the hours of darkness also and that the sheep are either 'netted' or 'penned' during the remainder of the time. Despite these safety precautions, the flock dog, has through the centuries, required extreme vigilance and, when called upon to deter a threat, great courage," Mr. Hammond states. "The Maremma-Abbruzzese had, therefore, an inborn sense of protectivity to what it is guarding, is ever alert and watchful, is quietly confident in its ability to deal with other animals, and, most importantly, is suspicious of human beings."

The Maremma-Abruzzese is a beautiful dog. He has a broad head, is slightly longer than tall, and has a powerful and majestic appearance. He is characterized by his luxuriant white coat, which is somewhat harsh to the touch. A thick, dense undercoat often makes the dog appear larger and more imposing than he actually is. The coat is generally all white, although fawn, biscuit, or lemon colored markings are common. These small markings are generally found at the base of the tail or on the ears. His pigmentation should always be jet black. The average Maremma-Abruzzese male measures in at an impressive 27 inches, while bitches average 25 inches at the shoulder. It Italy, you will often see males that exceed 30 inches at the shoulder. His size seems all the more impressive when the Maremma is aroused. Then the dog will puff himself up, become stiff-legged and his hackles will rise, emphasizing his magnificient ruff. At these moments, few people would doubt that the Maremma is well equipped to deal with any intruder. Owners say that when the Maremma-Abruzzese is unhappy, however, he will often curl up and appear to be half his original size. Despite his large body, the Maremma is agile and lithe and, when kept as a housepet, he seldom knocks anything to the floor. Individuals of this breed are slow maturing and often do not attain their full physical and mental maturity until they reach two to three years of age. At about 18 months, the Maremma-Abruzzese will begin to demonstrate his protective instincts. Owners report a definite personality change at this point, and the dogs become more protective as they attain complete maturity.

Don and Sue Drummond of Freeport, Michigan, say that their Maremma-Abruzzeses have given them "peace of mind" by protecting their flock of 250 angora goats, and their white and colored sheep. When the Drummonds moved to Freeport, in 1982, many of their neighbors warned them to expect loses from attacks by stray dogs. "Since angora goats are rather 'pricey,' we decided to investigate the possiblility of getting one of the breeds of dogs called guardian dogs," Sue says. "We began investigating guardian dogs in general. We spoke with breeders, talked with people who were actually working these breeds, read magazine articles and studied the reports from livestock projects in this and other countries. We began to zero in on the Great Pyrenees and the Maremma because of their reputations for being more friendly to humans than the other breeds. We have many people here looking at goats and we did not want dogs who displayed unfriendly temperaments, and we certainly didn't want to have to worry that anyone would be bitten." Finding that most of the Great Pyrenees stemmed from show bloodlines, the Drummonds decided the Maremma was the breed for them. They were fortunate in obtaining the help of Major Arthur Hammmond, who not only provided them with much information, but helped them in acquiring the best foundation stock available.

"All in all, working with the Maremma has been an adventure," Sue reports. "The dogs give us good lessons in patience, and remain unfailingly cheerful and outgoing. This type of dog lives with the livestock, primarily sheep, and protects them against anything that the dog perceives as a threat. The dog is

This Maremma is right at home with his charges, at Don and Sue Drummond's Stony Lonesome Farm, in Freeport, Michigan.

International and Nordic Champion Sonyer White Eagle of Maremmano. "Jodie" is owned by Arthur Hammond, Kennel Maremmano, Torup, Sweden.

waiting patiently for her owners to rouse themselves. Then, like a child calling for his buddy, I asked if Gemma was coming out to play! I have since learned that Gemma was all wrong, but she was beautiful and all I ever wanted. I contacted various people and, within a few months was the owner of a dog, Chico, who turned out to be an absolute treasure. Quite by accident, I found myself the owner of a Maremma male that was something special in the breed and is, perhaps, more widely known than any other specimen of the breed." Chico's likeness is featured on the logo and T-shirts of the Maremma Clubs in both Sweden and England. Arthur Hammond became fascinated with the Maremma and began to research both this and other livestock guarding breeds. He is now an internationally licensed judge who is much in demand, and has, twice, had the distinction of judging Maremmas at Crufts. He is also the author of a book on the breed's history in England.

fiercely territorial, large and LOUD so that intruders are largely frightened away rather than fought." Indeed, the Drummond dogs have never had to battle another animal, although two close neighbors recently lost a number of sheep to dogs. "We haven't even seen another dog near our farm. The Maremma's presence, their scent marking of the fields and their barking, keep other dogs far away by warning them that they are intruding on the Maremma's territory."

"This is not the dog for everybody," says Arthur Hammond, "but accept the breed for what it is, understand it, and be prepared to be taught the 'lore of the wild' by the dog, and you have the best companion ever." Major Hammond became involved with the breed quite by accident. In 1971, he was diagnosed as having vascular disease and doctors advised him to remain active. They suggested that he take up golf or purchase a large dog that required exercise. He considered Dobermans, German Shepherds, Rottweilers and other commonly known breeds. "Whilst debating which breed, I went down to Cornwall for the August Bank Holiday weekend and stayed overnight for Bed and Breakfast in a private home." One of the other families staying at the same home were accompanied by their dog. "Yes, by now you have guessed it," Arthur Hammond says. "They had a six month old Maremma bitch. I had never even heard of the breed at that time. I fell in love with her and six the next morning found me waiting outside Gemma's (that was my first love's name) room

While many Maremma-Abruzzese's are in working homes in this country, in England the breed is kept primarily as a home companion. Owners find in the Maremma a loyal friend who is an unfailing and diligent guard. The breed is very wary of strangers but extremely affectionate with his family. British Maremma owners, however, state that "the male is, at times, ashamed to admit that he has a need for any physical reinforcement of the bond that exists between himself and his master." The Maremma-Abruzzese is not a dog given to wandering. He much prefers to stay close to home and protect his master's property. Intruders will be warned to stay away, and the new Maremma owner should realize that this breed considers trespassing a very serious offense. Major Hammond warns that new owners should believe and respect the breed's nature and inherent protectiveness. "That is not easy when a puppy comes into the home, for he is a cuddly, white bundle of fluff that charms with its innocence even when it is being naughty. It is hard to imagine that that little pup, totally free of guarding instincts, and dependent upon a human for everything, could develop into an independent and protective adult. It is important to correct the pup consistently from the first. This is much easier when he is three months old. They accept training, and all should be socially trained as youngsters. Basic obedience should also be given to them and they will respond well enough, although you should never expect them to be as obedient as a German Shepherd or a Collie. Their characters are basically against such blind obedience. They also have a sense of humor which they especially use when recalled!" This is a common characteristic among the guardian breeds and can be frustrating to first time owners. These independent dogs think for themselves and decide if and when they will come. "Patience, the ability to 'make a game of things' and an understanding of the dog's need for dignity to be left intact," says Major Hammond, "helps to overcome the dog's horrible reluctance to come when called."

Understanding the Maremma-Abruzzese's sense of dignity is essential for new owners. "The dog's sense of dignity should never be forgotten and has to be experienced to be understood," Arthur Hammond explains. "Let's say the dog shows a reluctance to come out of the back of a car. Put a lead on him and take him out and that is fine. But, reach in and grab him by the scruff of the neck and you have trouble. You may be an old friend, of many years standing, but he will quickly warn you. Scold him, if you must, and he will accept it. Raise your hand to him and he will immediately react, even though you should, at least the first time, escape with a warning. If your dog, for example, wants to share the sofa with you and you do not approve, you can get up and encourage the dog off or attach a leash and lead him off. Getting up will usually suffice. But, continue sitting down and try to shove the dog off and you will quickly see what happens. Yes, again you have offended his dignity and you will pay the price with a warning."

The Maremma-Abruzzese is a loud breed that is very alert and barks quite often. This is seldom a problem in country homes but can be a nuisance if you live in a city environment. It is best to make the dog understand, in puppyhood, that such behavior is unacceptable. The Maremma is a very intelligent breed and becomes easily bored when left at home for long periods. Owners should provide him with diversions so that he does not dig holes or become destructive.

While the Maremma may accept non-family members, the breed is extremely wary of strangers, and new owners should fully understand this. "Remember," says Arthur Hammond, "that the Maremma makes its own decisions in all things, and that includes the question of whom it selects as friends. It is always better to let the Maremma make the approach to a stranger, rather than allow the stranger to approach the dog. It takes time, but it pays its own rewards. Put companion Maremmas away when people call, and allow the dog or dogs to see the visitors only when they are in the house and seated. Remember that the Maremma relies on HIS judgement and not YOUR judgement as to who is a reliable visitor. Once visitors have been admitted by the owner, he will accept that they have a right to be there, even if he does not agree that they are trustworthy. With most breeds, it is recommended that a stranger, meeting a dog for the first time, go down on his knee to the level of the dog, to show the animal that there is nothing to fear. DON'T do this with a Maremma. Meet it standing and allow the dog to make the approach. Never force yourself or another person on the dog."

Maremmas are reported to be very devoted to family children. Parents should understand, however, that this breed is very playful when young and could unconsciously inflict damage. If there are frequent juvenile visitors to your home, make sure you introduce them formally, as you would with an adult, and supervise the situation until you are sure that your dog has accepted the child.

When the Maremma lacks a working environment, he will adopt other family pets. There are many reported cases of Maremmas living in close harmony with cats, other dogs, birds and all manner of animals. Owners should be aware, however, that the Maremma-Abruzzese feels that it's his duty to look after and guard these companions. Owners report that housing more than two Maremmas together, and having them live side by side peacefully, varies from individual to individual. Some seem to establish a close rapport and work out their own pecking order, while others are loathe to share their masters and their

Maga Circe Neve plays with two year old Steven Grasso. Neve is owned by Dr. Louis and Lorraine Grasso.

153

Nordic Champion Bacco delle Grandes Murailles of Maremmano. Bacco is the sire of champions at Arthur Hammond's Kennel Maremmano, in Torup, Sweden.

Maga Circe Neve, owned by Dr. Louis and Lorraine Grasso, at 4 months of age.

guarding duties with another of their own breed. New owners are often astonished to see their large males bow in subservience to a bitch, but this is generally the case. To avoid potential problems, Maremmas should always be fed separately.

The Maremma-Abruzzese is a hardy dog that is generally free from disease or illness. This is a very fast growing breed and, from his initial birthweight of just over one pound, he can be expected to tip the scales at some seventy pounds by the time he reaches six months of age. He, therefore, requires a quality diet and will eat rather heavily during this initial growth phase. Once the dog attains his full growth, however, he is a very economical eater. With his weather resistant coat, the Maremma- Abruzzese is at home outdoors in all types of weather. In the hot summer months he becomes less active and will seek a shady spot in the yard. In winter, he will delight in playing in the snow. A simple brushing keeps his white coat in pristine condition, as dried dirt will easily flake off and fall away. The breed seldom requires baths. Owners report that the Maremma is a very clean dog by nature and, so, housebreaks easily. He has little doggy odor, except when wet.

"Essentially, the Maremma-Abruzzese is independent," Major Arthur Hammond says. "He is wary of strangers, and given to accepting humans as equals. The Maremma is a breed that responds to responsibility and consistent treatment, rather than one who slavishly looks to a master to control his

every move." With his great beauty, it seems inevitable that the Maremma-Abruzzese will gain a following in this country both as a household companion and a working breed. There are currently about 500 dogs in Great Britain with about 75 new entries to the fold yearly. Over one hundred Maremmas now make their home in Sweden, where the breed is attracting great attention. We do not know precisely how many Maremma-Abruzzese's reside in the United States, although the number is, certainly, in the hundreds. No club has yet been established in this country, although one individual has begun an informal registry, and Sue Drummond periodically prints a newsletter to maintain contact with other Maremma owners. One hopes that those interested in the breed will understand and accept the qualities that breeders, like Major Hammond, so appreciate and that they will not seek to alter the breed's inherent nobility and dignity.

Chapter 40

The Miniature Bull Terrier

"The Mini is a born entertainer, always on stage, a natural clown, and it may be that they sleep a lot (a breed characteristic) in order to store up energy and dream up ways to delight and amuse their owner," says B.J. Andrews, of Asheville, North Carolina. "They will frustrate you, fascinate you, and give you long years of utter and unquestioning devotion. In return they ask only to be loved and given a warm bed."

The standard size Bull Terrier has long been well known in dog circles. With his muscular, well-knit body and distinctive head, the Bull Terrier is a unique breed. Some find his oval, or egg shaped, head and the small, dark, triangular shaped eyes unattractive, but those who have been fortunate enough to share their homes with a Bull Terrier are quickly won over by his charm. His true terrier character, intellegence, humor and courage have gained many admirers. However, for some people, the standard size Bull Terrier, with his abundant energy, is just too much dog to handle. The Miniature Bull Terrier maintains all the physical and temperamental qualities of the standard size dog in a compact and convenient size. For those who appreciate Bull Terrier looks and personality, but would like a smaller animal, the Miniature is the perfect solution.

The Bull Terrier's roots lie in that period when man found pleasure in baiting any number of animals with dogs. Bull baiting was a popular diversion among royalty, noblemen and common folk. When bull baiting was finally made illegal, devotees turned their interest to dog fighting. Dog fight enthusiasts discovered that the breeding of the heavy bodied Bulldog to the smaller and leggier terriers of the time produced an unbeatable combination. These early Bull and Terriers, as they were called, combined the determination and legendary courage of the Bulldog with the speed and agility of the terriers.

The early nineteenth century was the most exciting period in terrier development. Experimental crosses developed new breeds, and forever changed and altered older ones. It was in 1862 that James Hinks, of Birmingham, England, introduced his strain of pure white dogs to the public. His dogs attracted great attention for they displayed soundness and grace. Mr. Hinks had extensively used the now extinct English White Terrier and, probably, the Dalmatian in an effort to stabilize color. These new white terriers, for all the attention they attracted, were the subject of much controversy. Other Bull and Terrier owners doubted that these dogs, with their cleaner, less "bulldog-type" faces, would be able to hold their own in the fighting arena. Mr. Hinks settled that question once and for all. He pitted a forty-pound bitch of his breeding against a sixty pound bitch from the old bloodlines. The prize was a five pound note and a case of champagne. Within a half hour, Mr. Hinks' white bitch had slain her opponent. In addition, her own wounds were so minor that she entered and won a dog show the following morning. Mr. Hinks' white Bull Terriers, as they would come to be known, were accepted. In coming years, these dogs would, many times over, prove their courage, their tenacity and endurance, and their incredible resistance to pain. Furthermore, the "White Cavalier", as he was nicknamed, had the ability to quickly size up a situation and think innovatively for himself. This made him an uncanny adversary in a fight. He was also renowned for keeping his head in the heat of battle. Many owners of fighting dogs were bitten and

An outstanding Colored Miniature Bull Terrier, Graymor Genghis, better known as "Tommy," is owned by Ms. Donly Chorn, of Crescent Bull Terriers, Deerfield, Illinois.

scarred from attempting to separate two dogs at the conclusion of a match, but the Bull Terrier never turned on his owner.

The Miniature Bull Terrier, although too small for the fighting pits, was often the star in ratting contests. In such events, the lone dog was placed in a pit and rats were released. The winner was the dog who could kill the greatest number of rats in a specified time. This may seem an unusual pastime to present day dog fanciers, but we must remember that the England of that day was much different from our modern world. People were crowded into cities, sanitation was poor and refrigeration was not in common usage. Rats, along with the diseases that they carried, were a significant problem. Most pub owners maintained kennels of small terriers. After they closed their doors to business, the terriers were released into the pub, and it was their duty to maintain a vigil and kill all rats that entered. Ratting contests were a natural outgrowth of these daily duties and they were a source of entertainment for working class people.

It was not until the early 1900's that the Colored Bull Terrier came into being. White Bull Terriers were bred to Staffordshire Terriers to produce colored dogs. There was great controversy over the appearance of these dogs, and clubs in England and the United States enacted policies that called for the expulsion of members engaged in breeding to colored dogs. The Colored Bull Terrier was eventually recognized as a separate variety and accepted as a full-fledged member of the Bull Terrier fraternity. The first Colored Bull

Terrier to complete a championship in the United States was Beltona Brindigal. Mr. W. J. McCortney had imported her mother, in whelp, from England, and Brindigal was one of the puppies from this breeding. Mr. McCortney stated that the Colored Bull Terrier was actually a by-product of the breeding program of Mr. Edward Lyon. Mr. Lyon was intent on breeding Miniature Bull Terriers and, in an attempt to achieve this, he crossed a small Staffordshire with a white Bull Terrier.

In the early days of the breed, type and size varied greatly. In England, classes for Bull Terriers were, at one time, divided by weight. In the middle 1880's Bull Terriers were judged in classes for small dogs (those under 20 pounds), the middle-weight division (for dogs 20-30 pounds), and the heavy weight class (for dogs which tipped the scales at over 30 pounds). Since the days of the earliest Bull and Terrier crossbreedings, size had fluctuated greatly, with both small specimens and heavy weights often produced in the same litter. There were even some devotees who preferred "Toy" Bull Terriers, which often weighed in at less than ten pounds. One bitch, Pony Queen, was said to weigh three pounds when fully mature.

It is unfortunate that the Toy and Miniature Bull Terriers were lumped together under the title of "Miniatures." While the Minis maintained the true Bull Terrier type, the Toys were often poor respresentatives of the breed, with prominent, bulging eyes. As a result of this fad breeding, the reputation of the Miniature Bull Terrier also receded.

The Miniature Bull Terrier declined in popularity, probably because the big dogs did the lion's share of winning in the show ring. The Kennel Club removed the variety from their register. A few determined breeders, however, loyally maintained their kennels of small dogs. In 1938, those few remaining fans of the Miniatures formed a club and began working to garner publicity for the small dogs. They tackled the problem of size head-on. In previous showings of the Miniature, when dogs had been limited by weight, off-type specimens had been starved to permit them to fit into Miniature classes. Instead, The Miniature Bull Terrier Club mandated that all dogs should measure no more than 14 inches at the shoulder. This move

An excellent Miniature Bull Terrier head study. Alcydion of Warbonnet, affectionately called "Butch," is owned by Patty and Ross Voorhies, Wilko Kennels, Edwardsburg, Michigan.

was a wise one, and did much to improve the lot of Miniatures in the show ring. To improve type, the Kennel Club allowed the breeding of Miniatures to small size Standard Bull Terriers, although Minis from such breedings were registered with the Club as "interbred." The Kennel Club mandated that this practice would be allowed for a period of five years and then discontinued.

There were a few small specimens in the United States. Toy Bull Terriers gained some popularity, but in 1916 the American Kennel Club ruled that Winner's Classes would not be offered until there was an increase in numbers. At that time, the maximum allowable weight was 12 pounds. The last appearance at Westminster of a Bull Terrier that could be classified as a Miniature came in 1928. There were probably a few Minis brought to this country through the years, but it was not until 1961 that a serious attempt to work with the Miniature Bull Terrier was begun. In that year, Mrs. Ralph Gordon, of Pass Christian, Mississippi, imported two dogs. Champion Navigation Pinto and Freesail Simone joined the Gordon home. In 1963, the American Kennel Club admitted the Miniature Bull Terrier to Miscellaneous Class status. The Miniature Bull Terrier Club of America was organized in 1966, and Jackie McArthur, of Imperial Kennels, was elected President. The MBTCA has recently been reorganized, and is a vital and thriving Club.

The Miniature Bull Terrier of today is an alert and vital dog with the best qualities of his standard size counterpart. He is a strong, active, muscular and agile little dog with a keen and intelligent expression. He displays the classic terrier fire and courage, but is even tempered and delightful. The approved standard calls for the Miniature to be 10 to 14 inches, with his weight in proportion to his height. Today's most outstanding Minis generally fall in the 20 to 30 pound weight range. The Miniature Bull Terrier is a healthy, hardy animal that should provide a family with a world of fun.

"A proper Bull Terrier is bold, courageous, inquisitive, stubborn, willfull and loves people, children in particular," says B.J. Andrews, of Asheville, North Carolina. B. J., or Barbara, as she is formally known, and her husband, Bill, have been involved with purebred dogs for more than twenty-five years. They are this country's most prominent breeders of Akitas, and their top winning and producing dogs have garnered them a world-wide reputation. In the mid-1970's, the couple became enchanted with the Bull Terrier, and purchased show and breeding stock from top kennels. They were successful, producing several champions, including Group and Specialty winners. However, they "became more intrigued with the concept of a smaller, more 'lap-sized' Bull Terrier". After an extensive study of available bloodlines, the Andrews obtained several top English imports. Mrs. Andrews is extremely enthusiastic in her support of the Miniature Bull Terrier. "They are extremely quick witted and intelligent, and surprisingly obedient," B.J. says. "He is tenacious, always hungry, an accomplished hunter and prone to swallow a mouse! They don't like baths or dirt, hard floors and cold beds, but they will jump in the pool with the family, romp in mud puddles with the children, fall asleep on a bed of nails if their owner does, and nap when you do!" B.J. stresses that the Miniature Bull Terrier is extremely intelligent and she considers this breed "a thinker," but, she warns, "they are also natural clowns. They are highly trainable, but inclined to be stubborn and known to delight in bending or inventing new rules."

"Miniature Bull Terriers are absolutely adorable!" says Patty Voorhees of Edwardsburg, Michigan. "They are very comical. My first pair have been referred to as 'Heckel and Jeckel', from the cartoon. Their noses and beady little eyes look a lot like those crows. And they're just as ornery," Patty laughs. "They are very muscular in a tight, compact little body, and they love to run and play. Our Lucy likes to ambush her sister, Maybelline, from the top of the dog house." Patty and Ross Voorhees had never owned a registered dog before they acquired their first Mini Bull Terrier. The couple did love dogs though, and they performed volunteer duties for Pet Refuge. The Voorhees household became a foster home for unwanted animals, and the couple successfully found homes for approximately 100 puppies. "We always liked Bull Terriers, but preferred the smaller size of the Mini," Patty says. The couple had a significant advantage as Ross' parents lived outside London. Trips to England enabled them to visit and talk with breeders, and see all the available bloodlines before making their purchases. They've never regretted the choice of the Mini Bull Terrier, and they take special delight in providing information on the breed to newcomers. "Mini Bull Terriers are cuddlers," Patty says. "They love to take a nap with a person or another dog, and will sleep in bed, but I must warn you, they snore!" "Bull Terriers, Standard or Minis, are not a breed for everyone. They are demanding of one's time and attention. They are not suited to kennel life," says B.J. Andrews. "They fit nicely in a lap or a favorite sofa or chair. They want to be with you, to touch you, to snuggle with you. Owners should have a firm hand, a forgiving nature and a strong sense of humor."

"The Miniature Bull Terrier owner should be a particularly responsible person with a lot of tolerance," says Donly Chorn, of Deerfield, Illinois. "They crave affection, and need to be near people. I suggest rudimentary training, at least. The owner must be a person who is willing to be dominant, particularly with males. A fenced yard is a must as the Bull Terrier cannot be allowed to run loose. They need to be kept happy as they can become easily bored," Donly says. Miss Chorn was already a Standard Bull Terrier breeder when she became interested in the Mini. "They were a natural extension of the breed I already raised," she says. "Creating a 10-14 inch Bull Terrier that is as typy as the Standards is a great challenge. Many show Standards are, in my opinion, too large to fit the Bull Terrier standard of the maximum power and agility in a compact package."

Patty Voorhees suggests that new owners invest in a dog crate. "I recommend a crate because the dogs like a little privacy and the security that a crate offers. Most of ours seek out their own crate at some point during the day, for a little quiet time. The Mini Bull Terrier is easy to house train and eager to please. They require plenty of exercise and a couch, if not your bed, to sleep on," says the Michigan resident. "The Mini Bull Terrier must be taught who is boss," Patty advises, "and refresher courses are sometimes necessary."

Bull Terriers are known for their allegiance to their family, and the Mini is no exception. "They are devoted to their friends, both human and canine," says B. J. Andrews. "Generally speaking, they have a terrier aggressiveness with strange dogs, but can be deeply devoted to family pets. They are not aggressive to people." Donly Chorn agrees. "People must understand that they may or may not get along with other animals. They are highly individual in this regard. They are not, and should never be, aggressive toward people. They are very fond of children and very tolerant with them. I do suggest, as with any other breed, that small children and dogs be supervised when playing." Patty and Ross Voorhees discovered the breed's suitability with children when they recently had their first child. "The Mini Bull Terrier is ideal with children. Our dogs are devoted to our four-month old son and he loves to pet them. He laughs in delight when they lick his feet."

"While the Mini Bull Terrier is an excellent watchdog, they are not dependable guard dogs," advises B. J. Andrews. "They will alert and bark at any intrusion, but may regard a burglar as a guest, and assume the role of host or hostess, showing them just where to find the family silver." Donly Chorn thinks it's because Bull Terriers "are overly friendly with strangers. Some will protect their person when

The impressive Erenden Ephraim O'BJ, owned by B.J. Andrews, Mini-Bulls O'BJ, Asheville, North Carolina. "Effy" exemplifies the nickname "White Cavalier."

threatened, but not all. It depends on the individual dog."

Arthur Yanoff, of Concord, New Hampshire, is another Mini Bull Terrier lover. Mr. Yanoff shares his home with a bitch he has cristened, "Maude the Magnificent." "When we first got Maude the Magnificent, the iron-jawed Miniature Bull Terrier, we were living in a two-hundred year old farm house with ten acres on one of those inconvenient dirt roads. Although we were, by no stretch of the imagination, real farmers, we did keep some chickens, ducks, geese and a few dairy goats. Maude proved to be especially valuable as a protector of our livestock," says Mr. Yanoff, who is a strong advocate of working terriers. "Even at the time she first came to us, at three and a half months, she appeared to have strong guarding instincts and, with a minimum of training, she became most trustworthy around the other animals. She developed something of a maternal and territorial possessiveness, especially with the goats. Strange dogs were not permitted to go near them, and many a large dog beat a hasty retreat from this twenty-five pound fireball." Maude proved invaluable in controlling rodents around the Yanoff poultry pens. "At rat killing Maude became so adept that she could go into the poultry house at night and perform her job without so much as disturbing a single sleeping chicken." Arthur Yanoff is convinced that the Bull Terrier makes an ideal all-around farm dog. "Now twelve, Maude is still eager to rout predators, and her dispostion is as stable as ever. She is completely trustworthy with our sheep, poultry and cats, and is still a wonderful children's companion."

The Miniature Bull Terrier is an easily cared for dog. "They are extraordinarily hardy dogs that are seldom ill," says B.J. Andrews. "They have stomachs like cast iron!" Patty Voorhees agrees, "Mine will eat almost anything that falls on the floor." They require only occasional baths, must have their ears periodically cleaned and their toenails clipped to be ready for the show ring. Some individuals do suffer from a condition known as lens luxation, and the Miniature Bull Terrier Club of America has formed a Genetics Committee that diseminates information on this abnormality. In this condition, the lens of the eye displaces, or dislocates, from its normal position. It is an inherited disorder and generally arises when the dog is from three to seven years of age. Total blindness can be the end result, and the Club has taken a wise stand with the formation of the Genetics Committee.

All in all, the Miniature Bull Terrier is a delightful and fun companion that can add many hours of enjoyment to your home. One prominent Bull Terrier breeder told a story of a judge he encountered at a show. The man was staring at his bitch and struck up a conversation when he approached. He told the owner that he would never own a Bull Terrier. The breeder became alarmed as this individual was scheduled to judge the Terrier Group that very day, and he asked why the man had this opinion. "They get under your skin too much, and you feel too badly when they check out." The man's eyes filled with tears as he talked of the Bull Terrier he had once owned. Miniature Bull Terrier owners would understand. Somehow this breed has a way of "getting under your skin" and engendering fierce devotion and loyalty in owners.

Neapolitan Mastiff puppies, sired by Italian Champion Squarcione, owned by Robert G. Yarnell, Kimbertal Kennels, Kimberton, Pennsylvania.

Chapter 41

The Neapolitan Mastiff

"I was born and raised in Italy, and I always admired the Neapolitan Mastiff," says Jerry Schiano, of Guilford, Connecticut. "I grew up in a small town and only heard stories about these dogs. When I was a little older, I traveled to Naples. There, I was finally able to see the Neapolitan Mastiff for myself. Their massive size, power and intelligence overwhelmed me. I would stare at those dogs, with monstrous faces and huge bodies, and they almost seemed like great statues that were unable to move. They were always alert, but moving ever so slightly until the occasion would demand action, and then they would spring like great bears. All the stories I had heard were true, and I saw that the Neapolitan Mastiff was one of the greatest animals that lived. I fell in love with the breed. Twenty years ago, when I came to the United States, I pledged to myself that if I was ever successful in business and started a family, I would fly back to Italy and purchase a Neapolitan."

The Neapolitan Mastiff is a very ancient dog and, as such, it is difficult to accurately pinpoint his origins. In all likelihood, as with so many of the Mastiff breeds, he is descended from the Tibetan Mastiff. Many authorities believe that the breed made his first appearance in Italy when he accompanied Alexander the Great on his journeys of conquest in about 300 B.C. From these early imports the Roman Molossus evolved and became well known. We are thankful to Lucien G. M. Columella for giving us information on so many of the Italian breeds. Writing in the second century A.D., he provides us with a picture that, except for the references to coat length, sounds remarkably like the present Neapolitan Mastiff. "The guard dog for the house should be black (or dark) so that during the day a prowler can see him

and be frightened by his appearance. When night falls the dog, lost in the shadows, can attack without being seen. The head is so massive that it seems to be the most important part of the body. The ears fall toward the front, the brilliant and penetrating eyes are black or grey, the chest is deep and hairy, the hind legs are powerful, the front legs are covered with long thick hair and he is generally short-legged with strong toes and nails."

Before the invention of gunpowder and modern weaponry, dogs were important adjutants to soldiers. With their natural proclivity to protect their masters, it was logical that the dogs would accompany and assist their owners in battle. They were tremendously successful in this endeavor, and early armies were often accompanied by a very large canine corps. The Greeks may well have been the first people to employ war dogs. We know that when the Roman Consul, Marius, fought at the battle for Versella, he was confronted by a vast horde of wardogs. These dogs, surprisingly led by women, delayed his victory and almost cost him the battle. After several encounters with war dogs and many casualties from the ferocious beasts, the Romans adopted the practice of using dogs themselves. The Romans added a few innovations of their own. They equipped their dogs with spiked armor, or heavily padded their bodies and mounted firepots on their backs. The dogs would then run under mounted soldiers, causing their horses to rear and throw the riders. Then, the dogs would set upon the fallen men.

The wardogs were often attractions in the sand bottomed arenas of the *Panem et Circenses* or "circuses" where the discontened masses could appease their lust for savagery and blood. We have evidence

Thundermugs Marianna del Nolano, an outstanding Neo bitch, owned by Garry and Lynn Travers, Thundermug Kennels, Cheltenham, Ontario, Canada.

that no less a person than Julius Ceasar wrote about them, and in paintings and drawings, such as those at the church of Santa Chiare in Naples, we see the predecessors of the Neapolitan Mastiff as we know him today.

The famous Italian writer and naturalist, Aldrovandus, discussed these dogs in the 1500's. "The war dog...should be a terrifying aspect and look as though he was just going to fight, and be an enemy to everybody except his master; so much so that he will not allow himself to be stroked even by those he knows best, but threatens everybody alike with the fulminations of his teeth, and always looks at everybody as though he was burning with anger and glares around in every direction with a hostile glance." Aldrovandus goes on to give us what must, certainly, be one of the earliest accounts of attack training. "This dog ought to be trained up to fight from his earliest years. Accordingly, some man or other is fitted out with a coat of thick skin, which the dog will not be able to bite through, as a sort of dummy; the dog is then spurred on against this man, upon which the man in the skin runs away and then allows himself to be caught, and falling to the ground in front of the dog, to be bitten. The day following he ought to be pitted against another man in the same manner, and at the finish he can be trained to follow any person upon whose track he has been placed. After the fight the dog should be tied up, and fed while tied up, until at the end he turns out to be a first class defender of human beings."

Through the centuries, the Neapolitan Mastiff continued to be bred, in small numbers, throughout much of southern Italy. He was esteemed as an estate guardian. However, it was not until the 1940's that

Italian dog lovers began to take notice of this native breed. Suprisingly, interest began at the height of World War II, when suffering in Italy and the rest of Europe was at its very peak. In those bleak days of 1942, with Italy firmly entrenched in the worsening conflict, perhaps the people looked for some way to express their sense of national pride. In that year, amidst the destruction wreaked by air raids, Dr. Durante, began to draw up a standard for the Neapolitan Mastiff. In 1946, at Naples' first dog show, eight huge Neapolitans entered a show ring for the first time. They attracted great attention, and spawned much interest from experts. In 1947, the esteemed Professor G. Solaro began a study of the breed. The next year, several experts including Piero Scanziani, considered the breed's reconstructor, completed and revised Dr. Durante's original standard. It was Mr. Scanziani who searched Italy for the most excellent specimens, and established his prestigious and successful kennel in Naples.

Breed popularity continued to grow. In 1961, Dr. R. Soldati, Mr. Conti and Dr. Fabio Cajelli, together with other breeders, once again revised the standard. They were concerned that Mr. Scanziani's standard was too vague and left too much to interpretation. It was their keen desire to insure that type would remain as it had through the centuries. In one of the most thorough attempts ever undertaken to quantify a standard, these men assembled twenty-four of the nation's leading champions. Carefully, they examined and measured each dog's body parts, and tabulated their findings. According to one authority, "Their calculations were so precise that, should the

Turco, a young male, from Gennaro (Jerry) Schiano's Kennels, in Guilford, Connecticut.

Neapolitan Mastiff ever become extinct, as long as researchers were able to ascertain the dog's height, they would be able to reconstruct the whole dog from only one discovered bone." The Italian standard, though cumbersome by American standards, is extremely detailed, calling, for example, for the length of the head to be 35 percent of the shoulder height. We owe these gentlemen a debt of gratitude for their conscientious work.

The Neapolitan Mastiff, *Mastino Napoletano*, Italian Mastiff or simply, the "Neo," as those familiar with the breed call him, is one of the world's most distinctive dogs. No other breed could ever be mistaken for a Neo, and those seeing the breed for the first time, are frequently startled by its unusual appearance. The breed is characterized by a massive head, with an abundance of folds and wrinkles that extend down the neck to form a dewlap. These hanging folds become even more prominent and exaggerated as the dog matures. His ears are cropped very short, which tends to accentuate the broad head. Neos are huge dogs with great bone, tremendous power and unbelievable strength. Their body is rectangular in shape and this, coupled with their massive bone, gives the breed a short legged appearance. The Neo's very thick tail is generally docked to about two-thirds of its original length. The hindquarters should be broad and powerful, and a distinctive feature of the breed is its bear-like gait. With his short coat, the Neo is easily cared for, and he comes in an attractive array of colors. A blue grey is the most commonly seen shade, although black or a bluish-fawn shade, known as *fulva*, are also seen. White markings may be found on the chest and toes. Pigmentation and eye color correspond with coat color. The Neapolitan Mastiff is one of the giant breeds with weights averaging between 100-160 pounds. Males weighing two hundred pounds are occasionally seen in Italy.

Despite his fierce looking scowl, the Neapolitan Mastiff is a loving family companion. They are alert, intelligent and they bond very closely with their families. It is generally conceded that this breed tends to be a one owner or one family dog. One owner reported that when she acquired her first Neo, the bitch went through a period of mourning before she accepted her new home. Most Neo owners are impressed with the breed's calm and steady nature. The Neo is not a hyperactive dog, and the breed is not given to incessant barking. "My wife and I prefer to sell our Neapolitans to a good family home, where they will receive much love and devotion," Jerry Schiano says. "They need to be a part of the family and they thrive on love. They care for you, they protect you, they love your kids and your home, and heaven help the person that tries to come between you and your Neo. This breed is very laid back with

The impressive Thundermugs Cattiva el Nolano, owned by Garry and Lynn Travers, of Canada.

your family. They must be a part of everything you do, be it watching television, taking a walk, or going for a ride in the car. The Neo is the kind of dog you dream about for your family. Even when my children take their baths, the dog has to be right in there and part of the action," Jerry laughs.

Indeed, the breed seems to have a special affinity for children. Garry and Lynn Travers breed Neos in their Cheltenham, Ontario, Canada, home. "Visitors with young children will set them down on the floor. The dogs immediately gravitate to the kids. They may be wary of the adults, but they lay down beside the babies and lick them." The Travers have, perhaps, the most knowledgeable perspective on this rare breed of anyone in North America. The couple was afforded the privilege of living in Italy for several years. Lynn worked in one of the most prestigious Italian Neo kennels and, on weekends, the couple was able to travel to dog shows throughout Europe. This experience afforded them an invaluable look at all the major Italian bloodlines, and they gained an in depth

Thundermugs Monaciello relaxes at Garry and Lynn Travers' Thundermug Kennels, in Cheltenham, Ontario, Canada.

knowledge of the Neo's character. "I have a daughter," Garry said, "and she frequently brings home friends. Our Neos are great with the kids."

Jerry Schiano would certainly agree. "They are gentle with babies and children. They will become intensely protective of your children. They'll let you talk with another grown-up, but don't let an adult try to mess with your kids or watch out!" The Schianos have two children and share their Connecticut home with a number of Neos. "My three year old has a whole set of toy characters that he plays with. He will set them up all around our female Neo's body. She realizes that he enjoys this and will lay there the entire time he wants to play, without moving."

In recent years, the Neapolitan Mastiff has gained in popularity. Their legendary prowess as a watchdog has, largely, accounted for the tremendous interest. "In Italy," Garry Travers says, "all the homes have fenced courtyards. During the day, they leave the gates open and chain the Neo outside the front door. At night, the gate is closed and the Neo has the run of the yard. No one would dare to break into a home protected by a Neo."

"The Neo has become the businessmen's dog in Italy," Jerry Schiano tells us. "To own a Neo is a sign of distinction. They are recognized as being very intelligent, trustworthy and devoted. In Naples, department stores and car dealerships will have a Neo guarding their establishments at night. Anyone who can afford them and feels that they have anything worth protecting, will buy a Neo. And, tell me," he smiles, "who of us don't feel that our families are worth protecting? I own a pizzaria and don't come home until four in the morning. We live in the country and our house is not far from a main road. It gives me a great feeling of security to know that I need not worry. The dogs are a valuable asset to our family. I will come home late and find my wife sleeping on the couch with one of our dogs lying across her legs to keep her feet warm. They are very alert at night. The bitch that shares our home goes from bedroom to bedroom at least a dozen times a night. She checks on the kids, the doors. If there is anything even slightly suspicious, I will be awakened with a big lick on the face. Neo's aren't really attack dogs," Jerry explains. "They're very cautious. They are much more likely to pin someone down, or corner them and hold them. They would probably bite, but only if there was extreme provocation."

"Neos are phenomenal as guard dogs," says Garry Travers. The couple recently discovered just how vigilant a Neapolitan Mastiff can be. "My wife and I were busy around the house and didn't notice a meter reader from the electric company, who entered the yard. Our Neo certainly noticed him, though, and she was doing her job. She went right through a plate glass door. The meter reader ran for his car. Her front legs were, literally, shaved down to the skin by the broken glass. Thank goodness, there were no lacerations." Impressively, the Neapolitan Mastiff comes by his guarding instincts naturally and requires no aggression training. "I don't want to promote the Neo as an overly aggressive breed. I feel that they have the sense to assess the situation and decide on appropriate action. With my daughter and her friends in and out of the house all the time, I can't afford a vicious dog. We have seven Neos living together in our home. My daughter also has three Australian Terriers. We also have three cats and a ferret. The dogs live peacefully with our entire menagerie. In fact, the little Aussies rule the house. Our Neos love the cats and ignore the ferret, even when it jumps all over them. I have to chase the dogs off the sofa when I want to sit down. The only precaution that I take is to separate my dogs at feeding time. I don't want to start any rivalry or disputes over food."

Garry Travers feels very strongly that the Neapolitan Mastiff needs a firm and consistent hand. He is concerned by the temperament of some dogs he's seen. "I believe that, with this breed, temperament is ninety percent environmental. They must understand that we are the owners. At our house, this training starts when they are puppies. For instance, if we find a puppy chewing on its bowl, then the food is quickly taken away. If the dog attempts to growl or grumble about this action, they are yelled at and very firmly reprimanded. They learn quickly that we gave them the food and we can take it away. With the Neo you must establish a pack order and you have to be the leader. Don't accept bad behavior when the Neo is a puppy, and you won't have an uncontrollable dog as an adult." This is sage advice that is well worth heeding. The Neapolitan Mastiff is a large and powerful dog, and he must be taught that he cannot dominate or dictate to the family. Bear in mind that the Neo must be taught his place, and that he must be subservient to every member of the family. Because of this need for consistent handling, the Neo is not the breed for everyone. Proper socialization and obedience training will help to make your Neapolitan Mastiff a well behaved and much loved family member.

Visitors to the Travers' Thundermug Kennels, quickly find themselves surrounded by barking dogs. "They invariably decide to wait in the car until we come out," Gary Travers says. Those interested in the breed must understand that the Neo is extremely wary of strangers. Responsible owners will exercise caution when inviting strangers, particularly adults, into their home. "When people come to visit our home," Gary says, "our Neos will sit next to me and, initially, they will grumble at the visitors. They're not nasty with them. They are just our dogs and are aloof to strangers. They will calm down and remain quiet if the visitors sit back, but if they make a sudden move, the dog will growl." You should be aware that some Neos do not tolerate strangers. "The bitch that lives in our home," says Jerry Schiano, "does not like visitors at all. We have to literally talk to her for about ten minutes and explain that everything is all right. We then lead her out on the patio and, even then, she glares through the sliding glass doors. If the strangers tried to harm us she would lunge through the glass in a minute."

"As a rule, the Neapolitan Mastiff is an intelligent dog," says Garry Travers. "We recently brought a bitch back from Italy. She had never before lived in a house. On her first day here, she had an accident on the floor and we reprimanded her. That night this dog grabbed Lynn's wrist and demanded to be let out. She had quickly learned her lesson."

With his ever increasing popularity, one hopes that the Neapolitan Mastiff will find a host of loyal and devoted owners who appreciate his character. Since Neos command high prices, those interested in purchasing one of these dogs would be well advised to speak to a number of breeders. Don't hesitate to ask questions. Those seeking to import stock from Italy are advised to deal with responsible and knowledgeable parties. Neo breeders are replete with horror stories of very expensive dogs who did not live up to their promise. It is heartbreaking and frustrating to go to the time and expense of importing, only to be disappointed. Dog care in Italy, as in so many countries, is primitive by American standards, and vaccinations and wormings that are routinely done here are often nonexistent there. Your money will be much better spent by dealing with a reputable breeder or importer who can help you with the purchase.

Many people, around the world, are discovering this ancient Italian breed. Those who want an uncommonly devoted dog that will become a treasured and protective family member, would do well to consider the Neapolitan Mastiff.

An exceptional head study of a Neapolitan Mastiff. Thundermugs Polenta, a ten month old bitch, is owned by Garry and Lynn Travers, Thundermug Kennels, Canada.

This outstanding dog, International and Scandinavian Champion Cato Eier, is owned by Rudolph Hagland, of Norway.

Chapter 42

The Norwegian Buhund

The Norwegian Buhund is one of many beautiful and sturdy breeds that come to us from Scandinavia. The breed is very popular in the Scandinavian countries, where he often garners top show awards. He can be seen around farms and homes in the region, where he is esteemed for his abilities as a watchdog. He is quite adept at herding and, in some areas, is still used for this purpose. The standard calls for the breed to be slightly less than "medium size." This convenient size allows the Buhund to adapt equally well to city or country life.

The breed takes its name from the Norwegian word *bu*, which means homestead. Often these dogs were the companions of Norwegian mountain shepherds, who lived in crude huts during the summer months, while their stock grazed on the lush pastures. While the Buhund is, undoubtedly, a very ancient breed, few authorities can agree on his exact derivation. Some have suggested that he is related to the more popular Norwegian Elkhound and his less flashy cousin, the *Jämthund*. Most likely he is closely related to the Iceland Dog, brought to the Scandinavian countries by Viking marauders. Authorities have been unable to decide which breed originated first, but the two share many characteristics. The ancient Icelandic Sagas do make mention of dogs which accompanied Norwegian immigrants to that country in approximately 874 A.D.

For many years, the breed entirely escaped the notice of dog fanciers. Only in this century has this ancient breed been recognized. The Norwegian Buhund was considered such an excellent farm dog that no attempt was made to breed them selectively or to enter them in dog shows. Indeed, their first appearance was made in an agricultural show.

Mr. John Saeland became quite interested in the Buhund in the 1920's and was instrumental in promoting the breed. He sought out typical specimens and instituted a breeding program. His Ch. Flink was considered outstanding, and quickly became a sought after stud. Norwegians began to take notice of Mr. Saeland's work, and there was much demand for the Buhund. As has happened so many times in the annals of dog history, this sudden popularity was not good for the breed. Poor Buhunds were bred and sold to an eager public, and breed quality declined. However, dedicated breeders like John Saeland and Toralf Raanaas refused to give up. They struggled for many years to educate dog lovers on the correct qualities of the Buhund. Finally, in 1936, they formed a club for the breed.

The Buhund is recognized by the Kennel Club in England. The breed was first brought to England in 1947. Mrs. Powys Lybbe and Gerd Berbom are credited with introducing the breed. They imported a male and a pregnant bitch in that year. Due to Britain's six month quarantine law, England's first litter of Buhunds arrived in the quarantine kennels. Several other imports have contributed to the breed's numbers in England, where over 100 dogs are registered annually. The breed was first recognized in 1968, and in 1970 they were granted the right to compete for championship certificates.

The Norwegian Buhund makes a stunning show dog, and it is no wonder that the breed is often seen in the winner's circle. He has a lively, smart look that is hard to ignore. The Buhund has a short, compact body, with a strong topline and deep chest. Males stand a little over 17 inches and bitches are proportionally smaller. Like the other Spitz breeds, Buhunds have prick ears and tails that curl over their backs. The tail is set high and often has a tight double curl. Buhunds have double coats that come in a lovely array of colors. The wheaten shades range from a pale cream to light brown. Dark red is not preferred. Wolf-sables are occasionally seen and blacks are exceedingly rare. A black mask and black points on the tail are allowable.

The Buhund is a highly recommended companion. Owners report that the breed still retains herding instincts and is quite capable of rounding up any livestock. They make good watchdogs and are very alert. The breed has great stamina and is quite strong for a small dog. The Buhund is very intelligent and more easily trained than many of the Spitz breeds. Furthermore, he is less boisterous than other Spitz breeds. He becomes very attached to his family and is remarkably loyal. Buhunds are alert dogs who are full of energy. They have a keen sense of hearing and their ears are quite mobile. They are said to clean themselves like cats and have very little doggy odor. They love children, and owners say that they are very trustworthy and not prone to wandering. Like all other Spitz breeds, the Buhund can be stubborn, but the trait is certainly less pronounced in this breed and they seem to have more desire to please.

Buhunds are vital and hardy dogs. They rarely suffer from health problems, and you can be assured that veterinary expenses will be minimal. The breed's beautiful and very natural coat is easily maintained. It does not mat, although your Buhund will benefit from a daily or weekly brushing. The breed does shed seasonally and all dead hair should be stripped out during this period.

A new addition to the breeds being promoted in this country, few Norwegian Buhunds have yet been imported. As Americans see and learn more about this delightful breed, their popularity is sure to grow. They have the alert and impressive features of many of our sled dogs and their countryman, the Norwegian Elkhound, but in a smaller package. Their size would make them adaptable to many American homes and lifestyles. The striking appearance of a top-quality Buhund would certainly command attention in rare breed shows.

Chapter 43

The Nova Scotia Duck Tolling Retriever

"I may be prejudiced, but I feel that the Nova Scotia Duck Tolling Retriever is the ideal dog," says Shirley Bishop (not her real name). "They are wonderful companions, great children's playmates, super obedience dogs, flashy show dogs and great retrievers. In short, Tollers are fun to own."

The smallest of the retrieving breeds, the Nova Scotia Duck Tolling Retriever has, of late, been attracting much attention. While the breed has been recognizable in type for more than 100 years, it did not gain official recognition until 1945. In that year, the Canadian Kennel Club admitted fifteen Tollers to its files. Dedicated and proud Canadians have continued to perpetuate the breed, and during a one-month period in 1980, two Tollers went Best in Show in Canada. The breed was recognized by the Federacion Cynologique Internationale in 1982, and Tollers now make their homes in several European countries. A small but staunch group of devotees are working for American Kennel Club recognition.

Some believe that Tolling Dogs were known, in England, as early as the 1600's. Indeed, the term Toll comes from the Middle English word *Tollen* and refers to the dog's ability to lure or draw waterfowl into shore. Most authorities believe that early hunters observed foxes running back and forth along the shoreline, all the while wagging their bushy tails. This action attracted the attention of curious ducks, who swam closer for a better look. Hunters quickly saw the advantage of these actions and trained their dogs to imitate the foxes' game.

These early European dogs were not of a distinct breed, but they were, nonetheless, valuable to their owners. In the early days, hunters netted their ducks rather than shooting them. Large nets were suspended across a small stream, adjacent to a larger body of water. When the net was in place, the dog would begin his merry dance, running back and forth on a the bank until he had attracted the attention of the waterfowl. While pretending not to notice them, the tolling dog was keenly aware of their every movement. Gradually, he would shorten the length of his run until he had successfully lured the fowl into the waiting nets.

Today's hunting style is different, as Shirley Bishop tells us. "The hunter will take his place in a blind, which is generally located downwind from the birds. He throws a stick, sometimes called a 'tolling stick', down to the shore. The Toller rushes to retrieve the stick. He does this with flashy style, and his tail wags joyously all the time. These little dogs have great stamina, and could chase and retrieve sticks all day long. He will then deliver the stick to his master, who repeats the procedure. The hunter keeps his eye on the birds and when he feels that they are close enough for a good shot, he calls the dog to his side. Once he has shot the birds, the Toller springs into action once more and retrieves them for the hunter."

This is the pattern of hunting developed long ago by sportsmen of Nova Scotia. H.A.P. Smith, of Digby County, in Nova Scotia, often used his Tollers on ducks. In 1918, however, he recounted his experiences with the Toller on the large, wild Canadian geese. "I ran my tolling dog out on the marsh behind me, and he played for some minutes before the birds noticed him. At last two or three old ducks woke up and stretched their necks, announcing to the others with loud quacks that something unusual was in sight on shore. In a second, every

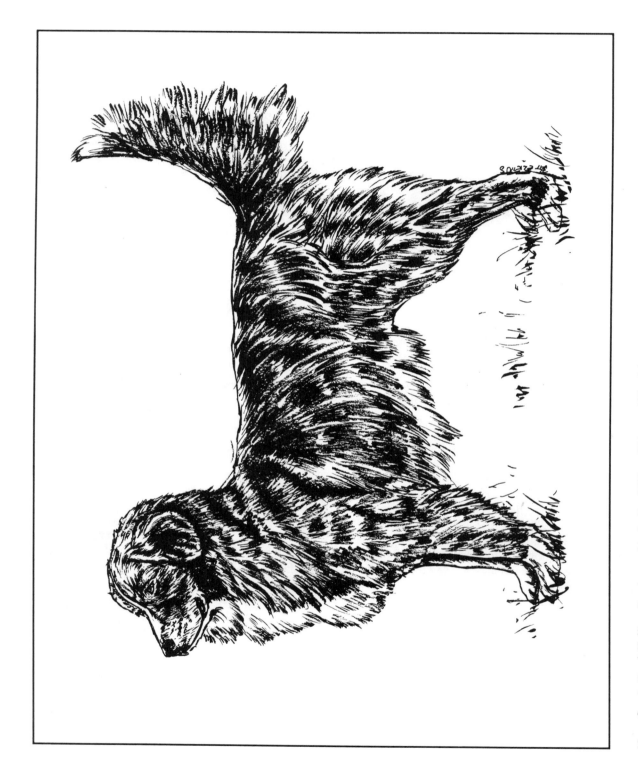

Nova Scotia Duck Tolling Retriever (Artist Pat Elkins, Chicago, Illinois)

duck was interested, and soon the tip end of the flock 'broke off' and swam for the shore. Reaching the sand, three birds stepped on shore." While Mr. Smith was preparing to take aim at the ducks, he noticed that several large geese were following the duck's example. With a quick motion, he commanded his dog to come to the blind. "However, as soon as the dog was out of their sight they began to swim away. Suddenly it dawned upon me that it was the dog they wanted. Picking up the 'tolling stick,' I tossed it out across the sand to the marsh. Like a flash the dog was after it. A glance through the peek-hole in the blind confirmed my guess. There came the four 'honkers' as straight and fast as they could swim for the dog...In a few seconds every duck was on shore, standing with extended necks looking at the dog. In all my former experience in tolling ducks, I had never seen birds step out of the water upon the shore. These ducks not only stepped out, but began to waddle up toward me like a battalion of recruits on parade. So curious became some of the birds that they waddled up within 15 feet of the blind, a few of them even walking around trying to peek into it, to see where the dog had disappeared. Every second I feared this inquisitive advance guard would discover me and take alarm." Needless to say, Mr. Smith had a very successful day of hunting. He bagged several geese and his Toller retrieved them.

We do not know the precise background of the Toller. For many years he was known as the Little River Duck Dog, and the primary breeding took place in Yarmouth County. It is said that a Mr. Allan crossed a Flat Coated Retriever with a Labrador Retriever or a Lab mix. Bitches from this litter are believed to have been bred to a brown Cocker Spaniel. The story of the Toller's ancestry becomes somewhat sketchy after this point, and it may be that there were later crosses to Irish Setters, Brittany Spaniels, Golden Retrievers, Chesapeake Bay Retrievers and possibly a local farm-type collie.

The Nova Scotia Duck Tolling Retriever is a medium size breed, the smallest of all the retrievers. At maturity, males measure 19-20 inches and weigh 45-51 pounds. Females stand 18-19 inches at the shoulder, and weigh 37-43 pounds. Like most retrievers, he has a deep chest and is strongly muscled. His sturdy body appears square. His tail, an essential breed characteristic, is heavily feathered. As befits a breed developed to retrieve in very icy waters, the Toller has a double coat that is quite water repellent. Some Tollers have a slight wave on their backs and, when in full winter coat, may have a loose curl at the throat. They come in various shades of red or orange, and many have white markings. These are generally found on the feet and chest, and sometimes as a white blaze on the face. Some dogs also have a

bit of white on the tips of their tails, and old time hunters are said to prefer this, as it aids in attracting the ducks' attention. In motion, the Toller is a delight to watch. These dogs have a springy gait, and with their wagging tails and beautiful color they are very eye-catching.

"Tollers are wonderfully playful dogs," Shirley Bishop says, "and they retain this quality all their lives. They are very good house dogs, as they keep themselves remarkably clean. I do not find that they smell, like so many other retrievers do when they've gotten themselves good and wet. They are an ideal dog for someone that lives in a small home and still wants a hunting dog for the weekends. They are tremendous retrievers and they are very speedy. In general, as a breed, Tollers have excellent temperaments. They get along great with children and become very devoted to them.

"Like most of the other retrievers, Tollers are very intelligent. They learn quickly and retain what you have taught them. I am very well acquainted with all the other retrieving breeds, and I believe that the Toller is a better watchdog than most. In my opinion, only the Chesapeake is on a par with the Toller, in this regard. I think that this breed is definitely suited to the colder climates and I worry that perhaps they will not fare well in the heat. Other than this, I find them very adaptable. Of course, they love to swim and if you have ready access to water, you couldn't ask for a more eager dog than a Toller."

With his wonderful qualities, the Toller has much to offer dog lovers. Retrievers have long enjoyed great popularity in this country, and the Toller is a worthy addition to this group of dogs. As Shirley Bishop says, he would seem to be ideal for the family living in a small house or apartment, who wants to spend their weekends hunting. Some owners have also taken their dogs hiking and backpacking, and the outing is enjoyed by all the participants. No wonder that Toller breeders are so loyal to their favorite dogs. With their lively and playful natures, owning a Nova Scotia Duck Tolling Retriever is just plain fun!

Head study of the Petit Basset Griffon Vendeén. (Artist Pat Elkins, Chicago, Illinois)

Chapter 44

The Petit Basset Griffon Vendéen

Rarely can one single dog be credited with introducing a entire breed to this country, but this was precisely the case with the Petit Basset Griffon Vendéen. It was in 1983 that a twelve week old puppy, Alexander of Gebeba, won Best Puppy in Show at the Professional Handler's Association Super Match. This adorable puppy, born in Canada and owned by Betty Barth, of Philadelphia, Pennyslvania, rocked the dog world. The Barths were offered $10,000 that very day for the little fellow, but they graciously refused the offer. Articles on this little hound appeared in dog publications, complete with photos of the bewhiskered Alexander, and the impact was electric. Thousands of requests poured in to magazine offices, and the phones of the American Kennel Club lit up with calls from dog fanciers eager for more information on the Petit Basset Griffon Vendéen.

While these small dogs are new to the United States, they have long been popular in their native France. The esteemed writer Adrian, in approximately 125 AD, saw a breed known as the Segusian Hound. These little dogs were in the company of Cynegii, the Roman Procurator. Adrian found them very different from the dogs he was familiar with, for he called them shaggy and ugly. The Segusians were a Celtic people who made their home in western France on the banks of the Rhone River. Some authorities believe that these hounds were the ancestors of the Griffon Vendéen. They may be correct, for the province of Vendée is located to the west of the Rhone, between Gascony and Brittany.

Vendée is a rough and rugged province. With its rock outcroppings, dense underbrush and brambly fauna, it presented challenges to the hunter. The ardent French hunter could only pursue his passion on foot, for horses were unable to traverse the rough terrain. Smooth coated dogs were easily injured on the jagged rocks and wicked thorns. What the hunter needed was a small sturdy dog with a coat that provided adequate protection. The Griffon Vendéen and his smaller brother, the Petit Basset Griffon Vendéen, provided the answer.

The Griffon Vendéen comes in two sizes. Intially, both the Grand (the larger size) and the Petit (the small size discussed here), were shown under the same standard. While the breed was predominately owned by hunters, owners also supported conformation shows. Reportedly, there was a large entry of these dogs at the Paris Exposition of 1895. A club was formed for the Griffon Vendéen in 1907. M. Paul Dezamy was elected president and he was to have an extraordinary influence on the future of both sizes. It was M. Dezamy who is credited with formulating the first standard. This blueprint for the breed acknowledged both the Grand Basset Griffon Vendéen (measuring 15-17 inches at the withers) and the Petit Basset Griffon Vendéen (which stood 13-15 inches tall). At the 1924 field trials in Venerie, M. Dezamy's Griffon Vendéen won the Grand Prize of Honor. In 1933, following the death of Paul Dezamy, his son-in-law, Abel Desamy (the variation in spelling is intentional), assumed the club presidency. M. Desamy was noted for his outstanding Grands, and these dogs are often referred to as "type Desamy." Finally, in the 1950's, the Petit and the Grand were separated and granted individual breed status. Still Grands and Petits continued to be found in the same litters. Abel Desamy's son, Hubert, next assumed the presidency of the club, and it was under his guidance that interbreeding of the Grand and the Petit was finally prohibited. Club rules called for the individual examination of every dog over one year of age, by a judge, before the dog was listed in the breed register.

The PBGV (Pee-Bee-Gee-Vee) or Petit, as the breed is known in this country, is still popular in France where he is esteemed for his hunting ability. In his native country, he is primarily used on rabbits. He is very energetic and enthusiastic, and some owners state that he is better hunted in small packs than with large numbers of hounds. The breed has a remarkably strong inherent desire to hunt, and, even in pet homes, owners will note how quickly he reacts to new scents and sudden movements. The breed has a good voice, although some hound enthusiasts have not found it as pleasing as that of other breeds. Interestingly, some writers have described the breed's manner of hunting as more typical of a terrier. Their enthusiasm is catching, though, for it is said that these little dogs are so anxious and enthusiastic that they will scramble over stone walls in pursuit of game.

Ten years before the advent of Alexander's notable win, the Petit Basset Griffon Vendéen was brought to this country by Mrs. Elizabeth Streeter, of Chester Springs, Pennsylvania. Mrs. Streeter established her Skycastle Pack with imports from France and England. She whelped the first PBGV litters in this country, but bred exclusively to contribute to her own working pack. Mrs. Streeter has little interest in obtaining American Kennel Club recognition for the breed. "This is a hunting breed, and show people don't understand hunting," she says. "These dogs are excellent hunters, very independent and sensitive. They are very intelligent as hounds go."

Vero Shaw, writing in 1881, said, "They are powerfully built,...and possess a speed which is extraordinary for their shape." In France, the breed competes for Certificates of the Hunt. To participate, a hound must be at least one year and less than six years of age. He is judged on his ability, including use of his nose, how true he holds to the line and the quality of his voice.

The shaggy little Petit has an extremely appealing appearance. Fanciers describe the breed as "rustic" and are dedicated to preserving the Petit's natural qualities. "He has a natural, rather unkempt, devil-may-care appearance," the Petit Basset Griffon Vendéen Club of America says. "His casual unaffected demeanor and appearance is part of the character and breed type. He should not be chiseled, shaped or primped...". The PBGV's large dark eyes peer from beneath his eyebrows. His houndy ears may reach the tip of his black nose. His harsh, scruffy coat comes in tricolor, lemon and white, grizzle and white, or orange and white. The breed must be shown in a natural state, completely untrimmed. The Petit has a strong, well muscled body and his front legs should be straight, although the standard allows for a "slight crook". PBGVs stand 13-15 inches at the withers, but the standard allows for 1/2 inch over or under these heights.

Despite his unkempt appearance, the Petit's coat does require consistent care. The breed seldom requires a bath and, indeed, this may soften the harsh coat texture. Weekly brushing is recommended to prevent matting, and most owners use wire pin brushes or slickers. "The object is merely to make the dog appear freshly brushed or groomed," the PBGV Club of America explains. While the breed seems to be very hardy, some owners in this country have found that Petits suffer from flea allergy.

Mrs. Anne Snelling, of Ottawa, Ontario, Canada, calls the PBGV "the happy breed." Several Petits share her home, and Mrs. Snelling was instrumental in garnering Canadian Kennel Club recognition for the breed. A long time dog fancier, Mrs. Snelling's Irish Water Spaniel won Best in Show at Westminster in 1979, and her Pekingese topped this premier event in 1982. She is a strong advocate of this charming French hound.

"The PBGV should not be compared to the Basset Hound, his smooth-coated cousin, for he is completely different, not only in appearance but in temperament," says the PBGV Club of America. "The Basset Hound is calm, placid, doleful and generally low key, unless there is work to do. The Petit, in contrast, is always working, a bit terrier like, always looking for something with which to busy himself." These little hounds are quite affectionate and willing to please, but, owners report, somewhat independent and stubborn. While his cute looks may make you want to cuddle your Petit, those familiar with the breed advise that they should never be considered lap dogs. "His abundance of energy requires that he have plenty of room to wander, explore and exercise. And there is a need for great security, for the Petit is a digger and a jumper. He is extremely agile and quick," the PBGVCA warns. Even with these caveats, the breed's enthusiastic and outgoing personality is sure to win friends and influence those unfamiliar with his charming ways. "He is extremely intelligent and, above all, curious," the PBGVCA says. "And generally, he greets everything and everyone with a wag of the tail and complete confidence." The breed gets along well with other pets in the home, and the only rivalries are likely to occur over food or competition for your affection.

The Petit Basset Griffon Vendéen Club of America was formed in 1984 to contend with the tremendous interest in the breed. The Club now lists over fifty members, and they have formulated a standard, adopted a Constitution and By-Laws, and established a registry. In 1986, they held their first specialty. There are currently some 34 PBGVs in this country, but with imports arriving from France, Denmark, Sweden, Holland, England and Canada, this number is sure to grow.

Those looking for an engaging and affectionate breed, with a rather quaint look, are sure to find the Petit Basset Griffon Vendéen tremendously appealing. His shaggy, whiskered look will continue to attract attention in both pet and show homes. It is to be hoped that, from the very start, breeders will encourage owners to actively hunt their dogs. With his proven field ability, the PBGV should provide hours of fun afield and may attract many to the sport of rabbit hunting. It would be a shame if this essential aspect of the breed's character were ignored in this country. However, whether in the home or the field, dog lovers will certainly be hearing and seeing much more of this little French hound in the coming years.

Babette de la Garonne, owned by Kitty and Chuck Steidel, of Scottsboro, Arizona. Babette has points toward her Canadian championship.

Elzbieta's Pan Vladek and Krymka Z Kordegardy, a pair of PONS from Kaz and Betty Augustowski's Elzbieta Kennels.

A trio of Owczarek Nizinnies from Poland. These dogs were featured on a Polish calendar.

A group of Owczarek Nizinnies relax at Betty and Kaz Augustowski's Elzbieta Kennels, Severn, Maryland.

Krymka Z Kordegardy, a gold medal winner in Poland, imported to this country by Betty and Kaz Augustowski.

Chapter 45

The Polish Owczarek Nizinny Sheepdog

In recent years, the Polish Owczarek Nizinny has created much excitement in this country. It's no wonder, for this breed has a charming appearance and a winning personality. The first of the native Polish breeds to be introduced to the United States, he is off to a fine start. Although still rare, with his many wonderful qualities, the breed won't remain a secret for long. Indeed, the Polish Owczarek Nizinny may be the Polish people's gift to American dog lovers.

Purebred dogs have been known for centuries in Poland. Writings and paintings from the Middle Ages confirm the Poles' love of canines. Poland has been invaded time and time again in its long history, and yet, dog breeders have persevered through these extremely trying times. The Polish Owczarek Nizinny Sheepdog, sometimes called the PONS, has fortunately survived. While we know little about the origin of this breed, he has long been known as a herding dog on Poland's central plains. Historians believe that the breed is descended from the Puli and a herding dog bred by the Huns. This Hun herding dog, from the little information that we can find, sounds very similiar to the PONS. By the 16th century, the PONS had been stabilized as a distinct breed. He was a rugged dog with a shaggy coat, which suited him well in Poland's harsh climate.

The first Polish Owczarek Nizinnies arrived in Scotland in the early 1500's. Polish farmers wished to acquire some Scottish sheep, and a trade was arranged for a shipload of grain. Six PONS accompanied the shipment, to help load the foreign sheep. The Scots were tremendously impressed with these little working dogs, and they promptly offered a trade. They would give a prized ram for two of the sheepdogs. The Poles haggled, and finally a deal was struck. The

ram and a ewe were loaded aboard ship, and a male and two female PONS departed, to make their home in Scotland. When bred with native Scottish sheepdogs, they gave birth to the Bearded Collie.

No country was more devastated by World War II than Poland. Were it not for the efforts of Dr. Danuta Hrzniewicz, a Polish veterinarian, the breed would certainly have been lost. At the conclusion of the war, she searched high and low for any remaining PONS. In Povorze, she came upon a male and female, which she purchased. When bred, they produced an outstanding male, Smok, who became the foundation for the breed's revival. It took the veterinarian more than 15 years of selective breeding to firmly establish the breed once more.

A newcomer to the United States, the PONS was first imported in the 1970's. Moira Morrison, a Bearded Collie breeder, became interested in these dogs when she learned that they figured prominently in the Beardie's history. Although no longer active in PONS breeding, the progeny of her early litters can still be found in the breeding programs of several active PONS kennels.

The PONS has a charming appearance. He is a medium sized dog, with males measuring 17-20 inches and females standing 16-18 inches. He is well muscled and suprisingly strong for a dog of his size. His shaggy coat comes in a profusion of colors and markings. Brown eyes peer out from beneath overhanging locks, but often all you will see is his black nose. His soft, dense undercoat suits him well in any climate. While tails should be docked, some breeders report that naturally bobbed tails are common.

Kaz and Betty Augustowski are avid PONS

enthusiasts. Keenly proud of their Polish heritage, the couple has undertaken the task of introducing this delightful breed to American dog lovers. "One day my husband and I went through *The Complete Dog Book* and realized that there were no Polish breeds recognized in this country. We began to wonder if there were any breeds native to Poland," Betty Augustowski said. Then, as if in answer to a prayer, Betty saw an ad in a dog magazine for Polish Lowland Sheepdogs, as the Owczarek Nizinny has been called. Soon the Augutowskis owned their first PONS. Now, several of these Polish natives make their home at the couple's Elzbieta Kennels, in Severn, Maryland.

"I began to write to Polish breeders. My ability to speak the language was a tremendous advantage, and I was fortunate in still having relatives in Poland. It was a little difficult at first, but I stressed my committment to Polish breeders, and they've responded warmly. They have been understanding and wholly supportive, and they've aided us in acquiring excellent stock. We were invited to come to Poland, and were treated royally from the moment we arrived until our departure. We toured the country and met many breeders. Everywhere we went the Polish people were charming and hospitable. They have been wonderful to deal with. They are very trusting. They sent us one bitch that had been bred to a top champion, and told us not to pay for her until the puppies had arrived. They couldn't have been more cooperative." The Augustowskis still raise Dachshunds and Maltese, but it is the PONS that is very close to their hearts.

PONS are lively, confident and intelligent dogs. "They are really cute and easy keepers," Betty says, "but what we love most are their fantastic personalities. They have the ability to think for themselves. I love this, but it also means that they aren't the breed for everybody. They are a little aloof with strangers. This is not a breed that will jump all over everyone that comes in the door. They are incredibly intelligent even from a very early age. They truly think, and form their own decisions on the proper course of action. They do require a firm hand, as they have the ability to walk all over you. They are, however, very loving and affectionate dogs, and they seem grateful for everything you do for them.

"The Polski Owczarek Nizinny is a herding dog, and he shows these strong traits at an early age. Although most suited for sheep, they have been worked successfully on cattle and horses. There are some PONS in this country that are working on a dude ranch. The PONS can live peacefully with other breeds, as long as they will accept being herded. This breed is also quite devoted to children, but sometimes feels obliged to herd them, too," Betty laughs.

With his quick intelligence and excellent memory, the PONS is well suited to obedience work. "They are highly trainable, but they are also strong willed, and it's important for them to realize that you are the boss. They do require grooming, but a twice a week brushing will keep them in presentable condition. This breed is very adaptable. Some time ago, I received a call from a woman living in an apartment in Brooklyn. She very much wanted one of these dogs, but I just wasn't sure how they would adapt to city living. I finally agreed to sell her a puppy. To my surprise, the dog adjusted very well to city and apartment life, and is healthy and happy. I have since placed other dogs in apartment situations, and they've all thrived.

"You must never underestimate the intelligence of this breed. I had a litter of five week old puppies. I had also recently received some three month old pups from Poland. It was one of the hottest summers in memory and, while I had allowed the older pups to go outside, I kept the young babies in the air-conditioned house. They begged me to let them out, and I finally gave in. I was working around the house when I heard this strange and horrifying sound. I ran outside and there stood my puppies in a circle around one of the younger pups. He was lying still on the ground. He was suffering from heat prostration, and I grabbed him and ran into the house. I administered first-aid and rushed him to the vet. There is no doubt that those little puppies saved his life. He recovered beautifully."

With his charming temperament, tremendous intelligence and beguiling appearance, the PONS is sure to win many friends in this country. The enthusiastic support of Polish breeders has provided Americans with access to top quality foundation stock. This is extraordinarily important in ensuring a good start for the breed in the United States. The Bearded Collie has earned an enviable position for himself in show rings in this country, and one can't help but think that, once recognized, the PONS will be a top competitor. With his convenient size and wonderful adaptability to country or city living, this breed is sure to acquire loyal devotees in the years to come. We owe a debt of gratitude to the Polish breeders for preserving such a unique and useful breed.

Chapter 46

The Shiba

"If I could only have one dog, it would be ten Shibas," one owner quips. Such enthusiasm would come as no surprise to owners of this small Japanese breed. This breed seems to inspire a special devotion and loyalty among his owners. The breed has a delightful personality, and is extremely sensitive to the moods and feelings of their masters. Those interested in the Shiba should be forewarned. These small dogs will charm their way into your heart, and they quickly become irreplaceable friends.

The Shiba may well be the oldest of all the native Japanese breeds. It is believed that the breed accompanied the country's original settlers on their migrations from Southeast Asia. Skeletal remains and fossils indicate that dogs were present in Japan during the Stone Age. Primitive drawings and other artifacts from the Bronze Age clearly show dogs with prick ears and curled tails.

The breed's name has been variously translated as "Little Brushwood Dog," "Little Ground Dog" and "Little Turf Dog." All bear tribute to the Shiba's use as a hunting dog for small game. The breed originated in the inland, mountainous areas of Japan, where he aided his master in pursuing birds and small game. There is some evidence that these little dogs were occasionally used to hunt deer and boar.

In 1854, the Japanese Government repealed its National Isolation Policy, and ships from the west arrived on Japan's shores. With them, foreigners brought their western dogs. These foreign canines became very popular, and there was a certain prestige in their ownership. Many of the native dogs were interbred with these newcomers, and the situation seriously endangered the perpetuation of the Shiba and other native breeds. Those animals residing in the

landlocked mountain regions were exposed to less crossbreeding. Those who loved and respected the Japanese breeds became alarmed. Japan's Education Ministry made a bold move. In the early 1900's, they declared the native Japanese breeds as National Monuments, to be respected and treasured. This innovative action was primarily responsible for saving the endangered native breeds.

The Shiba we know today is the result of a blending of three distinct strains of small Japanese dogs. While there is scant concrete evidence about these dogs, we know that the *San'in*, the *Shinshu*, and the *Mino* all contributed qualities to the present breed. The *San'in*, a mottled black dog, was larger than the present Shiba. The *Shinshu* dogs were predominately red, and possessed a soft, wooly undercoat and a harsh, bristly outercoat. The *Mino* was, perhaps, closest to the Shiba of today. They were characterized by upright prick ears, tails which curled correctly over the back and deeply set triangular eyes. The *Mino* was a brilliant rich red.

The Shiba enjoys great popularity in Japan today. Japan is a very populous country, and many people simply do not have room for a large breed. With his convenient size, clean nature and wonderful personality, the Shiba has become a popular choice. Small western breeds remain extremely popular today, and many toy breeds have very high annual registrations, but for the Japanese who wants to own a small native breed, the Shiba is usually the choice. Visitors to Japan have reported seeing Shibas in many parts of the country.

The Shiba is a very natural breed. "They incorporate the beauty of the wild with dignity," says Julia Cadwell, an avid Shiba supporter. With a

Yukihime of Gardenasow, a Shiba bitch. Natuso is owned by Janice Cowen. (Harkins photo)

Cowen's Autumn Mist C, a lovely female Shiba, owned by Janice Cowen, of Cowen III Kennel, Jeffersonville, New York.

median height of fifteen inches, the Shiba is well suited to either a country or city home. His body is well balanced and quite muscular for his size. The dark eyes are somewhat recessed and almond shaped. His prick ears are triangular in shape and inclined slightly forward, like his relative the Akita. The breed has a distinctly "foxy" appearance, and some Shiba owners have found it necessary to confine their red colored dogs during fox hunting season. His outer coat is hard and straight, and he has a soft undercoat. Grooming is minimal with the Shiba, and he can withstand extremes of temperature quite well. The breed comes in a whole range of beautiful colors, although reds remain the most popular. At Shiba gatherings you will see black and tans, sesames, fawns and brindles, in addition to the traditional reds. Occasionally one will see a white Shiba, but most breeders consider this an undesirable color.

Cheerful, energetic, beautiful, lively, faithful, obedient, friendly, considerate, gay, good natured...the list of Shiba qualities could go on and on. Shiba owners make liberal use of adjectives in describing their favorite breed. Whatever his innumerable list of qualities, it is clear that the Shiba inspires great enthusiasm and devotion in his human partner in life. A hardy and robust dog, the breed rarely suffers from illness. This very natural breed does not require coddling or pampering.

"I've found the Shiba to be a big dog in a small package," says Karen Raisanen, of Seattle, Washington. Karen raises Akitas and Shibas at her Benzaiten Kennels. "As a veterinary technician, I

work with all breeds of dogs, large and small. I've always been pretty much a big dog person. Shibas are not typical of small dogs. They're a rough, sturdy little dog, both structurally and temperamentally. They're built to withstand some pretty tough climates, but I think they largely prefer housedog status. I find that they're quite people oriented, and desire the companionship and attention of their human families. They are also very versatile dogs. Mine enjoy obedience, tracking, and just about any activity that I enjoy. They even accompany me in my kayak."

"Shibas are fun!" says Mary Malone, of Alliance, Ohio. Mary is a confirmed animal lover, and her Mini Meadow Farm and Kennel is home to an amazing array of rare animals. Her Shibas and Akitas share the Malone property with llamas, fallow deer, Norwegian blue fox, squirrels, ferrets, prairie dogs, pheasants, turkeys, guinea fowl, sheep, miniature and standard horses, pygmy goats, and a donkey that is the star of local Christmas pageants. School groups often visit Mini Meadows and, while Mary loves all the animals, she considers her Shibas special. "I can work around the house all day and not see the dog," Mary says. "They're with you, but they're not under your feet." This is obviously a benefit with Mrs. Malone's busy schedule. Mary enjoys showing her Shibas. One of her champions recently scored a Best in Show over not only rare, but also recognized breeds. At only eight months, that's an impressive achievement, and Mary can be justifiably proud.

"Since we have have owned and bred the Shiba Inu, we have become impressed with the breed's character, beauty and dignity," says Julie Jennings, of Waynesfield, Ohio. Julie and her husband, Bob, raise both Shibas and Akitas at their Arkee Kennels. "The Shiba is a very loving and loyal dog. This breed just seemed to be a natural choice for us. We already owned and loved Akitas, but were looking for a smaller breed that would be more suitable for the small home we owned at that time. We've found Shibas to be cheerful and they are loving with children. This was a most important quality to us as parents." Carol Harding of Hyrum, Utah agrees. "I especially like the Shiba for my children," she says. "This breed has an ingrown love for children and all people."

"Shibas are outgoing and extremely intelligent. You can almost see them think," says Julia Cadwell of Santa Rosa, California. Mrs. Cadwell is one of the earliest promoters of the breed in the United States, and a dedicated Shiba enthusiast. "This breed is hardy and robust, but very beautiful." Mrs. Cadwell's introduction to the breed came quite by accident. One day, Julia and her sons noticed a red dog on a busy four-lane freeway, in the middle of rush hour traffic. The dog seemed confused and bewildered. Mrs. Cadwell managed to coax the dog to her side, and she took him home. Her sons named the little male "Rusty" because of his red coat. They were struck by the breed's foxy appearance. The little fellow looked like a purebred, but he was like no breed with which Mrs. Cadwell was acquainted. She made a trip to the local library and, in one book, found a mention of the Shiba Inu and a picture. It looked just like Rusty. She contacted several organizations, but no one could give her any further information on the breed, so Rusty remained a loved pet. Finally, she contacted the Japanese Consulate, in San Francisco, in hopes that they could provide her with information. They were astonished to learn that she had a Shiba as they thought there were no specimens of the breed in this country. The Japanese Information Service provided

Bamboo and Cinnamon are owned by Mary Malone, of Mini Meadow Farms and Kennel, Alliance, Ohio.

her with the address of the Japan Kennel Club. Julia dashed off a letter asking if it would be possible to secure registration papers for Rusty. She included a photo of her pride and joy. In an extraordinary move, the Japanese Kennel Club sent a judge to this country specifically to evaluate Rusty. The historic meeting took place at the Information Service. The judge immediately declared Rusty a purebred Shiba and, shortly thereafter, his official papers arrived. It had been a long struggle, but Mrs. Cadwell's perseverance paid off. After almost a year of negotiations, Kojika (Japanese for "Little Deer") joined the Cadwell household. From Rusty and Kojika's first litter, the seeds were sown for Mrs. Cadwell's Shosha Shibas ("Elegant Little Dog" in Japanese), and Julia's life was changed. This energetic woman has done much to

Uchida's Yume No Benzaiten, better known as Yume, accompanying his owner, Karen Raisanen, of Seattle, Washington, on a kayaking trip.

promote the Shiba in this country, and her Rusty was the first of the breed to participate in San Francisco's prestigious Cherry Blossom Festival.

All owners stress that the Shiba is gay, active and alert. The breed's alertness to all manner of things in the home is one of the qualities that impressed Julia Cadwell. "My daughter-in- law fell asleep one afternoon, and a pot boiled empty, to the burning point, on the stove. Her little Shiba jumped on her and pawed at her chest until she woke up and took care of the situation." This inherent alertness makes the Shiba an ideal watchdog. "They will bark to let you know someone is around," says Julie Jennings, "but they don't carry on with nonsense barking. They are cautious with strangers."

Some owners report that their Shibas still show evidence of the breed's hunting heritage. "The Shiba can catch birds and rabbits with no problem at all," says Julie Jennings. Julia Cadwell agrees. "Shibas show a desire to hunt and retrieve even in pet homes. I have a bitch that jumps straight up in a six-foot high kennel to kill birds. They will also kill rats, and are very proud of their accomplishment."

With repect to their relationship with other dogs, Shibas seem to be individual in their response. Some are aggressive. "Bitches especially are aggressive with other dogs," says Julia Cadwell. "The males in this breed are 'softer.'" Most breeders have found some individuals to be aggressive, while others are quite comfortable in a pack. "Shibas tend to be more of a pack dog than the Akitas," says Karen Raisanen. "Generally, when more than two Akitas are together, someone will instigate a fight, whereas we can run five or six Shibas together with no problems." Indeed, some Shibas can become quite devoted to other dogs, as Janice Cowen discovered recently. The Jeffersonville, New York resident had a horrible experience. Her show bitch, "Autumn," broke away from her handler, and escaped from an upstate New York dog show. This is precisely the type of situation that all dog owners fear. Janice offered rewards, and Autumn was pursued by many people, but, although spotted many times, she eluded the searchers for three days. "On the third evening, I arrived at the show site with another Shiba. Within a few hours, Autumn was back in my arms. Her love for her kennel partner and me brought her to us." The experience served to reinforce Janice Cowen's love for the breed.

For those seeking an active and alert small dog, that can adapt well to city or country living, the Shiba makes a delightful choice. A small and very beautiful breed, with a strong constitution, the Shiba offers much to dog owners in this country. Most Shiba enthusiasts are dedicated to maintaining the Japanese qualities that have produced this dynamic breed. "I warn you, there is no other breed quite like the Shiba. They're so wonderful that it's difficult to own only one. They get under your skin, and worm their way into your heart. Most people who purchase a Shiba, find that they can't wait to get another one!"

A trio of outstanding puppies from Julia Cadwell's Shosha Shiba Kennels, in Santa Rosa, California.

Mary Malone's winning bitch, Mama, makes her home at Mini Meadow Kennels. (Harkins photo)

Chapter 47

The Sloughi

The Sloughi is a proud member of the internationally recognized family of sighthounds. Larger, heavier and stronger than the Saluki, the Sloughi is fascinating and elegant. This companion to the Bedouin helped to brighten his master's austere and barren life. Like all the other sighthound breeds, he has been long treasured for his skill at hunting and his wonderful character. The recent introduction of the Sloughi, to the United States, has been greeted with a great deal of controversy, since Saluki breeders declare that these dogs are merely smooth coated Salukis. Sloughi owners vehemently disagree. Whatever the case, the Sloughi seems sure to grow in popularity here.

It seems likely that the sighthounds were originally bred in the Middle or Near East. Significant historical evidence has been found, in northern Africa, attesting to the fact that coursing hounds have been known for millenia. Whether the Saluki, the Sloughi or the Pharoah Hound is the oldest of these breeds will never be firmly established. However, evidence from Egypt, dating to 1500 B.C., does show the presence of smooth coated sighthounds with drop ears. Many Sloughi breeders have noted the amazing resemblance to their present day dogs.

Most Sloughi breeders believe that the breed originated in the region known as the Maghreb. This area includes the present countries of Algeria, Tunisia, Morocco and part of Libya. The Federacion Cynologique Internationale cites Morocco as the breed's homeland. Those who have traveled to the Maghreb, specifically to find and study the dogs of the region, believe that the purest bloodlines are still found in this area. They point out that in the Maghreb the Saluki is unknown.

Westerners first heard of these sighthounds in the early 1900's, when adventurers returned to Europe with tales of the noble animals. The sighthounds were treasured by their nomadic Bedouin owners, and history is replete with stories of their love for and devotion to these dogs. While the Bedouin tribesman scorned most other dogs and treated them with contempt, he respected and loved the sighthounds, and hunted them with unabashed joy. His revered dogs were permitted to share his tent, and he would go without his own blanket, if need be, to provide them with warmth. Several early accounts tell us that nursing puppies were often breast fed by Bedouin women, and that amulets, thought to have magical powers, were attached to their collars. In some parts of the region, the ears of the sighthounds were cropped, and some were branded with slash marks on their front legs. Ancient tradition held that this would make them swifter in the hunt. When a beloved sighthound died, the whole family and, sometimes, the whole settlement would mourn his passing. Occasionally we find that there were even elaborate funerals and public burials. Indeed, the Arabian horse and the coursing hound were the pride of any Bedouin fortunate enough to own them.

It should come as little surprise that these dogs were so valued, for their hunting skills provided meat for the Bedouin's meager existence. Most often, the dogs were fed a mixture of whatever grain was available, milk from camels and olive oil. Occasionally, an egg was added to their diet. Hunting was pursued with a passion, and the sighthound was taken to the hunt astride the Bedouin's Arabian horse. He would not be released until a gazelle was spotted, and then the dog would spring from the horse and

A Sloughi hunting a jackal in Tunisia. Note the dog's concentration and courage. Several minutes later, the Sloughi has killed the jackal.

overtake the animal. Laws in some countries, today, prohibit the hunting of gazelle and jackal, but old habits are hard to break. However, these days, the sighthound will usually prove his ability on rabbits.

The first Sloughi imported to Europe arrived in about 1900. A painter from Holland had spent many years living with the Bedouins, and they presented him with his own Sloughi. Naturally, the dog accompanied him on his return to Europe. During the early 1900's, France established colonies in northern Africa and soldiers brought Sloughis home with them when their tours of duty were completed. There were a few more imports over the years, and the Sloughi is now well established in Europe. Large entries may be seen at prestigious shows, particularly in Germany, Holland and France. They have also enjoyed success in coursing events.

Israel has recently become the source of newly available Sloughi stock. During the years that this small country has held the Sinai, dog lovers have been able to search this ancient land for dogs. Both Sloughis and Salukis have been discovered and purchased from their Bedouin masters. These ancient bloodlines, maintained by their Arab masters for thousands of years, have been incorporated into Israeli breeding programs. Several Israeli Sloughis have been imported to the United States. It is interesting to note that in Israel all the sighthound breeds are referred to as "windhounds."

A heated controversy rages as to whether the Sloughi is, in fact, a separate breed. The bulk of the criticism for the separate breed classification comes from Saluki breeders in the United States and England. Those involved with the Sloughi point out that the vocal opponents have not owned and lived with the Sloughi. Ermine Moreau-Sipiere and her family moved from France to the United States in 1979. The Moreau-Sipiere family breeds Arabian horses on their farm in Brenham, Texas. They selected their best Arabians, winners of many European championships, to bring with them to this country. Also accompanying them on their move were four Sloughis. Now ten of the breed make their home at the family's Raynes' Kennel. "We know both the Saluki and the Sloughi very well," Ermine says, "and they are not the same breed. They have so many differences in their temperament, their conformation, their obedience and their courage. The Sloughi is very obedient and a great friend. The Saluki is far more independent and aloof. There is growing interest in the Sloughi in the U.S.A. Breed interest is building slowly because of the controversy, and because the Saluki is well established in this country and is recognized by the American Kennel Club."

There are certainly conformational differences between the two breeds. "The standard for the Sloughi has never changed through the years, while the standard for the Saluki has been modified many times," Mrs. Moreau-Sipiere says. "The Saluki standard is, in our opinion, now a European standard." The Sloughi is definitely the larger of the two breeds and stands 22- 30 inches at the shoulder. The Sloughi is a heavier dog, which is said to have greater strength and power than the Saluki. "The beauty of the Sloughi is rigid and sober. His esthetic value lies in the beauty of a perfect build, and noble and graceful movement. These are hunting dogs and racing dogs. If you place a Sloughi alongside any of the other coursing breeds, you will see similiarities, but you will also see differences. In appearance, the Sloughi is closer to the Greyhound than the Saluki. You will never see a brindle Saluki and you will never see a Sloughi with long hair or white spots on his body." Indeed, Sloughis never come in the flashy parti-colors that are frequently seen on Salukis. "The Sloughi can be sand, black brindle, sand brindle, and grey brindle, with or without a black mask," Ermine says. "The Sloughi brindle color is from the mountains," Ermine explains. "while the sand is from the desert. These colors are a kind of camouflage for hunting." Indeed, observers who have traveled to the area would agree with Mrs. Moreau-Sipiere. In the area near the Sahara Desert, the dogs tend to be smaller and more compact in build, while mountain bred dogs are much larger and more powerful. The Sloughi is square in shape with a straight topline and a leggy appearance. Some breeders believe that he is not as angulated as the Saluki. Furthermore, the Sloughi generally has a wider and somewhat coarser head than the more refined Saluki. Sloughi ears are often smaller than those of the Saluki, and many have noticed that when the dogs race they pull them back against the side of the skull, in the fashion of the Greyhound. Much has been written about the speed of the Sloughi versus the Saluki, and there seems to be little agreement. Some authorities believe that both breeds are equivalent in speed, while enthusiasts believe that their respective breed is quicker.

"The Sloughi is very affectionate and loyal to his family, but reserved toward strangers. He is very alert and makes a good watchdog," Ermine Moreau-Sipiere tells us. "The Sloughi loves open spaces and running. His favorite game is 'catch', which is just a ritual reenactment of the hunt, in which one dog plays the part of the 'hare' and invites the others to give chase. When he's caught, he drops to the ground and gives himself over. The game stops until another dog challenges. It is terrific to watch the agility with which these dogs can radically change course at enormous speeds.

"The Sloughi is extraordinarily elegant and has a supreme distinction. While they love to run, they

Kalif de Raynes, an impressive brindle male Sloughi, owned by Ermine Moreau-Sipiere, of Brenham, Texas.

also appreciate comfort. The Sloughi is neat, silent, loyal, affectionate, courageous and superbly decorative. It is small wonder that the lovers of the Sloughi and the lovers of the Arabian horse find that they have so much in common. Some breeders, like us, raise both, just as the Arabs did. They are both the preserved remnants of a hard and proud era of fascination and mystery."

Indeed, the Sloughi does seem to have an aura of mystery and a lovely grace that is difficult to resist. Brindle dogs, in particular, look quite distinctive and entirely different than the Saluki. With his beautiful sleek lines and distinctive coloration, the Sloughi will continue to win friends. His outgoing and less aloof personality will attract many dog fanciers. The Sloughi is an impressive animal and should create a sensation in rare breed circles. He deserves wider attention in this country.

Chapter 48

The Slovak Tchouvatch

It is seven in the evening, and a group of children sprawl on the living room floor, watching their favorite television show. The cartoon show begins when a little old man, carrying a lantern, begins to light the evening stars. Accompanying him on his nightly skyward rounds is a large white dog. At the conclusion of the program, the man enters his house for the night and the vigilant dog lies down outside the door. This scene is repeated nightly in Czechoslovakian homes. This animated show, *Vecernicek*, is very popular with children, and the white dog that the children so love is a *Cuvac*.

The *Slovensky Cuvac*, or Slovak Tchouvatch, as he is known in this country, is rarely seen outside his homeland. He is a respected member of the large group of white livestock guarding breeds known throughout Europe. The breed is most closely related to the Tatra Sheepdog of Poland. In fact, while the Tatra originates from the Polish side of the Tatras, the Slovak Tchouvatch was developed on the Czechoslovakian side of this mountain range. A few Slovak Tchouvatches do make their home in Poland, primarily in Slovakian villages. This heavily coated breed is well adapted to his homes in the Tatra, the Liptovsky, the Beskids and the Carpathian mountains. The breed is said to have existed for centuries and to have developed by crossing native white dogs with wolf spitz dogs and the Hungarian Kuvasz.

The breed takes its name from the Slovakian word *cuvat* which means "to listen." This term says much about the breed's function. Originally, the breed was used to guard flocks of sheep and herds of cattle. As in other parts of Europe, livestock was harrassed by predatory wolves and bears. The Slovak Tchouvatch was known for his keen senses of smell and hearing, and he was a valuable deterrent. He took his duties as a livestock guardian very seriously, and it was said that, with his tremendous power and agility, he was capable of slaying a full grown wolf in a one- on-one battle. In the early days, it was even said that the Slovak Tchouvatch was used as a big game hunting dog. Some Cuvacs still guard livestock in the mountains, but they also serve other functions. They are esteemed watchdogs and companions. They have proven very trainable and have been used as guard dogs by the border patrols. The Slovak Tchouvatch is popular with alpine sportsmen, and has proved able in search and rescue work. A powerful swimmer, the Slovak Tchouvatch is reported to have saved many people from drowning.

The breed has long been known in Czechoslovakia and, following World War I, the Slovak Tchouvatch was officially recognized. Little attention, however, was paid to his breeding. Dr. Antonin Hruza is credited with rescuing the breed from extinction. A professor at Brno's Veterinary University, the doctor first made a comprehensive study of the breed in 1929. He did much to stimulate interest in this native breed, and in 1933 a club was formed, with Dr. Hruza as president. The Society of Cuvac Breeders was very active in and around Brno, the capital of Moravia, and members searched for owners and dispensed information on proper care of the breed.

World War II was a difficult time for the Slovak Tchouvatch. Czechoslovakia was occupied by the Germans, but breeders persevered. At the conclusion of the War, the Society of Cuvac Breeders resumed their work, and the number of Slovak Tchouvatches

A beautiful head study of a Slovak Tchouvatch, owned by Joseph and Maya Schön, of Nanuet, N.Y.

These Slovak Tchouvatch puppies are a real handful!

increased. While the breed is still not common, there are now members in many cities and towns.

Joseph and Maya Schön call the Slovak Tchouvatch the "Rolls Royce of Dogs." These Nanuet, New York residents own the only breeding kennel of Slovak Tchouvatches in North America. "These dogs are so beautiful that they always attract attention," Joseph says. "Wherever we go, people stop us and comment on the breed's beauty." The Slovak Tchouvatch is indeed an impressive animal. Males measure approximately 28 inches in height and weigh about 85-105 pounds. Females stand 26 inches at the shoulder and weigh approximately 70-90 pounds. Some individuals, however, may be larger.

A pair of charming Slovak Tchouvatch puppies from Joseph and Maya Schön's kennel.

The Slovak Tchouvatch has a broad backskull, high set ears and dark oval shaped eyes. He has a deep chest and medium length back. He is a powerful and well muscled dog. Hind dewclaws rarely occur and should always be removed. The breed is characterized by its luxurious coat, which should ideally be pure white. Some yellowish colored markings are permissible on the neck and ears, but they are not preferred. His nose is black, although in colder climates it may fade to a brownish black in winter. The harsh coat is truly beautiful, and males, particularly, have a noticeable mane or ruff on the neck. The coat is 2-4 inches in length and may be smooth or wavy. The standard says, "on the back it is gently waved, and toward the rump there are successive wavy stretches that overlap...In winter the thick undercoat grows to two thirds the length of the top coat, making the whole coat softer and limiting its tendency to become wavy." The Slovak Tchouvatch's tail is heavily furred. Dogs usually carry their tails down, although they may raise them to the level of the back when excited.

The Schöns describe the Slovak Tchouvatch as an "absolutely loyal family dog." Like the other livestock guardians, the breed is totally devoted to his family. He takes his duties as a family protector very seriously and will give his own life in their defense. Indeed, the breed is wary of strangers and very much a one family dog. "They are very easy to train, and sensitive to praise and blame," the Schöns say. Like the other livestock guardians, he is quite independent, and centuries of breeding have conditioned him to think and evaluate situations for himself. The Slovak Tchouvatch is very fond of children, a quality which the Schîns much admire. "They have an extremely strong instinct to protect children," the couple says.

An adult Slovak Tchouvatch and two puppies pose for the camera at the Schön's kennel in New York.

A Slovak Tchouvatch puppy gets a ride.

The Slovak Tchouvatch is very affectionate and has endless patience. "Because of their unsurpassed physical beauty, gentleness, politeness and obedience, they are being used in recent years as companion dogs," the Schöns say.

The Slovak Tchouvatch is still a rare dog, even in his homeland. There are only about 100 dogs in the United States, at this date, but the breed is attracting much attention. The Slovak Tchouvatch Dog Club of America was recently formed, and Maya Schön serves as President. She devotes herself to her breeding activities and maintains close contact with other Tchouvatch owners. While a typical litter usually consists of 6-8 pups, the breed's population recently increased when a litter of 11 pups arrived. The entire Schön family lovingly participates in raising the dogs, at their home north of New York City. They have patterned their organization after that of the Society of Cuvac Breeders, in Czechoslovakia. Importing dogs from Europe has been very expensive, but Joseph and Maya Schön have been fortunate in receiving the support and aid of Czechoslovakian breeders. They have obtained excellent foundation stock and have carefully selected their imports from the finest bloodlines.

The Slovak Tchouvatch is sure to attract attention in this country. With his great beauty, gentle personality, and wonderful protective qualities, he is admirably suited as a companion and working dog in this country. The recent introduction of so many of the white livestock guarding breeds is exciting. Long known in Europe, it is hoped that the breeds will become respected and better known in the United States.

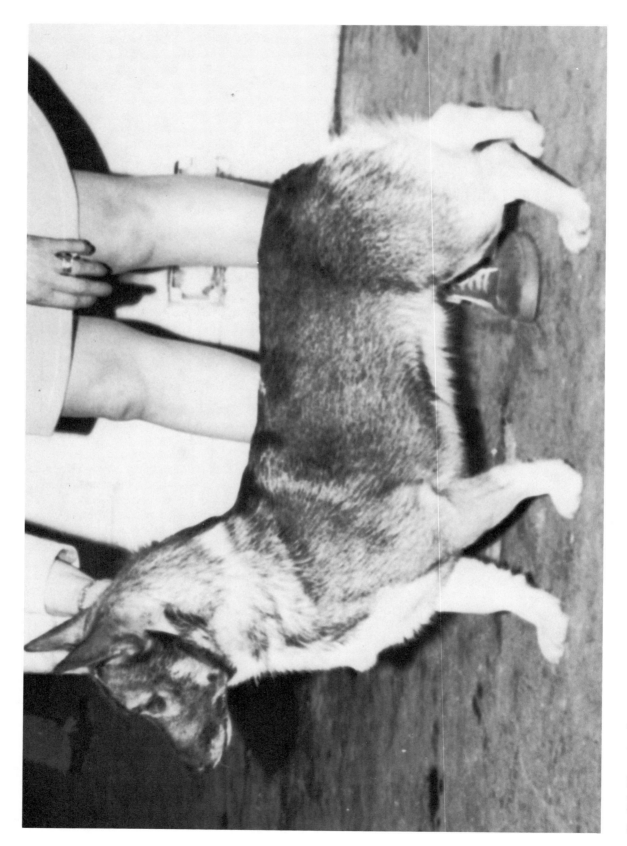

English Champion Starvon Andretti, the top winning Swedish Vallhund in Great Britain, from 1981-1985. Owned by Ada and Timothy West, England.

Chapter 49

The Swedish Vallhund

Dog lovers are sure to notice the resemblance of the Swedish Vallhund to the more widely known Pembroke Welsh Corgi. Although he has the low slung look of the Corgi, there is also a noticeable resemblance to the Norwegian Elkhound. This small, hardy breed from Scandinavia is an adept cattle herder and a very good watchdog. He is wonderfully eager to please and makes an ideal companion. Recently introduced to England, he is attracting a great deal of attention in that country. Before long, he should be seen in the United States.

Västgötaspets is the breed's Swedish name. Literally, it translates to "spitz of the West Goths." Fanciers who introduced the breed to Great Britain thought that English speaking people would have great difficulty pronouncing that name and dubbed the breed the Swedish Vallhund. The Vallhund has been known in Sweden for centuries. While many have pondered the relationship between this breed and the Corgi, the Swedes claim that the Vallhund is an indigenous breed. Found primarily in south and central Sweden, the Vallhund has long been esteemed for his work with cattle. He is related to the other smaller spitz-type herding breeds, and it is believed that his progenitors were brought to Sweden by the early Viking adventurers.

The breed escaped the attention of show fanciers until very recent times. The Swedish Vallhund was considered a farm dog, and it was there that he was appreciated. The sole concern of Swedish farmers was that he be able to perform his herding duties. Little concern was given to conformation, and crossbreedings were commonplace. As long as the rugged little dogs retained their ability to work, and

had the needed stamina and endurance, the stock raiser was satisfied.

In the late 1940's and early 1950's, a number of Swedish dog lovers became concerned about the state of the breed. They feared that if some action was not taken quickly, the Swedish Vallhund might become extinct. Björn von Rosen and other dedicated dog lovers searched the country for truly typical specimens. These enthusiastic people were able to bring a great deal of attention to their efforts to resuscitate the breed, and the ensuing publicity brought an increased awareness of this Swedish native. The Vallhund standard was formulated in 1948, and the breed has steadily gained in popularity. The Swedish Vallhund is now a frequent participant in shows and obedience trials.

Historians have long puzzled over the relationship between the Swedish Vallhund and the Pembrokeshire Welsh Corgi. The noted authority, Clifford Hubbard theorized that the Swedish Vallhund was the older of the two breeds. He believed that the Vikings took Vallhunds with them when they invaded Wales in the ninth and tenth centuries. The Vikings, who would eventually settle in South Wales, are believed to have arrived in an area south of Pembrokeshire. Here their Vallhunds are believed to have interbred with the native Welsh herding Corgi. Some authorities theorize that this may have been the point at which the Cardigan and the Pembroke Corgis parted in type. We may never know if this scenerio is real, but certainly, if the Welsh farmers found these new dogs to be capable herders, they wouldn't have hesitated to breed to them. There are some admitted difficulties with this theory. It is believed that the

Vikings launched their invasions from Denmark or Norway, and there is no evidence to suggest that the Vallhund is found in these countries. While some Swedish Vallhunds have reddish tones, they are primarily grey in color. Still both breeds have the same working style. The dart in and nip the cattle on their hocks, and then drop quickly to the ground to avoid the ensuing kick. Both breeds are agile, active and alert. Perhaps the story will always remain a mystery. With their abundant similarities, it does appear that the Vallhund and the Pembroke Corgi may have indeed crossed paths somewhere in the course of history.

Like the Corgi, the Vallhund is a low to the ground dog. He is leggier and not as long in body as the Corgi, though. He is quite strong and muscular for his size. This breed has a wedge- shaped head and prick ears. He has a jet black nose and very dark brown eyes. These little dogs have good bone and are quite substantial for their size. The Swedish Vallhund has a naturally bobbed tail and rarely needs docking. Although the standard allows a tail as long as four inches, this is rarely seen. The breed has a medium length, harsh coat that lies rather flat on the body. Their soft and wooly undercoat is often slightly lighter in color. The English standard says that the ideal height for a male is 13 inches, while bitches are 12 1/4 inches, and weights should range between 18-28 pounds. The Swedish standard allows for a larger dog who can be up to 16 inches in height and weighs up to 31 pounds. The English standard for the breed describes proper color as follows: "Desirable colours are steel grey, greyish/brown, greyish/yellow, reddish/yellow or reddish/brown with darker hairs on the back, neck and sides of the body. Lighter hair of the same shade of colour as mentioned above can be seen on muzzle, throat, chest, belly, buttocks, feet and hocks. Instead of these lighter shades, white markings are acceptable, but never in excess of one third of the total colour."

The standard describes the Swedish Vallhund as "watchful, alert and energetic," and this goes far in describing the Vallhund's temperament. They are very active and energetic dogs, and they require abundant exercise. With their convenient size, they are suitable to city homes, as long as their owner is willing to ensure that the dog receives proper exercise. Vallhunds are very intelligent and can be easily trained. In this respect, they are very much like the Corgi. They learn quickly and love to please their owners. They do tend to be barkers, and it's best to teach the puppy that excessive barking will not be tolerated. This breed, when given firm but consistent handling, will reward you with many years of devoted companionship.

With his small size, quick intelligence and wonderful adaptability, the Swedish Vallhund would make a marvelous addition to the breeds seen in this country. The Vallhund has a zest for life and is a wonderful companion. With his excellent herding instincts, he could be a valuable aid on American farms. Perhaps one day, in the future, a Vallhund will stand beside the Corgis in our show rings.

Chapter 50

The Tatra Sheepdog

The Tatra Mountains, in southern Poland, enjoy a reputation as a popular resort area. These peaks in the Carpathian range are a favorite with vacationers. Mountain climbing and other alpine sports lure many tourists to the area. The Tatras are also home to an impressive and very beautiful breed of dog. The Tatra Sheepdog, or *Owczarek Podhalanski,* originally served as a livestock guardian, a task for which he is most ably suited. Presently, the breed is most often seen as a companion of mountain guides, and as an effective watch and guard dog.

Bill Schrage, a former Foreign Service Officer, was stationed in Poland from 1977 to 1981. His job took him to all parts of the country, and he frequently vacationed in the mountains. It was there that he had the opportunity to see the large white dogs of the region. When he returned to the United States, Mr. Schrage decided to import several Tatras and begin promoting the breed in this country. "If I failed, I told myself, I would still have, as pets, the most fascinating breed I had ever seen."

Bill's Tatras arrived in December of 1981. His first three dogs left Poland on the very day that martial law was declared. Since then, other imports have followed, and Mr. Schrage and other fanciers have established the Polish Tatra Sheepdog Club of America. Mr. Schrage, who makes his home in Nine Mile Falls, Washington, believes that other Tatras may have preceded his to the United States, and he knows of a few others in Canada. The Club is working to establish contact with other Tatra owners. It is believed that the Tatra is the rarest of the livestock guardian breeds, with only 33 dogs known to be in this country.

The Polish Tatra Sheepdog is clearly related to the other large, white livestock guarding breeds. His Polish name, literally translated means "Podhale Shepherd," and it was in the Podhale area of the Tatra Mountains that he first achieved prominence as a livestock guardian. The breed has probably existed in this region for centuries, and the dogs were invaluable in defending flocks of sheep from predation by bears and wolves. Concerted breeding of the Tatra Sheepdog began after World War I, and a standard was formulated at this time. Like so very many of the European breeds, the Tatra was seriously endangered in the aftermath of World War II. But dedicated owners once more established breeding programs and, in 1967, the breed was accorded recognition by the Federacion Cynologique Internationale.

The Tatra is a large dog, often reaching twenty-six inches at the withers. He has heavy bone, a massive body and is powerfully muscled. His profuse coat is generally pure white, although some dogs have a pale creamy white color. "My Tatras are large, ranging from 100-130 pounds. They are remarkably easy to care for. They are easy to groom and never require bathing. Their coat is self-cleaning. They can truly withstand the most severe winter climate, yet adapt well to seasonal changes." The dogs do shed seasonally. For such a large dog, the Tatra does not have a huge appetite, and new owners are generally surprised by the breed's frugal eating habits. The breed is remarkably hardy. "They just don't get ill easily," Bill says. "In fact, mine have never been sick, and they have lived outside year round in the harshest weather."

The Tatra's exemplary temperament is sure to earn the breed more support in coming years. "The Tatras have a cheerful personality," Mr. Schrage says.

"They are not aggressive, except when they perceive a threat. And even then, they have a long fuse. They are not 'dangerous' dogs, nor could they be labeled 'mean' by any standard. But, they are courageous and formidable fighters when they see the cause for such behavior. Their normal behavior is very laid-back, and they just take life easy. They are great with children---patient, placid and sturdy to play with. But can they guard! They are intimidating without being aggressive."

Bill Schrage finds that the breed is very trainable. "The Tatra is also very adaptable. I have moved my dogs all around and they have been temporarily boarded with strangers. They have taken it all with equanimity and flexibility. They seem to accept anything their owners expect of them. A Tatra, I'm convinced, can be virtually ignored (as long as they are watered and fed) and will not become maladjusted. But, it is hard to ignore them because they are so sociable and interesting. They enjoy attention but do not demand it."

The impressive male, Goral, pictured with Sara Schrage. Owned by William Schrage, Tatra Canines, Nine Mile Falls, Washington.

With his wonderful temperament, beautiful looks, and commanding presence, the Polish Tatra Sheepdog should attract much attention. For those considering the purchase of a working livestock guarding breed, that can be trusted with visitors, the Tatra should fit the bill. For those who can provide a home with adequate room for exercise, the Tatra would be a wonderful companion.

Sara Schrage with Misz, a Tatra puppy, owned by Carol Wood, of Aspenwood Farms.

Chapter 51

The Telomian

The Telomian is unique among the rare breeds in this country. The breed was introduced and sustained, in its early years, by the scientific community. Only when they were successful with their breeding program were dog lovers, from the general public, invited to participate. The Telomian, however, remains rare, and many people are not familiar with this unusual breed. Originally from Malaysia, the Telomian may well be extinct in his homeland. The only viable breeding population exists in the United States, and it is here that the breed must be saved from extinction.

Early in 1960, a young anthropologist went to Malaysia to study the tree shrew. While there, Dr. Orville Elliot and his wife, Marjorie, learned of the existince of a native Malaysian breed from the aboriginal natives. With their natural curiosity about all animals, they hoped to see these aboriginal dogs, but, although they traveled extensively, they saw not one of these specimens. Finally, in one of the most remote areas of the country, near the border of Thailand, they caught their first glimpse of the Malaysian dogs. The Elliots were surprised to see that the dogs were very reminiscent of the Basenji.

The aboriginal natives were very fond of their pets, and the dogs seemed to be very much a part of their lives. These natives were so devoted to their canine companions that they sometimes referred to the dogs as children, and aboriginal women somtimes breast fed puppies. The aborigines were a primitive, semi-nomadic people. They survived by foraging, and employed slash and burn farming techniques. They would remain in their village until the soil in the surrounding area had been depleted, and then they would move on. Their diet was rather low in protein,

consisting primarily of rice, bananas, various berries, and tapioca. Sometimes fish and chicken were available. The natives explained to the Elliots that, on occasion, their dogs would wade into a stream and catch their own fish. Aboriginal homes were crude huts constructed on stilts and reached by five to eight foot ladders. Their small dogs were adept climbers that agiley scaled the ladders to be with their families. They were quite welcome in the huts. Even in this remote region, the natives realized that their beloved dogs were fast disappearing. They told the Elliots that many had been eaten by Communist rebels who hid in the deep jungles.

The Elliots were fascinated by these rare dogs and worried about their future. In fact the whole face of Malaysia was rapidly changing. The vast jungles were being cleared at an alarming rate. Large logging operations were stripping the land of trees, and huge farming operations were taking their place. With their traditional way of life destroyed, the natives were moving into towns, and their treasured pets were crossbreeding with the more popular European breeds. The Elliots quickly realized that the future of this native dog was in peril.

The Elliots became convinced that the breed would soon be extinct. They decided that the best course of action would be to send these Malaysian dogs to the United States. They discussed their idea with the aborigines and told them that this might be the only way to ensure the breed's survival. The couple assured the natives that their dogs would not be used for medical experimentation. With the cooperation of the natives, a male, Ahtong, was obtained from one village, and a female, Ahoing, from another. They contacted a friend and colleague,

Joy Joy Jimut, better known as Ruby, owned by Jody Nathan, of Tulsa, Oklahoma.

Dr. J. P. Scott, in Maine, who agreed to accept the Elliots' find. The dogs had no known name in Malaysia, so the Elliots dubbed the breed "Telomian," since they had first discovered the dogs near the Telom River.

The first Telomians arrived in this country in 1963. Dr. Scott already had a colony of Basenjis at Jackson Laboratory, in Maine, where he was Chairman of the Behavioral Studies Department. Dr. Scott held a respected position in the scientific community. With a master's degree in zoology, and a doctorate in zoology and genetics, he was the president of several scientific societies. He had also written several books on animal behavior and was the author of the *Encyclopedia Brittanica* article on the origin of dogs. It was this professional who conducted studies on the Telomian, and the first litter was born in Maine, in February, 1964. In 1965, Dr. Scott accepted the position of Director for the Center of Research in Social Behavior, at Ohio's Bowling Green University. The Telomians did not accompany him, as there were no facilities to house them. It was not until 1967 that he was able to offer the colony a home. Interestingly, Dr. Michael Fox had worked for Dr. Scott in Maine. Dr. Scott gave him several Telomians, but Dr. Fox had little success with them and eventually abandoned his research.

Progress with the Telomians had proved slow, for the dogs were not highly fertile. However, in 1969 and 1970, the Telomian's fate took an unexpected upward turn. Although artificial insemination had been tried, from time to time, it had met with little success. Allen Yates, however, developed a knack for working with the dogs, and he succeeded where others had failed. He successfully inseminated every female in the Bowling Green breeding colony, and soon the lab was filled with puppies. The expanding Telomian population totally

overwhelmed the staff, and it became apparent that something had to be done. Finally, with space at a premium, it was decided that some of the Telomians would have to be euthanized.

Audrey Palumbo (then Audrey Malone) came to the breed's rescue. A research assistant charged with caring for the lab's animals, Audrey had become fascinated with the Telomian. She strongly disagreed with Dr. Scott's decision to put any dogs to sleep and insisted that they should instead be placed in public homes. A determined woman, she finally convinced the skeptical Dr. Scott and was placed in charge of the project.

This industrious woman contacted the local press, but her efforts met with little success. Fortunately, the Telomian story was picked up by the Associated Press, and the report came to the attention of Ohio newspapers. Articles on the breed, and the studies being conducted at Bowling Green, appeared in papers across the state. Letters poured into the lab, and the phone began to ring. Soon Telomians were in private homes. It was not always an easy transition. While puppies quickly acclimated to the new surroundings, the adults were a different story. They had all spent their lives as kennel dogs, and the laboratory environment was quite different from that of a regular home. There were some early disappointments, and adult Telomians often taxed the patience of their new owners.

Luckily, many became entranced with their new and distinctive pets, and the number of enthusiastic Telomian owners grew. In July of 1970, they gathered to talk about their dogs and decided to form a club for the breed. In September of that year, the Telomian Dog Club of America was officially formed, and continues to this day. Audrey Palumbo remains a driving force in the Club.

Meanwhile, Dr. Elliot was teaching at a university in Singapore. He had kept abreast of the progress of the Telomian, and he was very impressed with the new club and the dedication of the owners.

Three week old Telomian pups bred by Jody Nathan.

He presented a proposal to club members. He and his wife would, once again, go to Malaysia to see if they could locate Telomians, if the club would pay their expenses. The news electrified the club, and the members quickly agreed. They considered the project essential, since all the breeding stock in this country descended solely from the original pair. The opportunity to expand the gene pool was irresistable.

It was a difficult search, and the Elliots traveled more than 1,000 miles in search of purebred Telomians. Letters arrived in the United States, but they were discouraging. The Elliots walked for days into the most remote regions, but it began to appear that the breed was now extinct in its homeland. Finally, a telegram arrived informing the group that two dogs would arrive soon by plane. An excited group assembled at the airport, but the dogs were not aboard the plane. No one knew what had happened to the precious cargo. Finally several days later, Kegan and Jimut arrived in the United States.

The Telomian is a distinctive dog. Dr. Scott believed that they had been purebred for more than 3,000 years, and might be the "missing link" between the Basenji and the Dingo of Australia. Indeed, they bear a striking resemblance to the Basenji. They are small and muscular. Like the Basenji, they have a furrowed brow, although their foreheads are less wrinkled, and they are longer bodied. Their tails, though carried over the back when the dogs are at play, lack the Basenji's tight curl. Telomians are 15 to 19 inches tall and weigh between 18 and 22 pounds. With commercial food they have prospered, for the original dogs imported into this country were significantly smaller. Like the Basenji, they have short sleek coats and strongly erect ears, although Telomian ears are somewhat smaller than their Basenji counterparts. They have dark almond shaped eyes that are set wide apart. The standard describes Telomian color as "any shade of sable, with white and ticking." Telomians vary greatly in color, from a blonde to a very deep red. Some have white markings on their chests, legs, necks and tails. They may be ticked with small spots on the white areas. Some dogs also have a black mask.

The Telomian is an affectionate dog, who makes an excellent pet. They become extremely attached to their human families and are quite good with children. The Telomian Dog Club of America says that the "Telomian is basically another child in the family." They do love their human families, and like to share the same room with them and be a part of family activities. An intelligent dog, the Telomian has been successfully trained in obedience, and it is reported that they learn very quickly. They can, however, become stubborn when they don't feel like working. Many owners report that their dogs are quite adept at learning new tricks. New owners are often taken with the Telomian's cat-like qualities. This breed will often bat balls around with their paws, and one owner said that her Telomian liked nothing better than to lie on the back of a couch near the window and sun herself.

Like the Basenji, the Telomain is generally a quiet dog. They are not silent, though. They make excellent and very alert watchdogs, and will let you know that someone is approaching, even before they arrive at the door. They create quite a commotion when strangers arrive. "Then," says the Telomian Dog Club of America, "all the howls, growls and crowing lets loose. If you've never heard a crow, it is a combination of a howl and a growl that makes an intruder think twice." Telomians may be small dogs, but you'll never convince them of that. They can be quite aggressive with strange dogs, but when reared with another breed they will adjust very well.

Jody Nathan's much loved Telomians, Astro and Ruby, relax in their Tulsa, Oklahoma home.

Like the Basenji, the Telomian was used for hunting in his native home and relies primarily on sight. While the breed has not had a chance to demonstrate its hunting ability in this country, some owners report that they are very good on woodchucks. The Telomian shares another trait with the Basenji. They are inordinately good climbers and can scale even the highest of fences with ease. With their amazing agility, a bored Telomian can become an accomplished escape artist. One of the many qualities that impress owners is the breed's natural resistance to disease. They are very healthy and hardy, and seldom need to see a veterinarian, except for routine innoculations. Also, like the Basenji, Telomians generally come in season only once a year.

Jody Nathan is an enthusiastic Telomian owner and a dedicated club member. Several Telomians live at her Tulsa, Oklahoma, home. "When I was looking for a dog, I saw a picture of a Telomian and fell in love," Jody says. "I was looking for a dog of that size and I just couldn't resist. I bought my first one before I had ever seen one in the flesh. Since I was not involved in showing, it really didn't matter to me that the Telomian was a rare breed. I did like the idea of helping to save a breed from extinction, though."

After obtaining her first dog, Jody was bitten by "the Telomian bug." "The Telomian is a very active dog and we are careful who we place them with," she says. "Crate training is highly recommended. Most placements that have not worked out were homes where the dogs were not crate trained. When left alone the dogs became destructive. It's not that they're bad dogs, it's just that they hate to be left alone. Actually, they're quite clever and learn quickly that if they misbehave when they're alone, they won't be left alone very often." The Telomian Dog Club of America would certainly agree, for they say that the breed may "behave badly if you don't pay attention to them." Because the Telomian bonds so closely with his new family, they recommend that puppies be placed with new owners before twelve weeks of age. To ensure that your Telomian becomes a friendly and self-confident dog, it is essential to fully socialize your new puppy. Growing Telomians do require exercise. "When young, Telomians need to have the opportunity to run off their excess energy," the Telomian Dog Club advises. "Run---that they do. Some have been clocked at 30 to 40 miles per hour and that's with no training." Who knows, perhaps some time in the future we will see the Telomian in coursing events!

The Telomian must still be considered endangered, and needs the widespread support of dog lovers around the world. Without the interest of Dr. Elliot and other Americans, the breed would certainly have become extinct. Telomian fanciers in this country hope that they will soon be able to reintroduce the breed to Malaysia. With the worldwide success of the Basenji, it seems only fair that the charming Telomian should take his place among the recognized breeds. To ensure that this happens, however, he will have to gain greater public acceptance, and the breed is still little known. The Telomian is distinctive and unusual, and he makes a marvelous addition to the group of rare breeds being promoted in this country.

Astro, a male Telomian, owned by Jody Nathan, of Tulsa, Oklahoma.

Chapter 52

The Tibetan Mastiff

If dog breeds were recognized on the basis of their contribution to the canine species, then surely the Tibetan Mastiff would qualify for registration in every country around the world. Indeed, he may well be the oldest dog breed still in existence. Behind many of our most popular breeds, you will find this noble dog of Tibet. He may, in fact, be the "grand daddy" of most of the Mastiff and livestock guardian breeds known around the world. Yet, somehow, the Tibetan Mastiff escaped notice, and some books speak of the breed as being virtually extinct. Fortunately, such is not the case, and these powerful dogs are attracting a host of loyal supporters in the United States and other countries around the world. It seems especially fitting for the beautiful Tibetan Mastiff to step into the limelight.

The Tibetan Mastiff hails from the Himalayas, those beautiful and awesome peaks where Mount Everest is located. It is a land of mystery and superstition, where the initial founder of the Yarlung Dynasty was believed to have descended to earth from the high heavens on a skycord. Travelers rarely ventured into the wild and hazardous mountain country. Tibet is a land of impressive peaks and deep valleys, where bitter cold alternates with steamy heat. It is no wonder that dogs developed in such a region have rugged constitutions and profuse dense coats.

In this remote country, the Tibetan Mastiff guarded flocks of sheep and yaks. He also stood vigil over the property of his master, and some reports say that Tibetan Mastiffs sometimes guarded entire villages. So proficient were these large dogs at guarding, that the Dalai Lama, ruler of the country, used eight Tibetan Mastiffs to guard his summer home, in Norbulinka. Two Tibetan Mastiffs were posted at the gates of each entrance to his estate.

Early visitors to this remote region were always impressed with these native dogs. So esteemed were they as guardians that early descriptions attest to the breed's savageness. On his home turf, the Tibetan Mastiff could be handled only by his owners. However, when away from his own territory strangers could approach safely. Marco Polo, the early explorer, mentions the breed and likens their size to that of a donkey. Several Tibetan Mastiffs were presented to Alexander the Great, to help him when he encountered elephants and lions on his conquests. Many believe that these dogs eventually made their way to Rome, where their descendants battled in the bloody Roman circus arenas.

Early visitors commented on the breed's deep bark. One French writer said it sounded like the roar of a lion. Samuel Turner traveled to Tibet, in 1800, on behalf of the East India Company. On the border of Bhutan and Tibet, he met a group of Tartars with a herd of approximately 300 yaks. The animals spent the days grazing the mountain pastures, but in the evening they were gathered in the valleys, and he saw two huge Tibetan Mastiffs guarding the entire herd. So impressed was he with the power of these dogs that he said that if their courage was as great as their size, they would surely have been able to battle with lions.

The hectic years of China's Cultural Revolution were hard on the Tibetan Mastiff. The new ruling Chinese considered dogs a bourgeois luxury, which took food from the mouths of the masses. Thousands of dogs were ordered killed, and their manner of death was not pleasant. Reports indicate that owners, including monks, were ordered to beat their own dogs

The beautiful Champion Dragonquest Mara v. Jamars is owned by Martha Reisinger. This outstanding bitch is a Group winner. (Harkins photo)

The impressive Champion Langtang Shuk-Sho-Sha-Man, owned by Martha Reisinger, Jamars Kennel, Bainbridge, Pennsylvania. (Harkins photo)

to death. If they did not acceded to the orders, they themselves would suffer the same fate. We may never know how many Tibetan Mastiffs were destroyed in this brutal and inhumane manner. Fortunately, some dogs did survive, but only in the most isolated and remote regions.

The first recorded importation of the Tibetan Mastiff, into the United States, came during the administration of President Dwight Eisenhower. The Dalai Lama presented the President with a pair of these rare dogs. Eisenhower gave them to his friend, Senator Harry Darby, who bred the pair. One of the pups was presented to Lowell Thomas, who had long

Jamars Kala of Stonenail, a Sweepstakes Specialty winner, owned by Linda Steinnagel and Martha Reisinger. (Harkins photo)

been fascinated with rare breeds.

The foundation stock, for today's Tibetan Mastiff breeding programs, came to this country in a most unusual way. Drug smugglers, from Nepal, hid caches of drugs in false bottomed dog crates. The largest and most aggressive Tibetan Mastiffs were shipped in the crates, to foil the efforts of customs agents. Unfortunately, the dogs were but mere pawns in the smuggling efforts, and little time was spent in finding them suitable homes. Fortunately, a few made their way into the hands of responsible and dedicated dog lovers, who appreciated the Tibetan Mastiff's unique qualities. They began to breed the dogs, and over the years new imports have enriched the bloodlines available in this country.

The Tibetan Mastiff is a large and powerful animal, with a broad and distinctive head. Indeed, it is impossible to adequately describe their noble look. Males must measure at least 25 inches at the shoulder, while bitches must be at least 24 inches. Many Tibetan Mastiffs, however, are considerably larger. These dogs have huge bone, broad bodies, and deep chests. They are well muscled, and the standard speaks of their unusual gait. "At the walk, which is distinct and unique in this breed, the Tibetan Mastiff should be considered to have a stalking, determined gait." Their profuse outer coat is harsh, and they have a soft wooly undercoat. The Tibetan Mastiff's coat is so dense that bathing one of these dogs is a challenge. Tibetan Mastiffs, particularly the males, have a pronounced ruff. The Tibetan Mastiff comes in a myriad of colors, and all are permissable.

"I heard of a Tibetan Mastiff that was going to be sent to the Humane Society," says Martha Reisinger, the Vice President of the American Tibetan Mastiff

A young male, Jamars Mo-Mo, owned by Martha Reisinger, of Jamars Kennel. (Harkins photo)

Association. "When I heard of his situation, naturally I had to see him. I had heard of the breed, but I'd never seen a Tibetan Mastiff. He was so very impressive that I fell in love with him. I brought him home, and he lived the rest of his life here." Marty, as friends call her, has years of experience with the giant breeds. She began to raise Saint Bernards twenty-one years ago. Sixteen years ago, she began breeding and showing Bernese Mountain Dogs. Both Bernese and Tibetan Mastiffs now make their home at her Jamars Kennels, in Bainbridge, Pennsylvannia.

"The temperament and personality of the Tibetan Mastiff is unique," Marty says. "They are aloof and independent, yet affectionate and playful. They are exceptionally clean dogs, and somewhat cat-like in the way they use their paws to play and in their manner of stalking. Yet, there's a touch of the wolf in their body language and everyday living habits. The Tibetan Mastiff possesses an uncanny understanding of human nature, and can size up a situation and decide on a course of action before acting. He is an alert dog of impressive size, courage and stamina, but has a temperament and disposition of patience, affection, gentleness and devoted loyalty to family. I like their calmness, cleanliness and the fact that they are different from other breeds.

"This breed seems to adapt well to any situation," Marty Reisinger explains. "They do need exercise, but not an excessive amount. They are most active in the early morning and at night." The American Tibetan Mastiff Association agrees. "The Tibetan Mastiff, being a large dog, does require enough room to romp and exercise properly. While they are an active dog out-of-doors, they are usually fairly quiet when in the house. Because of centuries of being bred for guarding flocks and homesteads, the Tibetan Mastiff does tend to be a 'night barker,' and this may be a consideration depending on where you live (close neighbors), and whether or not your Tibetan Mastiff will sleep outdoors or indoors at night."

"Grooming is minimal with the Tibetan Mastiff," Marty Reisinger says, "and they don't seem to have a doggy odor." Tibetan Mastiffs do shed once a year, and bred bitches will lose coat when their puppies are born. "I recommend socialization and basic obedience training for any breed," Marty says. "It's important that a dog have good manners. The Tibetan Mastiff can be stubborn in formal obedience work. This stems from his natural instinct to be independent and think for himself. They need no special training to be a watchdog. They are natural guardians of their territory and property. The Tibetan Mastiff was not bred to be an aggressive dog who kills, but rather as a protector who, if challenged, would not back down. First, they warn by barking ferociously. If the intruder persists, they will attack. Usually their bark is enough to frighten intruders or animals. When meeting strangers, they are very good judges of character. I never lock a door, day or night, home or away.

"I've found the Tibetan Mastiff to be very fond of children and exceptionally gentle with them. Many old books say that the smallest child can play with these dogs without fear," Marty tells us. The American Tibetan Mastiff Association says, "They are patient with children, when children and puppy are taught to be considerate of each other. They make an outstanding family dog."

The Tibetan Mastiff is still a very primitive breed in some respects. Females come in season only once each year, generally in late fall or early winter. If you are interested in purchasing a puppy, you should be advised that most are born from October through March. Recently, canine inherited hypertrophic neuropathy has been discovered in the breed. This recessive disorder is generally seen in 7-9 week old pups. The first signs are usually weakness in the hindlegs. The American Tibetan Mastiff Association has launched a testbreeding program, that should bring the situation under control. Needless to say, it is wise to deal with responsible breeders who are working to eradicate this disorder.

The Tibetan Mastiff is one of the most exciting breeds to come to the United States. These large dogs have scored some impressive wins in rare breed shows around the country. Certainly, the Tibetan Mastiff is deserving of recognition and he has attracted a host of loyal supporters who are working to better the breed. They hope to have breed type and size firmly established before stepping into the A.K.C. arena. We are all grateful for their work, and for introducing us to this ancient and worthy breed.

Toku, at 34 inches and 240 pounds, is the largest Tosa in Japan.

The superb Mutsu, decked out in his grand champion apron, is owned by Donald Lee, Jr., of Honolulu, Hawaii.

An outstanding Tosa puppy bitch, sired by Donald Lee's Mutsu, pictured at six weeks.

Chapter 53

The Tosa

The Tosa is the Sumo wrestler of the dog world. The Tosa-Ken or Tosa-Token has been used for years as a fighting dog in Japan. The breed is sometimes referred to as the Japanese Fighting Dog. His Mastiff-like appearance is quite distinctive and entirely different from the other native Japanese breeds. In the Japanese fight arena, the winning Tosa is the dog which can most quickly overpower his opponent. Breeders have specifically selected for size, speed, strength and tenacity. It was said that, in days of old, Samurai warriors attended dog fights so that they might learn courage and boldness from the Tosa. In spite of his dog fighting background, the Tosa is a quiet breed known for his patience and devotion to his human family. The Tosa has only recently been introduced into this country, but owners are finding that he is a devoted friend and an excellent home guardian.

The breed takes its name from Tosa, which is located on the island of Shikoku, in Kochi Prefecture. There, dog fighting is believed to have been a popular diversion for hundreds of years. The early Tosas were quite different in appearance from the modern breed. They had the erect ears and curled tail which characterize native Japanese dog types. It may be that both the Akita and the Tosa had common ancestors.

In 1854, the Government repealed its National Isolation Policy and Japan's doors opened to the world. Ships arrived on Japanese shores, and with them they brought strange and new items of trade, and foreign customs. Western dogs often accompanied the foreign travelers. It must be remembered that dog fighting was also a pastime in the west, and it was inevitable that the canine gladiators of the west would be pitted against dogs of the east. It soon became clear that the fighting dogs of the east were no match for their larger and stronger western counterparts. To gain a competitive edge, Japanese breeders crossed their native dogs with some of the new imports. Mastiffs, Great Danes, Bull Terriers, Bullmastiffs, Pointers, Bulldogs and Saint Bernards were combined with the traditional Japanese dog. Breed type was extremely varied during this period, and few Tosas looked alike. Japanese breeders had their own personal preferences as to combinations. The only arbiter of breed type was the success achieved in the violent dog pits.

The greatest challenge to the Tosa's existence came during World War II. The country was ravaged by the effects of the War, and in the Shikoku area food became extremely scarce. There just was not sufficient food to maintain the large Tosas. With heavy hearts, some Japanese breeders shipped their most outstanding Tosas to Aomori Prefecture in northern Japan. There, dedicated individuals kept the breed alive and, as conditions improved, Tosa breeding prospered. Aomori became known as the "Tosa Capital of the World." At the conclusion of the war, fight enthusiasts from Shikoku treked to Aomori to reacquire Tosas. The Tosa once again became king of the Japanese dog fighting arenas.

The Tosa is rare in Japan today. Truly top quality specimens are even harder to come by. Dog fighting is legal in Japan and the practice continues, although it seems to be declining. Only males compete in the fighting pits, while females serve as superb watchdogs for the home. Males that are being conditioned for fighting are walked six miles daily. In the Japanese style of dog fighting, the Tosa is expected to remain absolutely silent during the match.

The impressive Mutsu, the most outstanding example of the Tosa currently in the United States. This extraordinary male is owned by Donald Lee, Jr., of Foreign Gold Kennels, Honolulu, Hawaii.

No matter what the circumstances, he is not to scream or cry out in pain. Japanese breeders have, therefore, bred for a very quiet dog, who is not prone to excessive barking. On the rare occasion that a Tosa is seen in the show ring, he makes an impressive appearance. The large dog is accompanied by two handlers, who each hold stout leather leads to enable them to better control their charge.

Tosas are powerful dogs that have an agile and athletic appearance. There is a wide size variation in the breed, with males ranging from 25 1/2 inches at the withers to more than 30 inches. Males may weigh in at just over 100 pounds, or tip the scales at more than 200 pounds. The most outstanding breed specimens generally fall in the 130-160 pound range. Females are, of course, proportionally smaller. The Tosa has a huge Mastiff-type head. As with so many of the fighting breeds, his ears and eyes tend to be rather small. Tosas come in several colors, although red is highly preferred. Brindle, fawn and dull black Tosas are not excluded from the show ring. Some dogs will sport white markings on their feet and chests.

The Tosa has only recently been introduced to this country. The Tosa-Ken Association of America was formed in 1982, and has been successful in gaining the cooperation of Japan's top breeders.

Donald Lee, Jr., owner of Foreign Gold Kennels, in Honolulu, Hawaii, is the organization's President. Mr. Lee first became acquainted with the breed many years ago, in Hawaii, where Tosas were raised by a few prominent people. In an effort to learn more about the breed, he journeyed to Japan. "I made a personal committment to the Tosa. After many years, and investing a small fortune, I was very fortunate in meeting the right people. I now deal with the Government of Japan and several of the top Tosa breeders in all of Japan. I'm very proud to say that I'm the first American to be presented with Tosas of the highest quality from the Government." Under Mr. Lee's guidance, the Tosa-Ken Association has done much to inform the public of the Tosa's qualities. The Association is dedicated to preserving the qualities of this unique Japanese breed.

The Tosa makes a devoted and affectionate companion. Despite its great size, the Tosa is a very quiet and calm dog, and does well as a housepet. With his sleek, short coat, grooming is minimal. The breed, unlike some other heavily jowled dogs, is not prone to excessive drooling. The Tosa can be kept as an outdoor dog in warmer climates, but adequate shelter is necessary in colder sections of the world. Due to his aggressive nature with other animals, a fenced yard is a must. It is preferable that the new Tosa owner have experience with other large breeds.

As a watchdog, the Tosa is superb. He quickly becomes a family member, and will aggressively defend his owner's property. Proper socialization will

Two impressive Tosa pups from Japan.

204

insure that the Tosa will be manageable around other people. You do not have to worry that this will impede him as an effective guardian. This part of the dog's nature seems to be instinctive. While formalized obedience training has not yet been attempted with the Tosa, owners report that the breed is extremely intelligent and seems to enjoy learning. Tosas are gentle and loving with children. Due to the breed's great size and power, it is best to closely supervise dogs when they are engaged in play with very young children. The Tosa may not recognize his own strength and may, inadvertently, harm a small child.

Due to the breed's background as a fighting dog, owners must exercise extreme caution with the Tosa around other animals, most particularly dogs. The Tosa cannot be considered a good choice for a home which includes any other dog. The Tosa-Ken Association is very honest about this aspect of the breed's temperament. "Always remember that the Tosa has been selectively bred for many generations to view other dogs as the enemy, and do not expect your Tosa to ignore its instinct to fight with other dogs." Donald Lee, Jr. advises that males and females, if properly introduced, can live side by side successfully. On some occasions, a mother and daughter have shared the same home without difficulty. He warns new owners, however, that regardless of sex, no two Tosas should ever be fed together.

The Tosa can offer much to the person looking for a loyal companion and superlative guard dog. One hopes that the breed will attract only responsible and conscientious owners, who recognize the breed's aggression with other dogs and act accordingly. "While the Tosa-Ken Association of America in no way condones the organized fighting of Tosa dogs in the United States, it is our opinion that it would be a mistake to selectively breed Tosa dogs that do not display this aggressive fighting instinct. Aggression toward other dogs is the most definitive characteristic of true Tosa type, and to change this would be to produce inferior Tosa dogs."

These two Tosa pups are a real armful!

The superb Champion "PR" Hopkins' Gay Danny, owned by Mrs. Phil (Eliza) Hopkins, of Homer, Michigan. Danny is but one of the many outstanding champions that have been produced at Hopkins Kennels. Danny was the model for the National Toy Fox Terrier Association's logo.

Chapter 54

The Toy Fox Terrier

It may seem strange to class the Toy Fox Terrier as a rare breed, but recently these flashy little dogs have made appearances at rare breed events. The Toy Fox is registered with the United Kennel Club and continues to be one of their most popular breeds. Indeed, last year more that four thousand of these diminutive dogs were registered with that agency and Toy Fox Terriers make their homes in all of the United States, as well as several foreign countries. Still, because the breed is not registered with the American Kennel Club, there are some people who have yet to become acquainted with his abundant charms.

The Toy Fox Terrier owes his heritage to his larger relative, the Fox Terrier. Long enjoyed as an invaluable pet and superb show dog, the Fox Terrier was also an able hunter in the breed's early days. The breed evolved in the 18th century, in England, where he was used to hunt fox, badger and weasel, in the traditional go-to-ground terrier style. Fox Terriers were equally proficient on rats, and many a British homestead kept one of these versatile dogs near their barns. Their speed, agility, cunning and abundant courage made them wonderful helpmates for rural residents. The first English standard for the breed was established in 1876, and the British Isles have continued to turn out top-notch Fox Terriers, both smooth and wire-haired, ever since. The first Fox Terriers probably came to the United States in the early 1900's.

The breed proved popular in this country too, and Fox Terriers became common sights on many U.S. farms. Occasionally, there would be a particularly small puppy born in a litter. Country people called them "runts," but far from being fragile, they discovered that these little dogs were real scrappers, who could hold their own with their larger brothers and sisters. These smaller dogs became popular with farm wives, as their diminutive size made them ideal housedogs. Who could resist these little charmers, who had the character of the larger dogs and yet were so entertaining around the house? Certainly, they must have brightened the lives of the hard working farm families. They became such cherished favorites that many people began to selectively breed for smaller size. Over the years, they continued in their efforts and, gradually, a distinct breed emerged. He became, and remains, a uniquely American breed.

One writer says that the breeders of the Toy Fox Terrier applied to the American Kennel Club for registration in 1915. They were turned down. The breeders, then, turned to the United Kennel Club and were welcomed. The U.K.C. had registered the Smooth variety of Fox Terrier since 1912. The U.K.C. began registering the dogs, under the name Toy Fox Terriers, in 1936.

It's no wonder that those fortunate enough to own a Toy Fox Terrier become extremely devoted to the breed. They have the size of a toy dog and can easily accompany their owners anywhere, and yet they have the character of a much larger dog. They have abundant energy and a quick intelligence. They have even been used as circus dogs. Their innate playfulness and ability to entertain with their delightful antics, endears them to their owners. Yet, they are content to curl up and share quiet moments, as well. Furthermore, despite their small size, they make uncommonly good "burglar alarms," and thrive equally well in country homes or city apartments. The Toy Fox Terrier is a dog for all seasons.

Mrs. Eliza Hopkins has raised T.F.T's, as the breed is commonly known among fanciers, for more than thirty years. Many successful show winners have come from her Hopkins Kennels, in Homer, Michigan. Little did the Mrs. Hopkins realize, when her husband made a spur of the moment decision to purchase one of these little tykes, that it would lead to a lifetime of devotion to the breed. Phil Hopkins delivered some registered sheep to a buyer and, while there, saw two male Toy Fox Terriers. He was so impressed with the small dogs that he asked if they would part with one. Of course, they wouldn't, but these people took him to the home of a nearby breeder and he left with a female puppy. Although Mr. Hopkins died several years ago, Eliza has continued to raise the breed.

"The Toy Fox Terrier is an alert little dog," Eliza Hopkins says. "Most are friendly, if they are acquired as puppies and grow up with people around. Once in a while, you will find a shy or sassy one, especially if they have been teased or mistreated, but that's the case with most breeds. They are cute and amusing. Most people who've owned one want another. It's rare that they'll consider another breed. Many of my sales are to families where the parents had Toy Fox Terriers when they were children. A lot of senior citizens prefer them, since they make wonderful little watchdogs. Generally, this breed is a one person or one family dog. While they are friendly, some older dogs do not make up easily to strangers in their home.

Grand Champion "PR" Gorden's Little Rocky, owned by Betty and Doug Gorden.

The outstanding Grand Champion "PR" Gorden's Shamrock Lad, winner of the Fall 1985 National Grand Championship Show. Owned by Doug and Betty Gorden, of Crosby, Texas.

"The Toy Fox is easy to care for. They will pretty much self-exercise themselves in a normal home environment. They are short haired and require little grooming. Even though they are small dogs, they are, as a rule, hardy and strong. They're smart and easily trained, although they do have a mind of their own," Mrs. Hopkins says.

While the Toy Fox can become quite attached to children, parents with small youngsters must remember that this is a toy breed and should step in to prevent rough handling. "Children need to be taught not to hurt such small dogs," says Jenny Pandy of Frenchtown, New Jersey. "Their legs are most vulnerable, and Toy Fox Terriers quickly learn to be wary of children and stay out of the reach of rambunctious toddlers. Although not many people think of a Toy Fox Terrier as being a good dog for children, with close supervision a child is quite capable of being gentle to such a small dog. My daughter Ella has a dog named Barbie. Since Ella is younger than her teenage sisters and brother, she is often left behind when the older kids have chores to do or when their friends are over. On these occasions, I have Barbie to thank for keeping Ella occupied. Barbie will try just about anything to please her little mistress, including trips down the sliding board."

Mrs. Pandy is enthusiastic about the breed's ability as a watchdog. "Since T.F.T.'s are exceptionally bright, they can be trained to mind their manners when a stranger enters the home, but it takes little encouragement to teach them to bite, and they are apt to raise a ruckus when anything out of the ordinary occurs. This makes them great watchdogs," Jenny explains. Mrs. Pandy has many stories that demonstrate the breed's character and prowess as a watchdog. One little Toy Fox was killed when he foiled a burglary. Police apprehended the culprit when he showed up at the emergency room to have his wrist stitched. It seems that the owner's little Toy Fox had bitten him severely before being killed. Friends of the Pandy's told them of an incident in which their little dogs had prevented a break in. During the night their Toy Fox Terriers began barking, and in the morning they discovered that someone had unsuccessfully tried to pry their door open. The barking of the dogs had clearly been a deterrent.

The Toy Fox Terrier may be a small dog, but you'll never convince him of that! There's not one fearful bone in that little body. "For their size, Toy Fox Terriers can be quite aggressive with other dogs," Eliza Hopkins says. While your new Toy Fox may accept other dogs in the family, they are not likely to tolerate dog intruders, and it makes little difference that it may be a huge Great Dane or German Shepherd. Recently, Jenny Pandy received a request for a Toy Fox from a resident of Alaska. "During one of our conversations, she told us that her Toy Fox Terrier used to chase bear back into the woods next to their home. It isn't unusual for our dogs to protect their territory when a German Shepherd trespasses, but it takes unsurpassed courage for a dog as small as a Toy Fox Terrier to go after such big game."

Indeed, some owners have noted that the Toy Fox still retains his hunting instincts. "My husband's dog, Black Jack, is known for going down into a critters' burrow and flushing it out," Jenny Pandy says. "Bill was impressed when B.J. brought out three young fox in a field where he was working one day. Just last week the little guy went down a ground hog hole, while we were on a walk. The resident woodchuck started out his back door, but saw us waiting there for him. At that point, he turned around to face B.J. My husband was in a panic, but the dog held his ground. All we could hear was a muffled 'Woof Woof' from down in the ground. Bill could stand it no longer and sent our son, Wes, for a shovel. We were planning on digging the dog out of there, but before the shovel arrived, B.J. decided it was a useless crusade and came back up out of the hole." Indeed, such spunkiness, determination and courage, in this tiny breed, is part of the Toy Fox Terrier's character and personality.

The Toy Fox is a sleek dog with clean lines. They are true toys, weighing between 3 1/2 and 7 pounds. They have a square body, and are quite strong and athletic in appearance. Their short coats are a flashy black, white and tan. The main body color is white and the heads are predominately black, although some dogs have a white blaze. Rich tan markings on the cheeks and over the eyes complete the picture. Tan and white, or black and white dogs are acceptable, but they are not likely to triumph in the show ring. Toy Fox Terriers have strongly erect ears. Eliza Hopkins says those unfamiliar with the breed often ask about ears. "They are pointed and come up naturally," the Michigan resident says. "They are never cropped. Through years of selective breeding, we are now to the point where hardly any Toy Fox Terriers of good breeding don't get their ears up. Some puppies have theirs up by weaning time, while others don't come up until three or four months. If the ears aren't up by the time the puppy begins teething, then they generally won't come up until the milk teeth are shed. It's a little strange, but the smaller pups generally get their ears up faster than the larger ones." Newcomers often ask about tails too. The standard states that the Toy Fox Terrier's tail should be docked "with about a full three-fifths being

Little Gorden's Top Marc looks forward to a promising future. Owned by Doug and Betty Gorden.

taken off." "Some Toy Fox Terriers are born with natural bob tails. When mating dogs with natural bobtails, or ones whose close relatives had natural bobs, you sometimes get a puppy with no tail at all or one with a tail too short," Mrs. Hopkins says.

With his flashing appearance and smart personality, the Toy Fox Terrier makes an outstanding little show dog. They have an alert and self-confident manner, in the ring, that commands attention from judges and spectators alike. Betty and Doug Gorden, of Crosby, Texas, have been very successful with their show dogs. Dog showing has become a wonderful hobby for the Texas couple. Both come from "doggy" backgrounds. Doug's parents raised hunting dogs and quarter horses. Betty received much of her inspiration from her father who, prior to World War II, raised top Scottish Terriers. "I often think of my Dad and how he would have enjoyed the wonderful moments Doug and I have experienced while showing our Toy Fox Terriers," Betty says. "Who would ever have dreamed that that fat little girl, who sat on top of her Dad's six foot kennel fences with her younger brother, eating dog biscuits, would walk away with both the Spring and Fall 1985 National Grand Championship Awards!" This was the first time one owner had achieved both wins in the same year. The Gorden's became interested in showing Toy Fox Terriers after the death of their first beloved pet. They were so fond of the breed that they searched high and low for a replacement. They finally located a breeder, but were disappointed to learn that she had no available puppies. Luckily, this woman encouraged them to join the National Toy Fox Terrier Association and attend dog shows. They eventually purchased a female, but they really were bitten by the bug when they had the opportunity to buy their top winner Rocky. "I took the money I had saved to buy a new refrigerator and used it to purchase Rocky, and I haven't regretted it to this day," Betty laughs. This little guy was such a ham that he hooked the Gordens on showing. Since then, many Toy Fox Terriers have joined the couple at their Toy Circus Kennels, in Crosby, Texas, and they have become devoted Toy Fox Terrier lovers.

Whether he is a show dog, a beloved companion, a circus performer, a four-legged burglar alarm, or all of these, the Toy Fox Terrier is a neat little dog that has gained many admirers. This breed, with its 'take on the world' attitude, has an irresistible talent for getting close to its owners. Fortunately, these small dogs have a very long lifespan, and stay vital and full of vigor and energy into old age. Small wonder that the Toy Fox Terrier wins friends wherever he goes. He has a charm all his own. Just ask any Toy Fox Terrier owner!

Grand Champion "PR" Gorden's Madam Butterfly, an excellent bitch was the first Grand Champion for her owners, Betty and Doug Gorden, Toy Circus Kennels, Crosby, Texas.

Appendix

AKBASH DOG

AKBASH DOG ASSN. OF
AMERICA
P.O. Box 15238
Chevy Chase, MD 20815

AMERICAN BULLDOG

John D. Johnson
140 Hinton Street
Summerville, GA 30747

AMERICAN ESKIMO

NATIONAL AMERICAN
ESKIMO ASSN.
Karla Cole
P. O. Box 483
Keego Harbor, MI 48033

**AMERICAN HAIRLESS
TERRIER**

Edwin & Willie Scott
P.O. Box 79
Trout, LA 71371

**ANATOLIAN SHEPHERD
DOG**

ANATOLIAN SHEPHERD DOG
CLUB OF AMERICA
3620 Alpine Blvd.
Alpine, CA 92001

ARGENTINE DOGO

INTERNATIONAL
ARGENTINE DOGO CLUB
Cathy J. Flamholtz
Rt. 1, Box 180-A
Collinsville, AL 35961

AUSTRALIAN KELPIE

WORKING KELPIES
Susan Thorpe
Rt. 2
Oskaloosa, IA 52577

**AUSTRALIAN KELPIE CLUB
OF N.S.W.**
P. A. Townley
Glenfield Road
Cross Roads, N.S.W. 2170
Australia

**AUSTRALIAN
SHEPHERD**

AUSTRALIAN SHEPHERD
CLUB OF AMERICA
Joan Boice, Secretary
Rt. 2, Box 335
Timmonsville, S.C. 29161

BEAUCERON

BEAUCERONCLUB
NEDERLAND
Mme. Truus Manders
Raadhuisplein 4
6097 AS Heel (L)
Holland

CLUB LES AMIS DU
BEAUCERON
M. Collignon, Sec.
5, rue Etienne-Laurent
91700 Pussay
France

BOYKIN SPANIEL

THE BOYKIN SPANIEL
SOCIETY
P.O. Box 2047
Camden, S.C. 29020

CANAAN DOG

CANAAN CLUB OF
AMERICA
Lorraine Stephens, Sec.
Box 555
Newcastle, OK 73065

CASTRO LABOREIRO

CLUBE PORTUGUES DE
CANICULTURA
Praca D. Joao Da Camara, 4.3
Lisbon 2, Portugal

**CATAHOULA LEOPARD
DOG**

NATIONAL ASSN. OF
LOUISIANA CATAHOULAS
P.O. Box 1041
Denham Springs, LA 70727

**CAVALIER KING
CHARLES SPANIEL**

CAVALIER KING CHARLES
SPANIEL CLUB, USA
Mr. & Mrs. Gerald L. White
RFD 1, Box 21X
Strasburg, VA 22657

CHINESE CRESTED

AMERICAN CHINESE
CRESTED CLUB
Marjorie Rockwell, Sec.
106 Fraser St.
St. Simon Island, GA 31522

CHINESE SHAR-PEI

CHINESE SHAR-PEI CLUB
OF AMERICA
55 Oak Ct.
Danville, CA 94526

CHINOOK

Neil & Marra Wollpert
3400 Sunnycrest Lane
Kettering, OH 45419

CZECH TERRIER

FEDERALNI VYBOR
MYSLIVECKYCH SVASU V
CSSR
115 25 Praha 1
Stare Mesto, Husova 7
Czechoslovakia

DOGUE DE BORDEAUX

DOGUE DE BORDEAUX
CLUB OF AMERICA
301 South 72nd Street
Kansas City, KS 66111

DUTCH SHEPHERD

NEDERLANDSE
HERDERSHONDEN CLUB
Mrs. Th. F. M. Kolster-
Reckman
H. Reindersweg 28,
Bungalow 26
7933 TW Pesse
The Netherlands

ENGLISH SHEPHERD

ENGLISH SHEPHERD CLUB
1231 Stevens Ave.
Arbutus, MD 21227

FILA BRASILEIRO

FILA BRASILEIRO CLUB OF
AMERICA
P.O. Drawer 649
Manchester, GA 31816

FINNISH SPITZ

FINNISH SPITZ CLUB OF
AMERICA
Bette Isacoff, Sec.
4000 Houcks Rd.
Monkton, MD 21111

Joan Grant
Box 1423
Golden, B.C. V0A 1H0
Canada

GERMAN PINSCHER

GERMAN PINSCHER CLUB
OF AMERICA
33271 Windjammer
Laguna Niguel, CA 92677

PINSCHER-SCHNAUZER-
KLUB 1895 e.V.
Behringstrasse 26
5110 Alsdorf
West Germany

**GLEN OF IMAAL
TERRIER**

GLEN OF IMAAL TERRIER
OWNERS &
    BREEDERS
ASSOCIATION
21 Johnstown Road
Dun Laoghaire
Co. Dublin
Ireland

**GREATER SWISS
MOUNTAIN DOG**

GREATER SWISS MOUNTAIN
DOG CLUB OF AMERICA
Howard J. Summons
RD 8203
Sinking Springs, PA 19608

SCHWEIZER SENNENHUND-
VEREIN FUR
DEUTSCHLAND e.V.
Schwarzer Weg 62
4600 Dortmund 12 (Brackel)
West Germany

HAVANESE

HAVANESE CLUB OF
AMERICA
Dorothy Goodale
Box 1461
Montrose, CO 81402

HOVAWART

Rassezuchtverein für
Hovawart Hunde e.V.
Am Lagerberg 1
2740 Bremervörde
West Germany

ICELAND DOG

HUNDARAEKTARFELAG
ISLANDS ICELANDIC
KENNEL CLUB
P.O. Box 73
210-Garoabae
Iceland

JACK RUSSELL
TERRIER

JACK RUSSELL TERRIER
CLUB OF AMERICA
Ailsa Crawford
P.O. Box 365
Far Hills, NJ 07931

JACK RUSSELL TERRIER
BREEDERS ASSN. OF
AMERICA
Box 2326
Conway, NH 03818

JAGD TERRIER

KLUB FUR TERRIERS e.V.
Ohrensener Weg 18
2165 Harsefeld
West Germany

KARELIAN BEAR DOG

SUOMEN
KENNELLITTO-FINSKA
KENNELKLUBBEN r.y.
Bulevardi 14
00120 Helsinki 12
Finland

KYI-LEO

Harriet Linn
1757 Landana Dr.
Concord, CA 94520

LAEKENOIS

Mme. Liliane Lambert-
Equerme
6, rue de la belle Hôtesse
B- 5940 Huppaye
Belgium

LAPPHUND

SVENSKA KENNELKLUBBEN
Box 11043
161 11 Bromma
Sweden

LEONBERGER

LEOBERGER CLUB OF
AMERICA
Marlene Stuteville
P.O. Box 677
Kirkland, WA 98083-0677

LOWCHEN

LITTLE LION DOG CLUB OF
AMERICA
Leslie Healy
6 Homestead Circle
San Angelo, TX 76905

MAREMMA-ABRUZZESE

Sue Drummond
1451 Sisson
Freeport, MI 49325

Arthur Hammond
Kennel Maremanno
310 70 TORUP
Sweden

Maremma Sheepdog Club of
Great Britain
29A Manor Road
Brackley
Northants NN 13 6 ED
England

MINIATURE BULL
TERRIER

MINIATURE BULL TERRIER
CLUB OF AMERICA
Patty Voorhees, Sec.
68181 Elsie Lane
Edwardsburg, MI 49112

NEAPOLITAN MASTIFF

NEAPOLITAN MASTIFF
CLUB OF AMERICA
109 Old York Road
Bridgewater, NJ

USA-NEAPOLITAN MASTIFF
ASSOCIATION
21115 Devonshire St.
Suite 426
Chatsworth, CA 91311

NEAPOLITAN MASTIFF
CLUB OF CANADA
Garry & Lynn Travers
RR1 (General Delivery)
Cheltenham, Ontario L0P
1C0
Canada

NORWEGIAN BUHUND

NORSK KENNEL KLUB
Nils Hansens vei 20
Box 163-Bryn
0611 Oslo 6
Norway

NOVA SCOTIA DUCK
TOLLING RETRIEVER

NOVA SCOTIA DUCK
TOLLING RETRIEVER CLUB,
U.S.A
Marile Waterstraat
63 Blue Ridge Road
Penfield, NY 14526

PETIT BASSET
GRIFFON VENDEEN

PETIT BASSET GRIFFON
VENDEEN CLUB OF
AMERICA
Barbara Langlois, Sec.
2516 Lyndel Drive
Chalmette, LA 70043

POLISH OWCZAREK
NIZINNY

Kaz & Betty Augustowski
1115 Delmont Rd.
Severn, MD 21144

SHIBA

NATIONAL SHIBA CLUB OF
AMERICA
Mary Malone
8539 Schubert
Alliance, OH 44601

SHIBA CLUB OF AMERICA
Anita Regehr
758 S. Anderson Rd.
Exeter, CA 93221

SLOUGHI

Ermine Moreau-Sipiere
5191 Morgan Territory Rd.
Clayton, CA 94517

SLOVAK TCHOUVATCH

SLOVAK TCHOUVATCH DOG
CLUB OF AMERICA
Joseph & Maya Schön
49 Old Middletown Rd.
Nanuet, NY 10954

SWEDISH VALLHUND

SVENSKA KENNELKLUBBEN
Box 11043
161 11 Bromma
Sweden

TATRA SHEEPDOG

POLISH TATRA SHEEPDOG
CLUB OF AMERICA
N. 8325 Pine Meadow Rd.
Nine Mile Falls, WA 99026

TELOMIAN

TELOMIAN DOG CLUB OF
AMERICA
Audrey Palumbo
28765 White Road
Perrysburg, OH 43551

TIBETAN MASTIFF

AMERICAN TIBETAN
MASTIFF ASSN.
2425 Clark Lane
Paris, TX 75460

TOSA

TOSA-KEN ASSN OF
AMERICA
Donald Lee, Jr.
1691-A Kamamalu Ave.
Honolulu, Hawaii 96813

TOY FOX TERRIER

NATIONAL TOY FOX
TERRIER ASSN
Ann Mauermann
211 Exchange Ave.
Louisville, KY 40207

Index